CUSTOM WOODWORKING

The Home
Workshop

TIME® **LIFE** BOOKS

OTHER PUBLICATIONS

DO IT YOURSELF
Total Golf
How to Fix It
Home Repair and Improvement
The Art of Woodworking

HISTORY
Our American Century
World War II
What Life Was Like
Voices of the Civil War
The American Indians
Lost Civilizations
Mysteries of the Unknown
Time Frame
The Civil War

TIME - LIFE KIDS
Student Library
Library of First Questions and Answers
A Child's First Library of Learning
I Love Math
Nature Company Discoveries
Understanding Science & Nature

SCIENCE/NATURE
Voyage Through the Universe

For information on and a full description of any of
the Time-Life Books series listed above,
please call 1-800-621-7026 or write:

Reader Information
Time-Life Customer Service
P.O. Box C-32068
Richmond, Virginia 23261-2068

CUSTOM WOODWORKING

The Home Workshop

By the editors of Time-Life Books
and *Woodsmith* magazine

Time-Life Books, Alexandria, Virginia

The Home Workshop

WORKBENCHES 6

Cabinets and Bench..8

> *You can customize these simple cabinets with combinations of drawers and doors. Then join them together with a bench top designed for your needs.*

Fold-Down Work Center...18

> *This space-saving work center offers storage and security, plus its own light source. And the fold-down bench provides a work surface when you need it.*

Maple Workbench..27

> *In the classic European style, this workbench is massive, but affordable. The traditional dog system lets you clamp the largest workpieces with ease.*

Workbench Cabinet..44

> *This underbench cabinet not only increases your storage capacity, but when full of tools its weight also adds strength and stability to the workbench.*

Fold-Down Work Center

TOOL STANDS 50

Table Saw Cabinet..52

> *This sturdy but mobile cabinet will improve your table-saw setup with storage space, options for dust collection, and an outfeed support.*

Router Table..60

This stable router table can be built with a solid base of 2x4s. But you can also build the fence, clamping system and accessories to fit your own table.

Miter Saw Station..72

Fold-out tables extend the usefulness of your miter saw, and a stop block saves you the trouble of measuring and marking the workpiece.

SHOP STORAGE 82

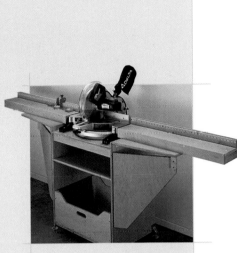

Miter Saw Station

Tool Cabinet..84

With special tool holders and adjustable shelves, you can customize this wall-mounted tool cabinet to organize and protect all your hand and power tools.

Pegboard System...94

Here's a tool rack you can customize to fit your needs. It features a different approach to using pegboard and holding your most commonly used tools.

Lumber Rack..100

This lumber rack is actually a complete storage system, providing easy access to boards and plywood. There's also an option for adding a sheet goods bin.

Finishing Cabinet..106

This cabinet's adjustable shelves let you tailor your storage space, but it's also a complete finishing station with a removable lazy Susan work table.

Modular Workshop...112

Not only can you adapt this system to fulfill all your shop requirements, but you can also modify the same design for storage in other areas of your house.

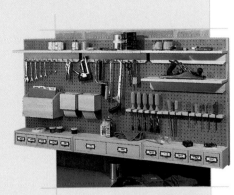

Pegboard System

Sources 126

Index 127

WORKBENCHES

The cornerstone of most home shops is a functional, convenient workbench. But the size and style can vary greatly, depending on space requirements and functional needs. So we give you options, beginning with a simple cabinet and bench top design that can be arranged in many different combinations.

Next is a space-saving fold-down version. Complete with its own light source and extra storage, it would be an ideal choice for a small shop.

If you would prefer a classic European design, you might consider the massive yet affordable maple workbench. Built to last, it features a traditional dog system for easily clamping large workpieces. And finally, a versatile cabinet can be built to add storage and stability to the maple workbench, or to any other open-based bench.

Cabinets and Bench — 8

Shop Tip: Drawer Rails and Filler Strips 11
Joinery: Drawer Joint Options 13
Shop Tip: Making Your Own Drawer Pulls 14
Shop Tip: Using Brackets 16
Designer's Notebook: Work Center or Benchtop Tool Cabinet 17

Fold-Down Work Center — 18

Shop Tip: Using a Story Stick 22

Maple Workbench — 27

Shop Tip: Cutting a Slab to Length 31
Shop Tip: Wooden Dogs 33
Shop Tip: Preventing Vise Rack 38
Designer's Notebook: Easy-To-Build Workbench Top . . . 42

Workbench Cabinet — 44

Shop Tip: Clamping Blocks 48
Designer's Notebook: Sliding Doors and Shelves 49

Cabinets and Bench

You can customize these simple, inexpensive cabinets with endless combinations of drawers and doors. Then join two or more together with a bench top designed for your specific needs.

Workshops never seem to have enough storage space or work surfaces. I solved both problems with these versatile cabinets.

The new cabinets had to meet three requirements. First, they had to be simple to build. Second, they should be fairly inexpensive. And third, it should be easy to customize the cabinets to fit different needs. By configuring the drawers and doors differently, each cabinet takes on a unique look and purpose.

The options are nearly endless, but we are showing a few different ways to configure the cabinets in the Designer's Notebook on page 17.

The trickiest part about designing these "custom-built" cabinets was coming up with a simple way to vary the placement of the drawers and doors. Instead of routing individual mortises for drawer rails, I cut grooves along the front stiles that the rails are set in. Then the grooves are filled above and below the rails with filler strips (see Shop Tip on page 11).

JOINERY. The basic cabinet is built using a frame and panel technique. A wood frame is joined together and holds a hardboard panel. The frames are joined with a stub tenon and groove — a simple joint to make, and one that's easy to set up on a table saw for making multiple joints.

For the drawers, I used simple nailed butt joints at the fronts and dadoes at the backs. But there are a number of joints you could use, as explained in the Joinery section on page 13.

MATERIALS. To keep the cost down, the frames, rails, and drawer parts are made from $3/4$" pine, and the panels and drawer bottoms from $1/4$" hardboard.

To bridge across a couple of the cabinets, I built a benchtop from plywood and hardboard, edged with pine.

FINISH. Finally, I applied two coats of tung-oil finish to the cabinets and top.

EXPLODED VIEW

OVERALL DIMENSIONS OF ONE CABINET:
35½H x 16W x 21½D

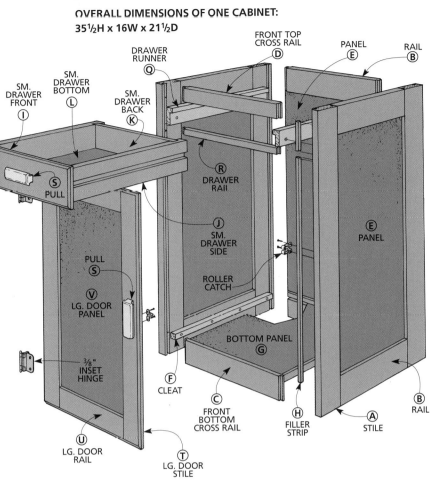

Labels on exploded view:
- SM. DRAWER FRONT (I)
- SM. DRAWER BOTTOM (L)
- DRAWER RUNNER (Q)
- SM. DRAWER BACK (K)
- FRONT TOP CROSS RAIL (D)
- PANEL (E)
- RAIL (B)
- PULL (S)
- DRAWER RAIL (R)
- J SM. DRAWER SIDE
- PANEL (E)
- PULL (S)
- LG. DOOR PANEL (V)
- ROLLER CATCH
- ⅜" INSET HINGE
- LG. DOOR RAIL (U)
- CLEAT (F)
- FRONT BOTTOM CROSS RAIL (C)
- BOTTOM PANEL (G)
- FILLER STRIP (H)
- STILE (A)
- RAIL (B)
- LG. DOOR STILE (T)

MATERIALS LIST

FOR ONE CABINET

BASIC CASE
A	Stiles (4)	¾ x 3½ - 35½
B	Rails (6)	¾ x 3½ - 15
C	Ft. Btm. Cr. Rail (1)	¾ x 3 - 15
D	Ft. Top Cr. Rail (1)	¾ x 1¾ - 15
E	Panels (3)	¼ hdbd. - 15 x 29
F	Cleats (2)	¾ x ¾ - 20
G	Bottom Panel (1)	¼ hdbd. - 14¼ x 20½
H	Filler Strips	¼ x ¼ - cut to fit

SMALL DRAWER (AS AT LEFT)
I	Front (1)	¾ x 4¼ - 15
J	Sides (2)	¾ x 3½ - 20⅜
K	Back (1)	¾ x 3½ - 12½
L	Bottom (1)	¼ hdbd. - 12½ x 19¼

LARGE DRAWER (OPTIONAL, SEE PAGE 12)
M	Front (1)	¾ x 8¾ - 15
N	Sides (2)	¾ x 8 - 20⅜
O	Back (1)	¾ x 8 - 12½
P	Bottom (1)	¼ hdbd. - 12½ x 19¼

DRAWER RUNNERS/RAILS/PULLS
Q	Runners*	¾ x 2⅛ - 20
R	Drawer Rail **	¾ x ¾ - 15
S	Pulls	¾ x 1 - 4

LARGE DOOR (AS AT LEFT)
T	Lg. Door Stiles (2)	¾ x 2½ - 26¾
U	Lg. Door Rails (2)	¾ x 2½ - 10½
V	Lg. Door Panel (1)	¼ hdbd. - 10½ x 22¼

SMALL DOOR (OPTIONAL, SEE PAGE 12)
W	Stiles (2)	¾ x 2½ - 17¾
X	Rails (2)	¾ x 2½ - 10½
Y	Panel (1)	¼ hdbd. - 10½ x 13¼

SUPPORT FRAME (AS IN PHOTO ON PAGE 8)
Z	Stretchers (2)	¾ x 3½ - 30
AA	End Members (2)	1½ x 3½ - 18½

BENCH TOP (AS IN PHOTO ON PAGE 8)
BB	Cores (2)	¾ ply. - 22½ x 76½
CC	Cover (1)	¼ hdbd. - 22½ x 76½
DD	End Edging (2)	¾ x 1¾ - 22½
EE	Frt./Bk Edging (2)	¾ x 1¾ - 78

* Two runners per drawer.
** One drawer rail per drawer.

HARDWARE SUPPLIES
No. 8 x 1" Rh woodscrews (2 per drawer)
No. 8 x 1" Fh woodscrews (4 per drawer)
No. 8 x 1¼" Fh woodscrews
4d Finish nails
⅜"-Inset hinges w/screws (2 per door)
Roller catch (1 per door)
¼" x 3" Machine bolts, nuts, washers
L-brackets for attaching top to cabinet

CUTTING DIAGRAM

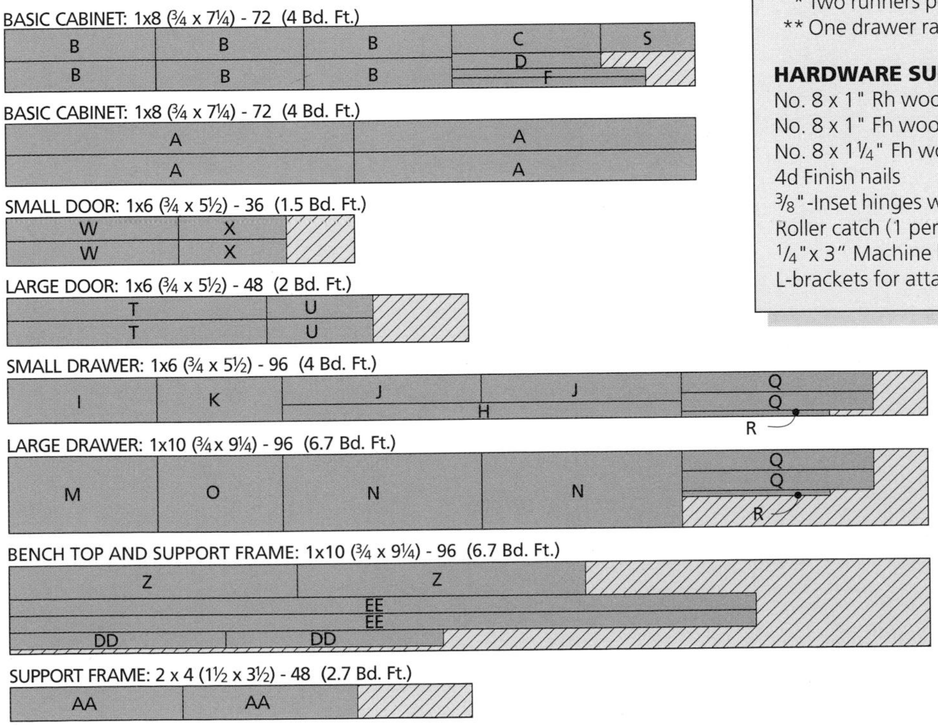

BASIC CABINET: 1x8 (¾ x 7¼) - 72 (4 Bd. Ft.)

B	B	B	C	S
B	B	B	D	
			F	

BASIC CABINET: 1x8 (¾ x 7¼) - 72 (4 Bd. Ft.)

A	A
A	A

SMALL DOOR: 1x6 (¾ x 5½) - 36 (1.5 Bd. Ft.)

W	X
W	X

LARGE DOOR: 1x6 (¾ x 5½) - 48 (2 Bd. Ft.)

T	U
T	U

SMALL DRAWER: 1x6 (¾ x 5½) - 96 (4 Bd. Ft.)

I	K	J	J	Q
		H		Q
				R

LARGE DRAWER: 1x10 (¾ x 9¼) - 96 (6.7 Bd. Ft.)

M	O	N	N	Q
				Q
				R

BENCH TOP AND SUPPORT FRAME: 1x10 (¾ x 9¼) - 96 (6.7 Bd. Ft.)

Z	Z
EE	
EE	
DD	DD

SUPPORT FRAME: 2 x 4 (1½ x 3½) - 48 (2.7 Bd. Ft.)

AA	AA

ALSO REQUIRED:
ONE 4' x 8' SHEET OF ¾" PLYWOOD FOR BENCH TOP PARTS BB (AS SHOWN IN PHOTO ON PAGE 8)

ONE 4' x 8' SHEET OF ¼" HARDBOARD FOR PARTS E, G, L (OR P), V (OR Y), AND CC

I started building the cabinet by making two side frames. Then I connected them with cross rails and a back panel *(Fig. 1)*.

Each side frame is made from two stiles (vertical pieces), two rails (horizontal pieces), and a panel. Holding these frames together is a groove on the inside edge of the stiles and rails. This groove holds the panel in place and forms a "mortise" for the tenons on the ends of the rails (refer to *Fig. 2*).

Since the groove is the same size on all of the pieces (¼" wide and 5/16" deep), I cut the stiles and rails to their finished dimensions. Then I cut the grooves.

STILES AND RAILS. First, using ¾"-thick stock, cut four stiles (A) to finished width and length *(Fig. 1)*. Then cut six rails (B) to size. Two of these rails are used as cross rails for the back.

GROOVES FOR PANELS. The next step is to cut the groove for a panel on the *inside* edge of each stile (A) and rail (B). These grooves are centered on the thickness of these pieces *(Fig. 1a)*.

GROOVE FACE OF STILE. After grooves for the panel are cut on the edges of the stiles and rails, another groove is cut on the face of each *stile*. These grooves are used to join the side frames with the cross rails *(Fig. 1)*, and to hold and position the drawer rails (see Shop Tip on page 11.) Each groove is located ¼" from the edge of the stiles *(Fig. 1a)*.

BACK BOTTOM CROSS RAIL. Now one of the rails (B) also needs a groove on the inside face *(Figs. 1b and 3)*. This rail will be used as the back bottom cross rail and the groove will hold the back edge of the bottom panel in place.

FRONT CROSS RAILS. To hold the front of the bottom panel, make a front

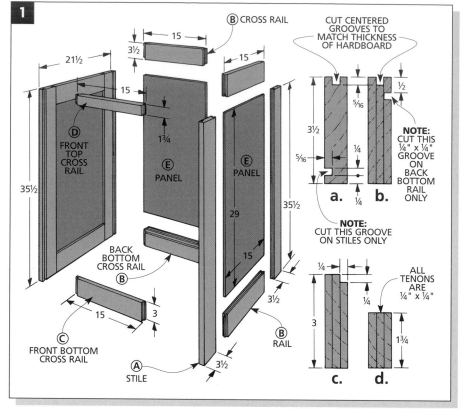

bottom cross rail (C) *(Fig. 4)*. This rail is the same length as the other rails (15"), but it's only 3" wide and it has a ledge for the bottom panel to sit on. To form the ledge, cut a rabbet on the top edge of the rail *(Fig. 1c)*.

There's one more rail to cut — the front top cross rail (D). This rail is narrower than the others (1¾" wide), but it's the same length (15") *(Fig. 1d)*.

TENONS. Now tenons need to be cut on the ends of all the rail pieces. All the tenons are the same size and are cut to fit the grooves in the stiles. Center all of the tenons on the thickness of each piece *(Fig. 2)*.

PANELS. The next step is to determine the size of the panels (E) *(Fig. 1)*. To do this, dry assemble one of the side frames from two stiles (A) and two rails (B), and then measure the opening. To allow for the grooves, add ½" to the width and height. Then cut three panels to these dimensions *(Fig. 1)*. (One panel is for the back.)

ASSEMBLY. After the panels are cut to finished size, assembly can begin. First glue and clamp the two side frames *(Fig. 1)*. Then add the cross rails and the back panel, making sure to check that the case is square before gluing them to the side frames.

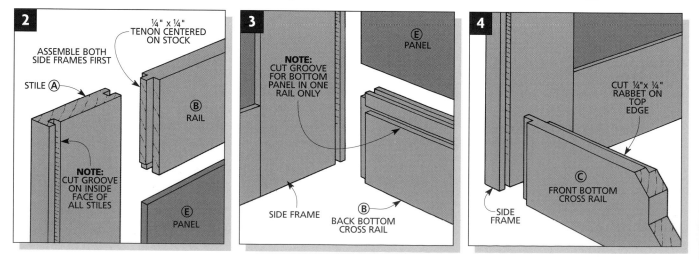

BOTTOM PANEL

After the glue on the basic cabinet is dry, you can begin working on the bottom panel (G).

I cut this panel from ¼"-thick hardboard. To keep it from sagging under the weight of heavy tools, I added support cleats under it *(Fig. 5)*.

CLEATS. Cut two cleats (F) from ¾"-thick stock to fit between the front and back cross rails. Then screw the cleats to the side frames of the cabinet. They should be flush with the bottom of the rabbet in the front cross rail, and flush with the bottom of the groove in the back cross rail *(Fig. 5a)*.

PANEL. Once the cleats are screwed on, the bottom panel (G) can be cut to size and glued in place *(Fig. 5a)*.

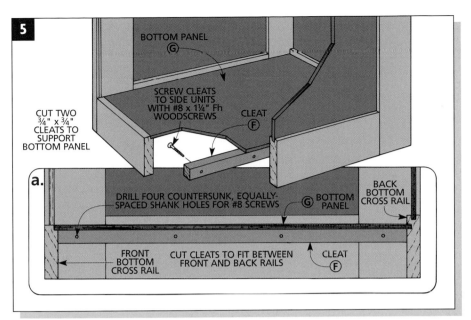

5

BOTTOM PANEL
(G)

SCREW CLEATS TO SIDE UNITS WITH #8 x 1¼" Fh WOODSCREWS

CUT TWO ¾" x ¾" CLEATS TO SUPPORT BOTTOM PANEL

CLEAT (F)

a.

DRILL FOUR COUNTERSUNK, EQUALLY-SPACED SHANK HOLES FOR #8 SCREWS

(G) BOTTOM PANEL

BACK BOTTOM CROSS RAIL

FRONT BOTTOM CROSS RAIL

CUT CLEATS TO FIT BETWEEN FRONT AND BACK RAILS

CLEAT (F)

SHOP TIP .... *Drawer Rails and Filler Strips*

When building a cabinet, rails are installed across the front to hold the sides together and establish the drawer opening.

Typically, the tenons on the ends of the rails are set into mortises. If the cabinet has several drawers, it can mean cutting quite a few mortises.

To make things simpler, I used a completely different technique on this project — I set the drawer rails in a groove. Then to create a "mortise," I filled the grooves above and below the rail with filler strips. This way the height of the opening is determined by the length of the strips *(Fig. 1)*.

After making the drawer rails (R) and cutting tenons on their ends *(Fig. 2a)*, the filler strips (H) are cut to fit the grooves in the side of the cabinet *(Fig. 2)*. I found it easiest to cut these pieces in long strips and then cut them to length to match the desired opening height. Note: I used two different

drawer sizes, and two different door sizes *(Fig. 1)*.

Now the drawer rails and strips can be glued in place. Starting at the bottom, glue a filler strip into the groove on each side of the cabinet. Then insert a rail *(Fig. 3)* and glue and clamp it in place. Continue this process right up the side of the cabinet.

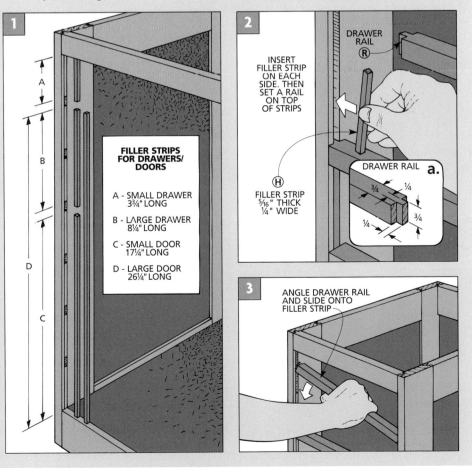

1

FILLER STRIPS FOR DRAWERS/ DOORS

A - SMALL DRAWER 3¾" LONG

B - LARGE DRAWER 8¼" LONG

C - SMALL DOOR 17¼" LONG

D - LARGE DOOR 26¼" LONG

2

DRAWER RAIL (R)

INSERT FILLER STRIP ON EACH SIDE. THEN SET A RAIL ON TOP OF STRIPS

(H) FILLER STRIP 5⁄16" THICK ¼" WIDE

a. DRAWER RAIL

¾   ¼

¼   ¾

3

ANGLE DRAWER RAIL AND SLIDE ONTO FILLER STRIP

The lipped-front drawers shown here are simply glued and nailed together. For other joinery options, see page 13.

FRONTS. To make the drawers, start by measuring the drawer openings. Then, to allow for the lip, cut the drawer fronts (I or M) $\frac{1}{2}$" longer and wider than these dimensions *(Fig. 6)*.

The next step is to cut a $\frac{3}{8}$"-deep rabbet around the inside face to create a lip. However, the width of this rabbet varies. On the top and bottom of the drawer front, cut a $\frac{3}{8}$"-wide rabbet (refer to *Fig. 7*). But on the ends of the drawer front, the rabbets are wider ($1\frac{1}{2}$") to allow for the thickness of the side pieces and the drawer runners.

Once the drawer fronts are rabbeted, rout a small chamfer around the outside face of each one *(Fig. 6b)*.

SIDES. After making the fronts, the drawer sides (J or N) can be cut to size. The length of the sides is $20\frac{3}{8}$". But the width of the sides is the same as the shoulder-to-shoulder dimension on the drawer front *(Fig. 6)*.

To provide a channel for the runners, cut a $\frac{1}{2}$"-wide groove in the outside face of each drawer side *(Fig. 7)*.

DRAWER BACK. After cutting the grooves, cut $\frac{1}{4}$"-deep dadoes on the inside face of all the drawer sides for the $\frac{3}{4}$"-thick back *(Fig. 6a)*. The width of the small drawer back (K) and the large drawer back (O) is the same width as the sides *(Fig. 6)*. To determine the length of the drawer backs, measure the width of the inside of the drawer face from rabbeted shoulder to rabbeted shoulder. Then, to allow for the dadoes, add $\frac{1}{2}$" to this dimension and cut the drawer backs to length.

BOTTOM GROOVE. Next, cut a $\frac{1}{4}$"-deep groove in each drawer piece for a

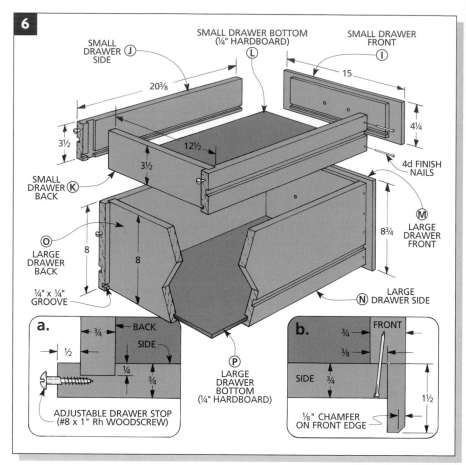

$\frac{1}{4}$" bottom *(Fig. 6)*. On the drawer front the groove is located $\frac{1}{4}$" from the shoulder of the rabbet *(Fig. 7)*.

CUT THE BOTTOM. To determine the size of the bottom (L or P), dry assemble the drawers and measure the distance between the grooves. Now cut $\frac{1}{4}$"-thick hardboard to these dimensions. Then glue and clamp the drawer pieces together. For extra strength, I nailed the sides to the front *(Fig. 6b)*.

RUNNERS. Now work can begin on the drawer runners. Each runner (Q) is cut from a piece of $\frac{3}{4}$"-thick stock to a width of $2\frac{1}{8}$" and a length of 20" *(Figs. 8*

and 9). Then cut it to an "L-shape" by cutting a $\frac{5}{16}$" x $1\frac{7}{16}$" rabbet on one edge.

ATTACH THE RUNNERS. Next, runners are mounted to the inside of the cabinet. To do this, drill two countersunk shank holes in each runner *(Fig. 8)*. Then position the runner so it rests on top of the drawer rail ($\frac{1}{2}$" from the front) and parallel with the top edge of the cabinet.

With the runner in position, mark pilot holes on the stiles. Then drill and screw the runner in place *(Fig. 9)*.

Finally, I screwed roundhead screws into the back ends of each drawer side to act as adjustable stops *(Fig. 6a)*.

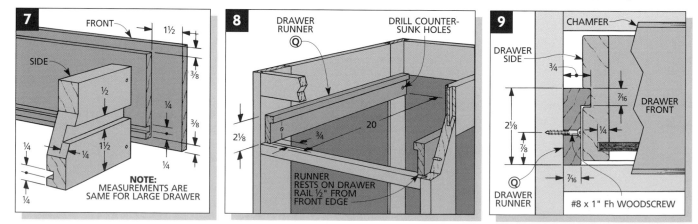

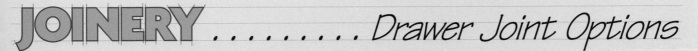

JOINERY .... Drawer Joint Options

Whenever we build a project that has several drawers (like the shop cabinets), we spend a great deal of time discussing how to build them. Most of the decisions involve two main points — the style of drawer front, and the joinery used to assemble the drawer.

LIPPED FRONTS. In the case of these cabinets, I decided to use a lipped front on the drawers. The most important factor here is covering the gap needed for the drawer runners.

To allow for the runners (or metal slides), the drawers require $1/2$" clearance on each side. I used the lip to cover this clearance.

This could also be accomplished by

using a false front. But that requires more material because you're actually making two drawer fronts.

JOINERY. The next step is to determine what kind of joinery to use to assemble the drawer. I consider three factors for the joinery: strength, the time and tools required to build it, and the appearance of the joint.

STRENGTH. It's not just a matter of making the joint strong enough to hold together. The key factor is that the joint be strong enough to withstand the weight that's in the drawer, especially if it's jerked open or slammed shut.

This is the most critical factor for the drawers on these cabinets because of

the heavy tools that will be in them.

SPECIAL TOOLS. All the joints below are strong enough, but they vary in the time and tools required to build them.

The nailed butt and locked rabbet joints can be cut easily on a table saw. But the sliding dovetail requires a dovetail bit and router table. And, of course, half-blind dovetails require a special jig.

APPEARANCE. Finally, how important is the appearance of the joint? On the shop cabinets, appearance is not critical, unless you want to show them off.

So what's the final decision? I decided to use the nailed butt joint because it's the easiest. But here are all four options.

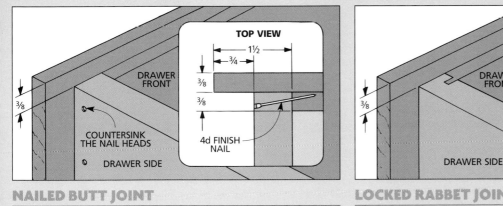

NAILED BUTT JOINT

Of all the joints shown, the nailed butt joint is the simplest to make, requiring no specialized tools. It should be glued to help prevent racking, but it gets virtually all its strength from the nails driven through the sides and into the drawer front. To keep these nails from working out, countersink the heads.

LOCKED RABBET JOINT

There are a couple of things I like about this joint. First, it provides a certain amount of interlocking strength. Second, it doesn't require any special tools, other than a table saw. The drawback to this joint is the glue surface — you're gluing mostly to end grain.

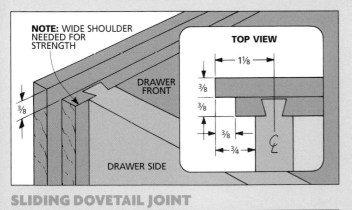

SLIDING DOVETAIL JOINT

All that's needed to make this joint is a router table and a dovetail bit. The pieces interlock and have good glue surfaces. However, it can be difficult to get the pieces to fit together well. And if the dovetailed dado on the drawer front is too close to the edge, the edge may break off.

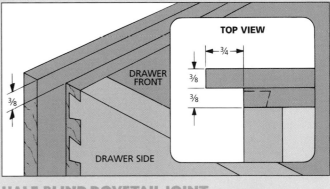

HALF-BLIND DOVETAIL JOINT

The half-blind dovetail joint stands out as one of the strongest and most decorative of all drawer joints. The pins and tails not only lock together, they provide an excellent glue surface. The only problem is that you need a special jig and a router, or you have to cut them by hand.

DOORS

If you don't need drawer space, you can easily add a door as the front panel. The cabinets I built use two door sizes. The finished width of each door is the same as the drawer fronts (15"). But the height of the doors will depend on the size of the opening.

STILES. To determine the finished height of the doors, add $1/2$" (for the lips) to the height of the door opening (*Fig. 10*). Now, cut two $2^1/2$"-wide stiles (T or W) to this measurement.

RAILS. After cutting the stiles to length, the next step is to make the rails (U or X). To determine the length of these $2^1/2$"- wide rails, take the width of the door (15") and subtract the width of both stiles (5"). To allow for tenons on the ends of the rails, add $1/2$" (*Fig. 10*).

CUT THE GROOVE. Once the rails are cut to length, cut a groove on the inside edge of each stile and rail. This groove is centered on the thickness of each piece and cut to match the thickness of the panel (*Fig. 11a*). Next, tenons are cut on the ends of the rails to fit the grooves in the stiles (*Fig. 11*).

PANEL. With the tenons complete, the panel (V or Y) can be cut to size. To do this, dry assemble the door frame and measure the opening. Add $1/2$" to the length and width (*Fig. 10*), and cut a $1/4$" hardboard panel to that size. Then glue up the pieces to make the door.

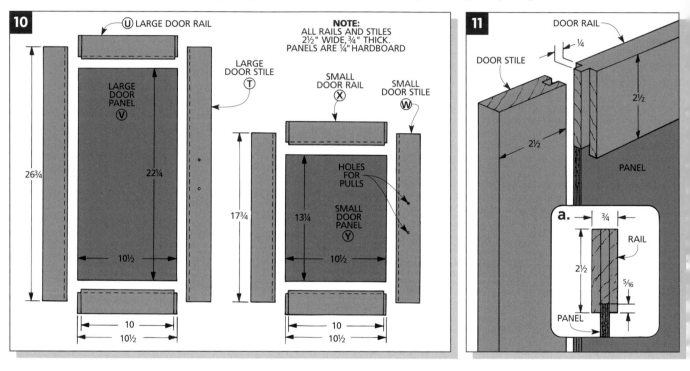

SHOP TIP . . . . *Making Your Own Drawer Pulls*

To safely make the pulls (S), I started with long strips and then cut each one to finished length. To do this, rip $3/4$"-thick scrap to a width of 1" (*Fig. 1*).

Then, rout finger grips on the back edges of each strip. I used a router table and a $1/4$" cove bit set for a $1/2$"-deep cut (*Step 1 in Fig. 2*).

Next, turn the strips over and round over the front edges with a $1/4$" round-over bit (*Step 2*).

Now the pulls can be cut to length (4").

Next, I wanted to rout a $1/4$" roundover on the *ends* of the pulls. There are a couple of tricks here.

First, to keep the pieces from slipping into the opening in the fence, I clamped on an auxiliary hardboard fence with a notch cut in it that was slightly larger than the bit.

Also, I used a backer board to hold the pieces square while routing.

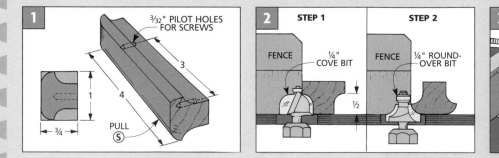

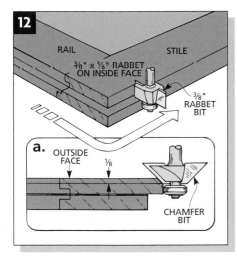

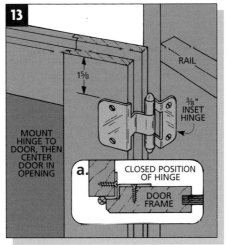

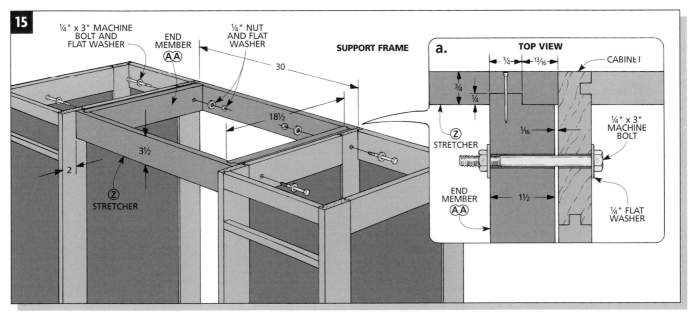

DOOR LIP. To form the door lip, rout a $3/8$" x $3/8$" rabbet around the inside face *(Fig. 12)*. Then rout a chamfer around the outside face *(Fig. 12a)*.

MOUNT THE DOOR. Once the doors are finished, I attached them to the cabinet with $3/8$" inset hinges. To do this, position each hinge $1^5/8$" from the shoulders on the top and bottom edges of the door. Then, drill pilot holes and screw the hinges to the door *(Fig. 13)*.

Now, center the door in the opening and mark the hinge hole locations on the inside of the cabinet. Then drill pilot holes and screw the hinges to the cabinet.

PULLS. Next, I made wood pulls (S) for the drawers and doors (see Shop Tip on opposite page). Each pull is centered on the width and length of the door stile *(Fig. 14)* or drawer front.

DOOR CATCH. To hold the door closed, mount a roller catch inside the cabinet behind the pull *(Fig. 14)*.

JOINING TWO CABINETS

After completing a couple of the cabinets, I decided to add a top to make a workbench. There are a variety of ways to arrange the cabinets and add a top. (Two different options are shown in the Designer's Notebook on page 17.)

SUPPORT FRAME. If you plan to mount a top over two cabinets with an open space between them (as shown in the photo on page 8), you'll want to add a support frame between the cabinets *(Fig. 15)*. To do this, I used two $3/4$"-thick stretchers (Z) that fit between the cabinets, and two $1^1/2$"-thick end members (AA) to connect the stretchers.

STRETCHERS. To make the frame, determine how much space you want between the cabinets. (I have a 30" opening.) Then cut two stretchers (Z) to this length *(Fig. 15)*.

Note: For convenience, I added

electricity to the workbench by installing an outlet box into the front stretcher (see photo on page 8).

The stretchers are joined to the end members with a rabbet and dado joint *(Fig. 15a)*. When cutting this joint, I positioned the dado so the end member would be set in $1/16$" from the ends of the stretchers. This allows the frame to pull tight against the cabinet *(Fig. 15a)*.

END MEMBERS. After cutting dadoes in the stretchers, cut the end members (AA) $18^1/2$" long. Then rabbet the ends to form a tongue that will fit in the dadoes *(Fig. 15a)*. Finally, glue and nail the frame together.

ATTACH THE FRAME. To attach the frame between the cabinets, align the frame flush with the back of the cabinets and temporarily clamp it in place. Then drill holes for hexhead machine bolts, and bolt the cabinets and frame together *(Fig. 15a)*.

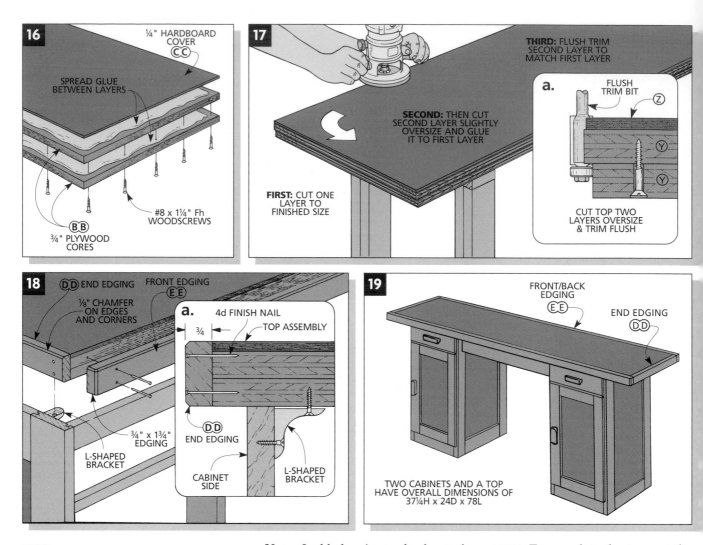

16 ¼" HARDBOARD COVER (CC)

SPREAD GLUE BETWEEN LAYERS

#8 x 1¼" Fh WOODSCREWS

(BB)

¾" PLYWOOD CORES

17 FIRST: CUT ONE LAYER TO FINISHED SIZE

SECOND: THEN CUT SECOND LAYER SLIGHTLY OVERSIZE AND GLUE IT TO FIRST LAYER

THIRD: FLUSH TRIM SECOND LAYER TO MATCH FIRST LAYER

a. FLUSH TRIM BIT (Z)

(Y)

(Y)

CUT TOP TWO LAYERS OVERSIZE & TRIM FLUSH

18 (DD) END EDGING   FRONT EDGING (EE)

⅛" CHAMFER ON EDGES AND CORNERS

¾" x 1¾" EDGING

L-SHAPED BRACKET

a. 4d FINISH NAIL   TOP ASSEMBLY

¾

(DD) END EDGING

CABINET SIDE

L-SHAPED BRACKET

19 FRONT/BACK EDGING (EE)

END EDGING (DD)

TWO CABINETS AND A TOP HAVE OVERALL DIMENSIONS OF 37¼H x 24D x 78L

TOP

After the support frame is attached between the cabinets, all that's left to build is the top. I built the top from two ¾" plywood cores (BB) (you could use particleboard), and a cover (CC) of ¼" hardboard *(Fig. 16)*. Then I trimmed the assembly with edging (DD, EE) made out of ¾"-thick pine *(Fig. 18)*.

BUILDING UP THE TOP. If you're building a small top for one cabinet (see page 17), the layers can simply be glued and screwed together, and the edges trimmed to size on a table saw. But if you make a larger top like the one in *Fig. 19*, it may be too heavy and awkward to be managed on the table saw.

There is a simpler method for getting the edges of all three pieces aligned flush. First, cut the bottom piece of plywood to final size. Next, cut the other two pieces oversize, and glue and screw them onto the bottom piece. Then trim the edges of all three pieces flush, using a router with a flush trim bit *(Fig. 17a)*.

Note: I added a vise to the front of the bench (see photo on page 8). To do this, cut a notch deep enough so the wooden back face of the vise will end up flush with the front of the edging. (The edging will then be cut to fit around and butt against the vise.) Add a filler piece below to make it flush with the top.

TRIM. To complete the top, cut the ¾"-thick pine edging (DD, EE) to width to match the combined thickness of the three top pieces, and glue and nail the edging to the glued-up top *(Fig. 18a)*. Then rout a ⅛" chamfer on each of the corners, and along the top and bottom of the edging *(Fig. 18a)*. ■

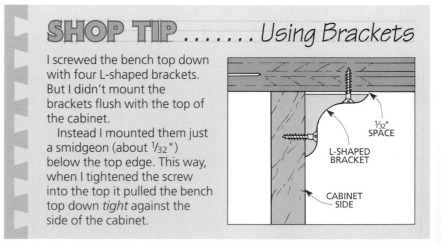

SHOP TIP . . . . *Using Brackets*

I screwed the bench top down with four L-shaped brackets. But I didn't mount the brackets flush with the top of the cabinet.

Instead I mounted them just a smidgeon (about ¹⁄₃₂") below the top edge. This way, when I tightened the screw into the top it pulled the bench top down *tight* against the side of the cabinet.

¹⁄₃₂" SPACE

L-SHAPED BRACKET

CABINET SIDE

DESIGNER'S NOTEBOOK

Whether you need extra storage space or a single-tool station, this versatile case design can be combined into many possibilities.

VARIATIONS

The thing I like more than anything else about these shop cabinets is the fact that they all start out the same — a basic, easy-to-build case as shown in the drawing at right.

But from this basic case design, you can come up with a number of possible variations and combinations. It's simple to change the number — as well as the size — of both the drawers and the doors to fit your own shop's individual storage needs.

And, once one cabinet is built, you can complete it with a smaller top that will hold a single benchtop tool such as a scroll saw (below right). This is an ideal design for small shops.

If you build a couple of cabinets and add a top, they can be combined into a workbench with an open area underneath (as shown in the photo on page 8), or four of them can be fastened together in a square shape to become a work center (below left).

BASIC CASE

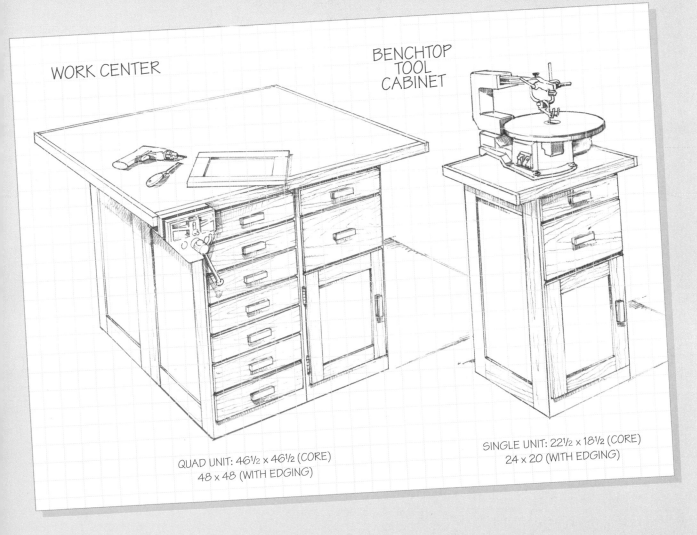

WORK CENTER

BENCHTOP TOOL CABINET

QUAD UNIT: 46½ x 46½ (CORE)
48 x 48 (WITH EDGING)

SINGLE UNIT: 22½ x 18½ (CORE)
24 x 20 (WITH EDGING)

Fold-Down Work Center

This space-saving work center offers both storage and security, plus its own light source. And the fold-down bench provides a large work surface when you need it.

This compact storage case and workbench was designed to fold down in a garage, but it would work just as well in a basement workshop or utility room.

The beauty of this project is its versatility. It's perfect for the craftsperson or model-maker in your family. It also makes a great potting bench for a gardener. Or it can be set up in your shop for wood carving or as a sanding or finishing station.

FOLD-DOWN. To take up minimal space wherever it's used, the work center mounts up out of the way on the wall (see photo on opposite page). When it's time to work, the front folds down to create a large, stable workbench.

STORAGE. To keep your tools right at hand, there are a pair of tool boards that swing out for easy access. Inside the case there are shelves and platforms designed to hold a vise, grinder, or other tools. There's even a set of drawers for hardware and accessories.

MATERIALS & FINISH. To build the work center I used maple plywood, hardboard, and solid maple. For protection, I finished it with two coats of satin polyurethane varnish.

EXPLODED VIEW

OVERALL DIMENSIONS:
Closed: 69½H x 58½W x 15¾D
Open: 69½H x 58½W x 38D

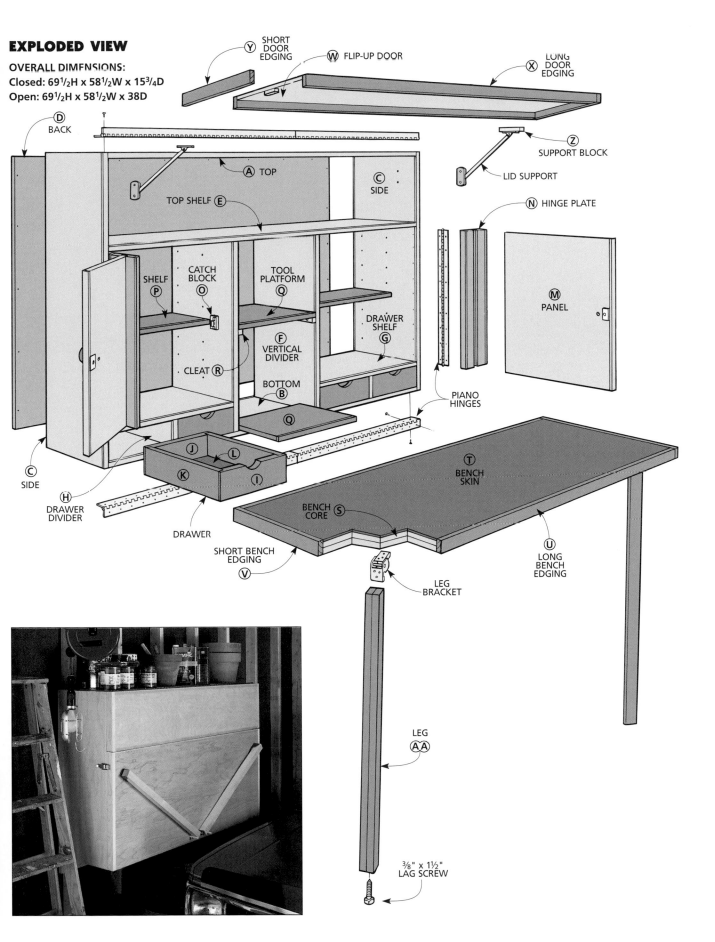

Y SHORT DOOR EDGING

W FLIP-UP DOOR

X LONG DOOR EDGING

D BACK

A TOP

C SIDE

Z SUPPORT BLOCK

LID SUPPORT

N HINGE PLATE

TOP SHELF **E**

SHELF **P**

CATCH BLOCK **O**

TOOL PLATFORM **Q**

DRAWER SHELF **G**

M PANEL

CLEAT **R**

VERTICAL DIVIDER **F**

BOTTOM **B**

Q

PIANO HINGES

C SIDE

H DRAWER DIVIDER

J **L**

K **I**

T BENCH SKIN

DRAWER

BENCH CORE **S**

SHORT BENCH EDGING **V**

U LONG BENCH EDGING

LEG BRACKET

LEG **AA**

⅜" x 1½" LAG SCREW

CUTTING DIAGRAM

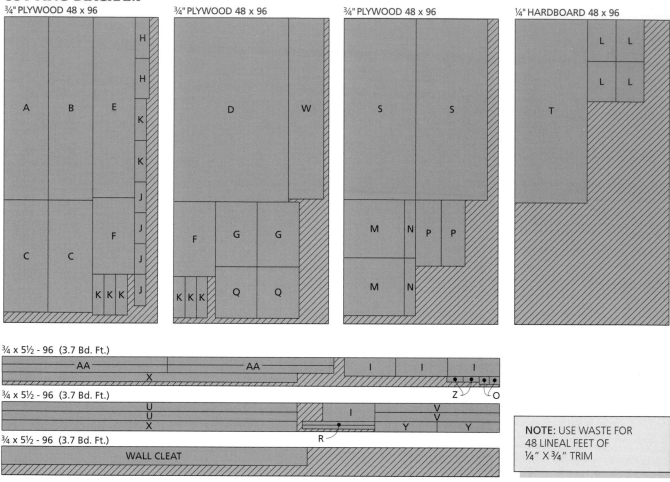

¾" PLYWOOD 48 x 96 ¾" PLYWOOD 48 x 96 ¾" PLYWOOD 48 x 96 ¼" HARDBOARD 48 x 96

¾ x 5½ - 96 (3.7 Bd. Ft.)

¾ x 5½ - 96 (3.7 Bd. Ft.)

¾ x 5½ - 96 (3.7 Bd. Ft.)

WALL CLEAT

NOTE: USE WASTE FOR 48 LINEAL FEET OF ¼" X ¾" TRIM

MATERIALS LIST

FOLD-DOWN WORK CENTER:
CASE

A	Top (1)	¾ ply - 13¾ x 58¼
B	Bottom (1)	¾ ply - 13¾ x 58¼
C	Sides (2)	¾ ply - 13¾ x 36
D	Back (1)	¾ ply - 35¾ x 58¼
E	Top Shelf (1)	¾ ply - 13 x 57½
F	Vert. Dividers (2)	¾ ply - 13 x 23⁷⁄₁₆
G	Drwr. Shelves (2)	¾ ply - 13 x 20¼
H	Drwr. Dividers (2)	¾ ply - 4 x 13

STORAGE

I	Drawer Fronts (4)	¾ x 3⁷⁄₁₆ - 9⁷⁄₁₆
J	Drawer Backs (4)	¾ ply - 3⁷⁄₁₆ x 9⁷⁄₁₆
K	Drawer Sides (8)	¾ ply - 3⁷⁄₁₆ x 12¾
L	Drawer Btms. (4)	¼ hdbd. - 8⁷⁄₁₆ x 12¼
M	Panels (2)	¾ ply - 18½ x 18
N	Hinge Plates (2)	¾ ply - 3¾ x 18
O	Catch Blocks (2)	⅜ x 1½ - 2

P	Shelves (2)	¾ ply - 7¾ x 19⁵⁄₈
Q	Tool Platforms (2)	¾ ply - 13 x 15⁷⁄₈
R	Platfm. Cleats (2)	¾ x ¾ - 13¼

BENCH

S	Bench Cores (2)	¾ ply - 22½ x 57
T	Bench Skin (1)	¼ hdbd. - 22½ x 57
U	Edging, long (2)	¾ x 1¾ - 57
V	Edging, short (2)	¾ x 1¾ - 24

FLIP-UP DOOR

W	Door (1)	¾ ply - 10⅜ x 57
X	Edging, long (2)	¾ x 1¾ - 57
Y	Edging, short (2)	¾ x 1¾ - 11⁷⁄₈
Z	Support Block (2)	¾ x 1 - 3
AA	Legs (2)	1½ x 1½ - 31¼

HARDWARE SUPPLIES
(6) No. 6 x ⅝" Fh woodscrews
(4) No. 6 x 1" Fh woodscrews
(6) No. 8 x 1¼" Fh woodscrews

(58) No. 8 x 2" Fh woodscrews
(12) No. 10 x 1¼" Rh woodscrews
(2) ⅜" x 1½" Lag screws
(1 lb.) 4d Finish nails
(2 oz.) 1" x No. 18 Wire brads
(2) 1½" x 30" Piano hinges
(2) 1½" x 28" Piano hinges
(2) 1½" x 18" Piano hinges
(8) Shelf rests
(2) Magnetic catches with screws
(2) Draw catches with screws
(2) Folding leg brackets
(1) ½"-Dia. x 6"-long dowel rod
(2) 1¼" Wood knobs with screws
(2) Self-locking lid supports (left and right)
Mounting hardware to attach work center to wall
Optional: Four foot shop light
　　　　　 Magnetic tool bars

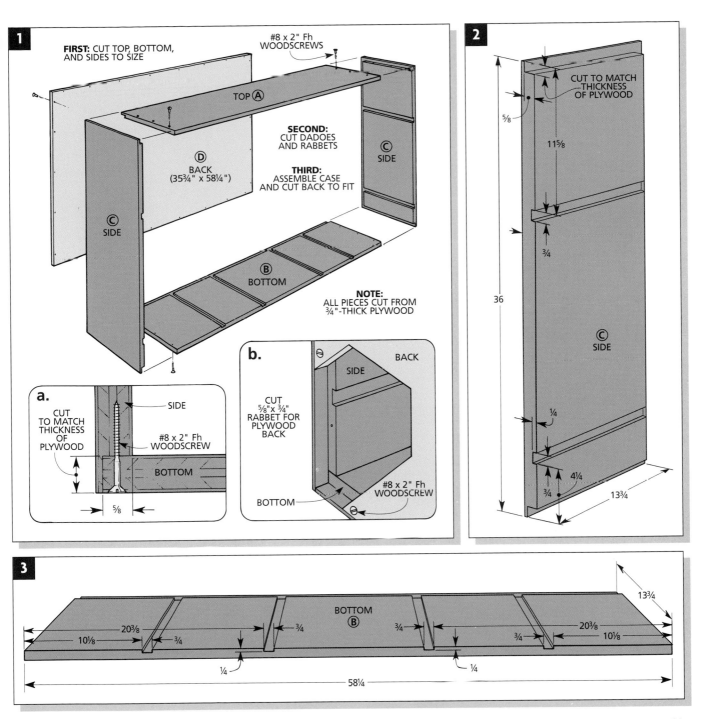

1

FIRST: CUT TOP, BOTTOM, AND SIDES TO SIZE

#8 x 2" Fh WOODSCREWS

TOP Ⓐ

SECOND: CUT DADOES AND RABBETS

BACK (35¾" x 58¼")

THIRD: ASSEMBLE CASE AND CUT BACK TO FIT

Ⓒ SIDE

Ⓒ SIDE

Ⓑ BOTTOM

NOTE: ALL PIECES CUT FROM ¾"-THICK PLYWOOD

a.
CUT TO MATCH THICKNESS OF PLYWOOD
SIDE
#8 x 2" Fh WOODSCREW
BOTTOM
⅝

b.
BACK
SIDE
CUT ⅝" x ¾" RABBET FOR PLYWOOD BACK
BOTTOM
#8 x 2" Fh WOODSCREW

2
CUT TO MATCH THICKNESS OF PLYWOOD
⅝
11⅝
¾
36
Ⓒ SIDE
¼
4¼
¾
13¾

3
13¾
20⅜
10⅛
¾
BOTTOM Ⓑ
¾
¾
20⅜
10⅛
¼
¼
58¼

CASE

The work center consists of a case, a fold-down bench, and a flip-up door. I started by building the case. It's just an open box with dividers.

CUT PIECES. To make the case, begin by cutting the pieces that make up the open box to size *(Fig. 1)*. The top (A), bottom (B), and sides (C) are all cut from ¾"-thick plywood (I used maple).

DADOES. The sides (C) and bottom (B) both have dadoes cut in them to accept shelves and dividers that will be added later *(Figs. 2 and 3)*. To make it easier to slip the shelves and dividers into the box after it's been assembled, it's best to cut these dadoes just a hair wider than the thickness of your plywood. (Since my plywood actually measured a little less than ¾" thick, I cut ¾"-wide dadoes.)

RABBETS. Since I planned on screwing the top and bottom of the case to the sides, the next step is to cut rabbets on both ends of the side pieces *(Figs. 1 and 2)*. These rabbets are cut extra deep (⅝") *(Fig. 1a)*. This way, I could use long screws (for strength) and run them straight in.

But before you can assemble the case, there's one more thing to do. You'll need to cut ⅝" x ¾" rabbets on the back edges of all the case pieces (A, B, and C) *(Fig. 1b)*. These rabbets are for a plywood back that's added after the case is assembled.

ASSEMBLY. Once all of the rabbets are cut, glue and screw the top and bottom to the sides. Then cut a back (D) from ¾" plywood to fit the case and glue and screw it in place.

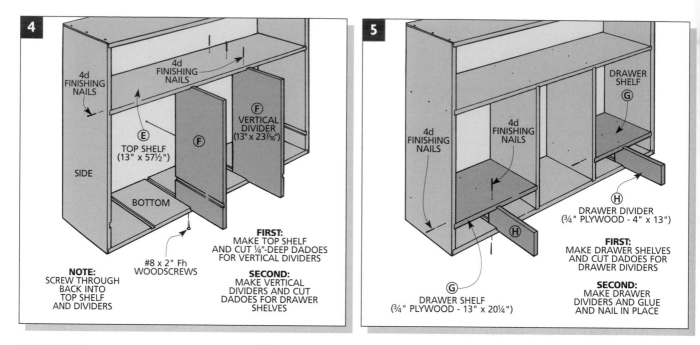

4

4d FINISHING NAILS

4d FINISHING NAILS

TOP SHELF (13" x 57½")

VERTICAL DIVIDER (13" x 23⁷⁄₁₆")

SIDE

BOTTOM

#8 x 2" Fh WOODSCREWS

NOTE: SCREW THROUGH BACK INTO TOP SHELF AND DIVIDERS

FIRST: MAKE TOP SHELF AND CUT ¼"-DEEP DADOES FOR VERTICAL DIVIDERS

SECOND: MAKE VERTICAL DIVIDERS AND CUT DADOES FOR DRAWER SHELVES

5

DRAWER SHELF

4d FINISHING NAILS

4d FINISHING NAILS

DRAWER SHELF (¾" PLYWOOD - 13" x 20¼")

DRAWER DIVIDER (¾" PLYWOOD - 4" x 13")

FIRST: MAKE DRAWER SHELVES AND CUT DADOES FOR DRAWER DIVIDERS

SECOND: MAKE DRAWER DIVIDERS AND GLUE AND NAIL IN PLACE

SHELVES & DIVIDERS

With the basic box complete, you can start adding the shelves and dividers *(Figs. 4 and 5)*. Since most of these pieces will have dadoes cut in them to match those in the case, they need to be cut in order using a simple method to locate the dadoes. The trick is to slip each piece into the case and mark the dado locations with it in place.

TOP SHELF. Start by cutting a top shelf (E) to length to fit between the upper dadoes in the sides *(Fig. 4)*. The width equals the distance from the back rabbet to the front of the case (13").

The next step is to cut dadoes in this shelf for the vertical dividers (F) that fit between the top shelf and the bottom *(Fig. 4)*. Since you've already cut the dadoes in the bottom (B), the tricky part is cutting a matching set in the top shelf. Note: The easiest way I've found to accomplish this is to use a story stick (see Shop Tip below).

Once the layout is complete on the top shelf, cut ¼"-deep dadoes at both of the marks.

Then the top shelf can be glued and nailed in place. Note: For extra strength, I screwed through the back (D) and into the edge of the top shelf.

VERTICAL DIVIDERS. Now you can cut a pair of dividers (F) to fit between the top shelf and bottom (B) *(Fig. 4)*.

Before you install them, use a story stick again to locate and cut dadoes for the drawer shelves. Then, glue and screw the dividers to the back and bottom of the case. (I used nails to secure the top shelf.)

DRAWER SHELVES & DIVIDERS. With the vertical dividers installed, use the same procedure along with the story stick to cut two drawers shelves (G) first and then two drawer dividers (H) *(Fig. 5)*. When they're cut to size, glue and nail them in place.

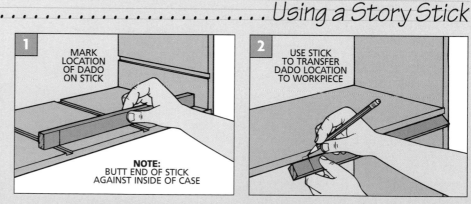

SHOP TIP .... *Using a Story Stick*

When laying out matching dadoes, I like to use a story stick. It's simply a piece of scrap that I use like a ruler, but it only has marks on it where the dadoes need to be cut.

The real advantage of a story stick is you don't have to measure anything. (It's easy to make a mistake when using measurements and adding them up.) With a story stick it's just a matter of marking the locations of the dadoes on the stick and then trans-

1 MARK LOCATION OF DADO ON STICK

NOTE: BUTT END OF STICK AGAINST INSIDE OF CASE

2 USE STICK TO TRANSFER DADO LOCATION TO WORKPIECE

ferring the locations to the matching piece.

To use a story stick on the work center, start by butting one end of the

stick against the inside of the case and marking the exact locations of the dadoes *(Fig. 1)*.

Then with the same end

of the stick against the case, move the stick to where the dadoes need to be cut and transfer the marks *(Fig. 2)*.

TRIM

All that's left to complete the case is to cover all of the exposed plywood edges on the front of the case with trim (I used maple) *(Fig. 6)*. The trim is $1/4$" thick and cut to width so it matches the thickness of the plywood. Then it's attached to the case with glue and brads.

Note: You will eventually need a total of about 48 lineal feet of this trim to cover all of the exposed plywood edges on the work center.

TOOL BOARDS

In order to keep all my tools handy, I mounted them on the T-shaped tool boards that swing out of the large openings on either side of the case (see photo at right).

Each tool board consists of a panel for mounting tools and a hinge plate for attaching the panel to the case *(Fig. 7)*.

PANELS. Both panels (M) are cut from $3/4$" plywood to a length (height) of 18". To determine the width, measure the width of your opening and subtract $1^{1}/_4$" for clearance. (In my case, I cut the panel $18^{1}/_2$" wide.)

HINGE PLATES. The plywood hinge plate (N) is $3^{3}/_4$" wide and cut to match the height of the panel (18"). Then a $1/4$"-deep groove is cut centered on the plate to accept the panel *(Fig. 7a)*.

ASSEMBLY. Once the grooves are cut, glue and screw one hinge plate to each panel. Then cover the exposed plywood edges by gluing and nailing on $1/4$"-thick trim *(Fig. 7)*.

MOUNT BOARDS. I used an 18"-long piano hinge to attach each tool board to the case *(Fig. 8)*. To do this, center a hinge between the top shelf and drawer shelf with the knuckle flush with the

front of the case *(Fig. 8a)*. Then screw it to the case.

Next, for each tool board to be able to swing open completely, insert a temporary $1/8$" spacer between the board and case before screwing the hinge to the tool board *(Fig. 8a)*.

KNOB AND CATCH. To pull open the boards, a wood knob is screwed to the front of each board *(Fig. 7)*. And to keep the boards closed, I used a magnetic catch *(Fig. 9)*. Note: Each catch is screwed to a catch block (O) that's glued to the case *(Fig. 9a)*.

TOOLBARS. Finally, I bought magnetic toolbars to hold my tools on the panels (for sources, see page 126).

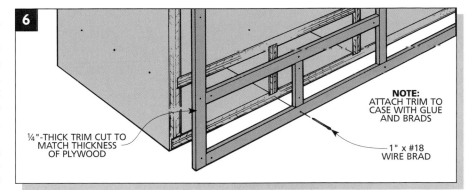

6

$1/4$"-THICK TRIM CUT TO MATCH THICKNESS OF PLYWOOD

NOTE: ATTACH TRIM TO CASE WITH GLUE AND BRADS

1" x #18 WIRE BRAD

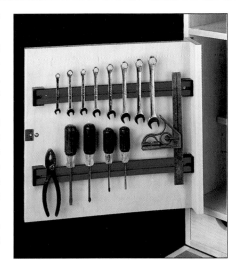

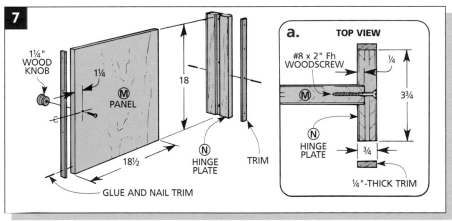

7

$1^{1}/_4$" WOOD KNOB

$1^{1}/_4$

(M) PANEL

18

$18^{1}/_2$

(N) HINGE PLATE

TRIM

GLUE AND NAIL TRIM

a. TOP VIEW

#8 x 2" Fh WOODSCREW

$1/4$

(M)

$3^{3}/_4$

(N) HINGE PLATE

$3/4$

$1/4$"-THICK TRIM

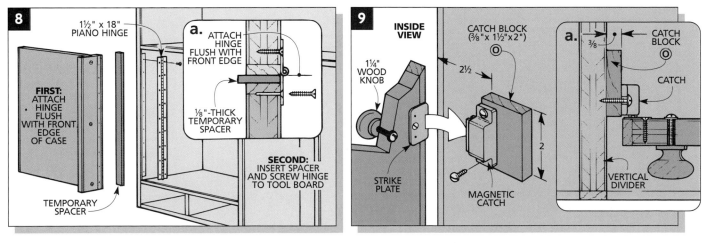

8

$1^{1}/_2$" x 18" PIANO HINGE

FIRST: ATTACH HINGE FLUSH WITH FRONT EDGE OF CASE

TEMPORARY SPACER

a. ATTACH HINGE FLUSH WITH FRONT EDGE

$1/8$"-THICK TEMPORARY SPACER

SECOND: INSERT SPACER AND SCREW HINGE TO TOOL BOARD

9 INSIDE VIEW

$1^{1}/_4$" WOOD KNOB

STRIKE PLATE

CATCH BLOCK ($3/8$" x $1^{1}/_2$" x 2")

$2^{1}/_2$

MAGNETIC CATCH

a. $3/8$

CATCH BLOCK

CATCH

2

VERTICAL DIVIDER

DRAWERS

With the case complete, I began working on a set of pull-out drawers that fit in the openings near the bottom of the case.

Each drawer consists of a hardwood front (I), and a back (J) and two sides (K) cut from $3/4$"-thick plywood (*Fig. 10*). For clearance, each piece is cut $1/16$" shorter than the height of the opening ($3^7/16$"). Likewise, the front and back are cut $1/16$" narrower than the width of the opening (in my case, $9^7/16$").

RABBETS. To join the drawer parts together, $1/2$"-deep rabbets need to be cut in the ends of each front and back piece (*Fig. 10*).

NOTCH. Before you can assemble each drawer with glue and nails, there are two more things to do. First, to make the drawers easy to pull out, a centered notch is cut in each drawer front (I) (*Fig. 10a*).

BOTTOM. Second, a $1/4$" x $1/4$" groove is cut near the bottom inside edge of each drawer piece (*Fig. 10b*). This groove is for a bottom (L) made from $1/4$"-thick hardboard that's cut to fit inside each of the drawers (*Fig. 10*).

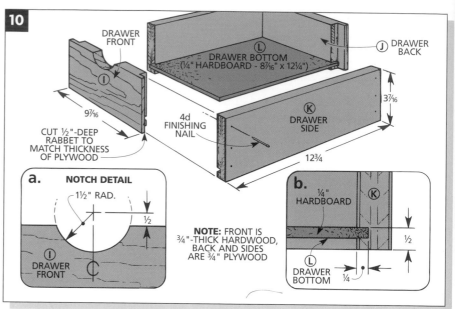
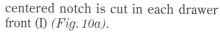

10

DRAWER FRONT

DRAWER BOTTOM (1/4" HARDBOARD - 8$7/16$" x 12$1/4$")

(J) DRAWER BACK

(I)

CUT $1/2$"-DEEP RABBET TO MATCH THICKNESS OF PLYWOOD

9$7/16$"

4d FINISHING NAIL

(K) DRAWER SIDE

3$7/16$"

12$3/4$"

a. NOTCH DETAIL

1$1/2$" RAD.

$1/2$

(I) DRAWER FRONT

b.

$1/4$" HARDBOARD

(K)

$1/2$

(L) DRAWER BOTTOM

$1/4$

NOTE: FRONT IS $3/4$"-THICK HARDWOOD, BACK AND SIDES ARE $3/4$" PLYWOOD

SHELVES & TOOL PLATFORMS

For additional storage, I added an adjustable shelf behind each tool board.

SHELVES. Each plywood shelf (P) is $7^3/4$" wide (deep) and cut to fit between the sides and vertical dividers, less $1/8$" for clearance ($19^5/8$") (*Fig. 11*). Once they're cut to size, the front edge is covered with $1/4$"-thick trim.

The shelves sit on metal shelf rests that fit into holes in the case. To drill the holes so they're evenly spaced, I made a template (*Figs. 12 and 12a*).

The template is a scrap of $3/4$"-thick plywood with a series of $1/4$" holes. Just press it against the case (or vertical divider) and with the aid of a depth stop, drill the holes. Note: Always butt the same edge against the back (D).

TOOL PLATFORMS. Finally, to make it easy to clamp a vise or grinder to the bench, I mount them on tool platforms (Q) that fit in the center opening of the case (see photo above left).

The lower tool platform rests in the bottom of the case. But the upper tool platform sits on a pair of $3/4$"-square tool platform cleats (R) that are screwed to the vertical dividers (*Figs. 11 and 11a*).

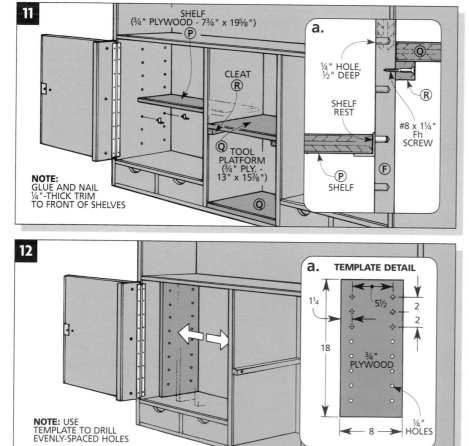

11

SHELF ($3/4$" PLYWOOD - 7$3/4$" x 19$5/8$")

(P)

CLEAT (R)

(Q) TOOL PLATFORM ($3/4$" PLY. - 13" x 15$7/8$")

(Q)

a.

$1/4$" HOLE, $1/2$" DEEP

SHELF REST

(R)

#8 x 1$1/4$" Fh SCREW

(F)

(P) SHELF

NOTE: GLUE AND NAIL $1/4$"-THICK TRIM TO FRONT OF SHELVES

12

NOTE: USE TEMPLATE TO DRILL EVENLY-SPACED HOLES

a. TEMPLATE DETAIL

1$1/4$

5$1/2$

2

2

18

$3/4$" PLYWOOD

8

$1/4$" HOLES

CASE FRONT

After completing work on the inside of the case, work can begin on the case front. The front consists of a fold-down bench and a flip-up door *(Fig. 13)*.

BENCH. To create a bench top that's solid and durable, I glued up a three-layer slab. Two pieces of $3/4$" plywood form a solid core (S). And a $1/4$"-thick hardboard skin (T) provides a durable work surface *(Figs. 13 and 13b)*. Note: For one technique to get the three layers the same size, see how it was done on the Cabinets and Bench as shown on page 16.

The width of the slab is $22^1/2$". The length is $1^1/2$" less than the overall width of the case *(Fig. 13)*. This allows for $3/4$"-thick edging (U, V) to be glued to the slab *(Fig. 13b)*.

DOOR. Once the bench is complete, the next step is to add the door. It covers the storage area at the top of the case. And it flips up to provide a handy place to mount a shop light (see photo above).

The door (W) is just a single piece of $3/4$"-thick plywood *(Fig. 13)*. And just like the bench, it's wrapped with hardwood edging (X, Y) *(Fig. 13a)*.

ASSEMBLY. Now the bench and door can be attached to the case. To provide as much support as possible, I used piano hinges. The easiest way to mount these hinges is to lay the case down on its back and clamp the bench and door in place *(Figs. 14 and 14a)*.

While I was at it, I installed two draw catches to hold the bench tight against the case when the work center is folded up *(Fig. 14b)*. Then to hold the door open, I used a pair of special self-locking lid supports *(Fig. 15)*. One end is screwed inside the case. The other screws into a support-block (Z) glued to the door *(Fig. 15a)*.

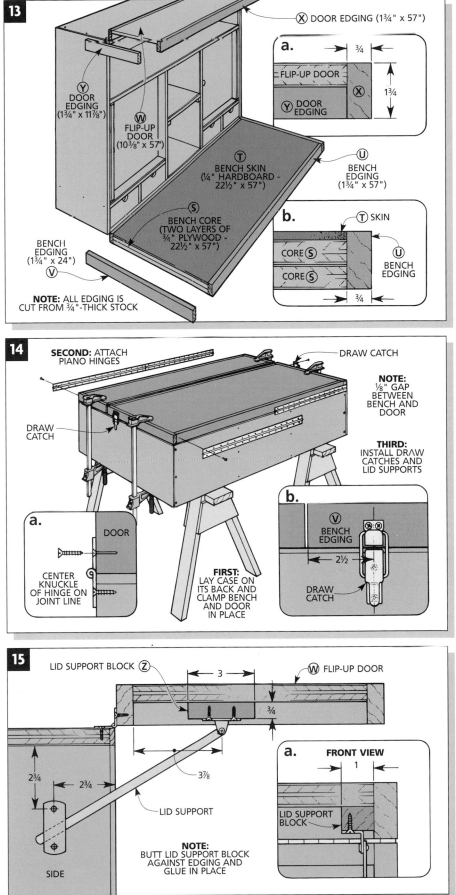

LEGS

To support the bench when it's in the open position, I added a pair of folding legs *(Fig. 16)*.

GLUE UP LEGS. The legs (AA) are glued up from two pieces of ³/₄"-thick stock. After the glue had dried, I screwed a lag screw into the bottom of each leg to act as a leveler on uneven floors *(Figs. 18 and 19)*.

MOUNT LEGS. With the levelers in place, the next step is to mount the legs to the bottom of the bench. The legs are attached with heavy-duty folding brackets that work similar to those found on a card table. The beauty of these brackets is that they can be locked in either the open or closed postion.

To attach the brackets, first screw one to each leg *(Fig. 16)*. Then position the legs correctly and screw them in place *(Fig. 17)*.

LEG STOPS. Once my work center was mounted on the wall with the bench folded up, I noticed the legs tended to droop a little low. So before mounting it on the wall, I would recommend adding a pair of stops made from ¹/₂"-dia. dowels *(Figs. 16 and 18)*.

MOUNTING THE WORK CENTER

Now that the work center is complete, it can be mounted to a wall. To support the case while attaching it to the wall, I used a cleat *(Figs. 19 and 19a)*. This cleat also allows you to accurately position the height of the work center and keep it level.

WALL CLEAT. The cleat is just a piece of ³/₄"-thick hardwood cut to match the width of the case (58¹/₂"). Bolt the cleat to the wall so it's level and the top edge is 33¹/₂" from the floor *(Fig. 19)*.

Note: If you're mounting the cleat to a wood framed wall, make sure that you screw into the wall studs. Then, with the help of a friend, lift up the case and set it on the cleat *(Fig. 19a)*.

Finally, to attach the case to the wall, lower the bench and lift up the door. Now it's just a matter of drilling holes through the back of the case, and installing lag screws and washers. (Here again, make sure you hit the studs.) ■

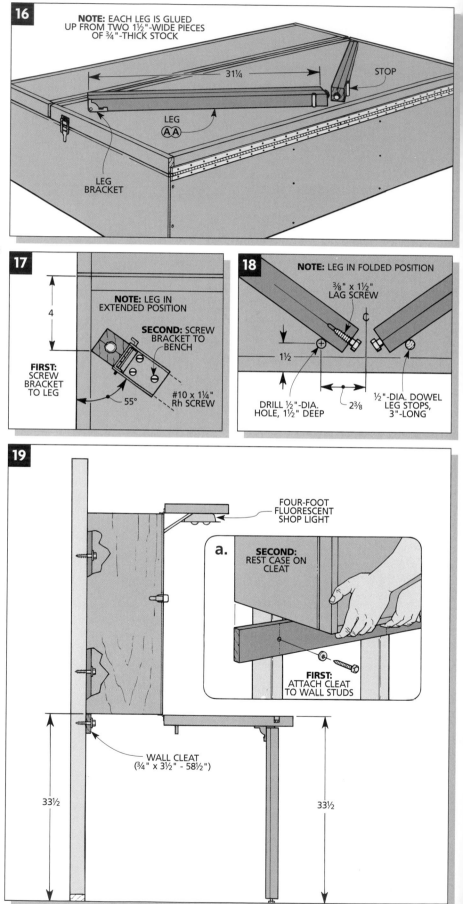

Maple Workbench

This classic European-style workbench is massive and stable, yet still affordable. The traditional dog system lets you clamp the largest workpieces with ease.

The main challenge I was faced with when I began designing this maple workbench was to start out with the classic European-style design, and end up with a project that was functional and buildable — but still affordable.

I wanted to keep all the features that contribute to a great heavy-duty workbench. A flat, stable, hardwood working surface. A convenient tool tray along the back edge. A front vise with a large wooden face. And finally, an end vise and a "dog" system.

DOG SYSTEM. That last feature is what I think makes this bench unique. Traditionally, benches like this have had a large L-shaped shoulder vise on one end of the bench. But this vise uses dogs (metal or wood blocks that fit into holes in the bench top) to hold the workpiece steady.

Shoulder vises tend to be expensive, and also have a tendency to get out of adjustment when changes in humidity occur. So for this workbench, I came up with a simpler end vise-and-dog block system. This system can actually be "adjusted" to better cope with those changes in humidity.

MATERIAL. Since I wanted my bench to be both heavy in weight and able to stand up to hard use over the years, I built it completely from hard maple and finished it with tung oil. Getting a maple benchtop flat was a challenge, but you'll find out how I did it on pages 29 to 31.

ANOTHER VERSION. If you want a less expensive and easier way to make the top, take a look at the laminated version on pages 42 and 43. It's built up from particleboard (or plywood) and hardboard.

EXPLODED VIEW

OVERALL DIMENSIONS:
34H x 65L x 29½D

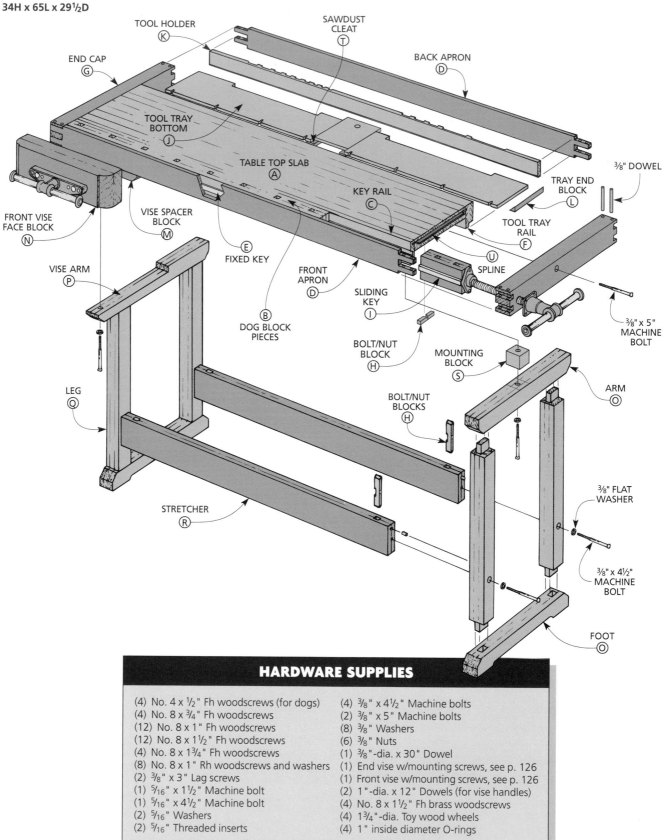

TOOL HOLDER
Ⓚ

SAWDUST CLEAT
Ⓣ

BACK APRON
Ⓓ

END CAP
Ⓖ

TOOL TRAY BOTTOM
Ⓙ

TABLE TOP SLAB
Ⓐ

KEY RAIL
Ⓒ

⅜" DOWEL

TRAY END BLOCK
Ⓛ

FRONT VISE FACE BLOCK
Ⓝ

VISE SPACER BLOCK
Ⓜ

FIXED KEY
Ⓔ

FRONT APRON
Ⓓ

TOOL TRAY RAIL
Ⓕ

Ⓤ

⅜" x 5" MACHINE BOLT

VISE ARM
Ⓟ

DOG BLOCK PIECES
Ⓑ

SLIDING KEY
Ⓘ

SPLINE

BOLT/NUT BLOCK
Ⓗ

MOUNTING BLOCK
Ⓢ

ARM
Ⓞ

LEG
Ⓠ

BOLT/NUT BLOCKS
Ⓗ

⅜" FLAT WASHER

STRETCHER
Ⓡ

⅜" x 4½" MACHINE BOLT

FOOT
Ⓞ

HARDWARE SUPPLIES

(4) No. 4 x ½" Fh woodscrews (for dogs)	(4) ⅜" x 4½" Machine bolts
(4) No. 8 x ¾" Fh woodscrews	(2) ⅜" x 5" Machine bolts
(12) No. 8 x 1" Fh woodscrews	(8) ⅜" Washers
(12) No. 8 x 1½" Fh woodscrews	(6) ⅜" Nuts
(4) No. 8 x 1¾" Fh woodscrews	(1) ⅜"-dia. x 30" Dowel
(8) No. 8 x 1" Rh woodscrews and washers	(1) End vise w/mounting screws, see p. 126
(2) ⅜" x 3" Lag screws	(1) Front vise w/mounting screws, see p. 126
(1) ⁵⁄₁₆" x 1½" Machine bolt	(2) 1"-dia. x 12" Dowels (for vise handles)
(1) ⁵⁄₁₆" x 4½" Machine bolt	(4) No. 8 x 1½" Fh brass woodscrews
(2) ⁵⁄₁₆" Washers	(4) 1¾"-dia. Toy wood wheels
(2) ⁵⁄₁₆" Threaded inserts	(4) 1" inside diameter O-rings

MATERIALS LIST

WOOD

A	Table Top Slab (1)	1⅝ x 12¼ - 60
B	Dog Blk. Pieces (3)	¾ x 3⅝ - 60 rough
C	Key Rail (1)	¾ x 3½ - 60
D	Fr./Bk. Aprons (2)	¾ x 3½ - 65⅛
E	Fixed Keys (2)	¾ x ¾ - 46
F	Tool Tray Rail (1)	1¾ x 3½ - 60
G	End Caps (2)	2½ x 3½ - 26
H	Bolt/Nut Blocks (6)	¾ x 1 - 4½
I	Sliding Keys (2)	¾ x ¾ - 7
J	Tool Tray Btm. (1)	½ x 8¼ - 62 rough
K	Tool Holder (1)	¾ x 2½ - 60
L	Tray End Blocks (2)	1¼ x 1¼ - 7¼ rough
M	Vise Spcr. Block (1)	1 x 3¹¹⁄₁₆ - 18
N	Vise Face Block (1)	3½ x 5 - 18
O	Feet/Right Arm (3)	2¼ x 2½ - 22½
P	Vise Arm (1)	2¼ x 2½ - 25½
Q	Legs (4)	2¼ x 2½ - 28½
R	Stretchers (2)	1⅝ x 4½ - 48½
S	Mount. Block (1)	1¾ x 1⅞ - 2⁷⁄₁₆
T	Sawdust Dr. Cl. (2)	½ x 1½ - 9⅛
U	Splines*	¼ " hdb. x ⅞

*Need approximately 12 feet.

CUTTING DIAGRAM

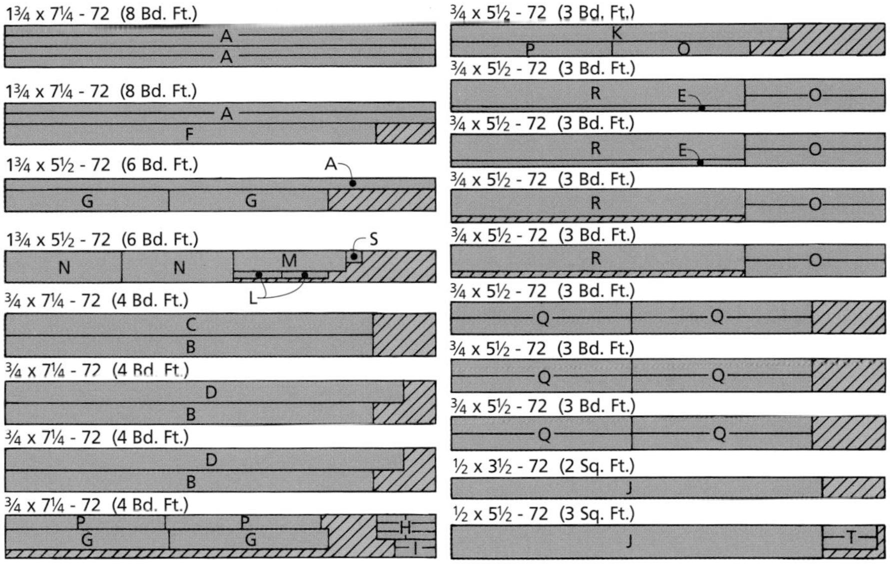

1¾ x 7¼ - 72 (8 Bd. Ft.) A / A

1¾ x 7¼ - 72 (8 Bd. Ft.) A / F

1¾ x 5½ - 72 (6 Bd. Ft.) A / G / G

1¾ x 5½ - 72 (6 Bd. Ft.) N / N / M / L / S

¾ x 7¼ - 72 (4 Bd. Ft.) C / B

¾ x 7¼ - 72 (4 Bd. Ft.) D / B

¾ x 7¼ - 72 (4 Bd. Ft.) D / B

¾ x 7¼ - 72 (4 Bd. Ft.) P / P / G / G / H / I

¾ x 5½ - 72 (3 Bd. Ft.) P / K / O

¾ x 5½ - 72 (3 Bd. Ft.) R / E / O

¾ x 5½ - 72 (3 Bd. Ft.) R / E / O

¾ x 5½ - 72 (3 Bd. Ft.) R / O

¾ x 5½ - 72 (3 Bd. Ft.) Q / Q

¾ x 5½ - 72 (3 Bd. Ft.) Q / Q

¾ x 5½ - 72 (3 Bd. Ft.) Q / Q

½ x 3½ - 72 (2 Sq. Ft.) J

½ x 5½ - 72 (3 Sq. Ft.) J / T

NOTE: ALSO NEED ¼" HARDBOARD (⅞" WIDE x 12 FEET) FOR SPLINES (U)

TABLE TOP SLAB

The most important feature of any bench is the top. (I'm calling it the slab.) It needs to be stable and strong, but most of all perfectly flat. In a factory this is easy — it's glued up in a gluing jig and then sanded flat on a wide-belt production surface sander.

In a home shop, it's another story — but it can be done. You need a little patience, a number of clamps, and a hand-held belt sander. (I didn't use a hand plane, more on this later.) By taking your time, the bench top can be made as flat and smooth as though it came from a factory in the Black Forest.

RIPPING THE STRIPS

To build the slab, I started by ripping 1⅝"-wide strips from 1¾"-thick stock to a length that was about a foot longer (6 feet) than what was needed. (Note: Cut the pieces long to allow for any end checks, imperfections, or planer snipes in the stock.) Since the main part of the workbench is 12¼" wide, I ripped seven boards (Fig. 1).

POSITIONING THE BOARDS. Before gluing up the boards to form a solid butcher block-type slab, there's a number of things to consider — especially when positioning the boards.

After ripping, two surfaces of each

board remain smooth and two will have sawblade marks. To create the best glue joint, flip the boards so the planed surfaces face each other (Fig. 1).

There's another reason for flipping the boards. If the edge grain faces up, there's less movement across the width of the slab with changes in humidity.

WHICH SIDE UP? Now, take a close look at each board and decide which of the sawn surfaces should face up. For the best appearance, choose the surface that has the straightest grain and the least chipout and defects.

CHECK FOR BOW. After ripping, the pieces will usually have a slight bow over their length. First, set the two straightest boards aside for the outside edges of the benchtop.

Next, line up the remaining pieces so the bow in one board opposes the bow in another when viewed from the top

(Fig. 2). Once they're glued up, the forces will neutralize one another and help keep the entire top straight.

Now, look at each piece from the end for any warp up and down. Once again, place the pieces so the warp (crown) on one faces up and the one next to it (sags) down.

A PROBLEM. Okay, I know, there's a problem. You can't get every piece where it's supposed to be. When you put all the opposing bows together, the crowns won't oppose each other. Or there's some chipout or a knot right in the middle of the top.

It turns into a puzzle — usually without a perfect solution. You have to find a solution that has the most desirable features. Once you find the solution that seems the best, mark the pieces so the whole assembly can be put back into order later.

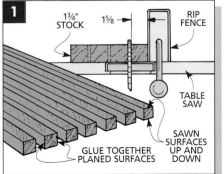

1 — 1¾" STOCK — 1⅝ — RIP FENCE — TABLE SAW — SAWN SURFACES UP AND DOWN — GLUE TOGETHER PLANED SURFACES

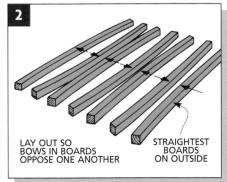

2 — LAY OUT SO BOWS IN BOARDS OPPOSE ONE ANOTHER — STRAIGHTEST BOARDS ON OUTSIDE

CLAMPING THE SLAB

Once the positions of all the pieces in the slab are determined, the clamps can be laid out. (Note: Now is the time to go out and beg for, borrow, or rent enough clamps to do the job. I used nine pipe clamps.)

SIGHTING. To produce a flat slab, the most important step is "sighting" the clamps. Start by finding the flattest surface available to clamp on. This might be a large table, a flat section of floor in the shop, or a couple sawhorses *(Fig. 3)*.

Now lay down two *flat* 8'-long 2x4s side by side about a foot apart. Then lay down two pipe (or bar) clamps across these base boards.

Before placing the pieces to be glued onto the clamps, stand back about five feet, get down until your eyes are even with the top of the clamps, and look for any twist from one clamp to the other *(Fig. 3)*. Both clamps should be aligned with each other. If they're not, shim under the base board at the low corner until the clamps are aligned.

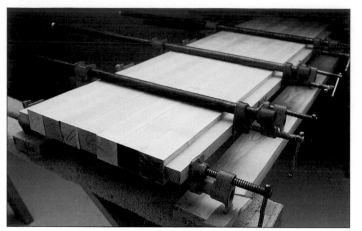

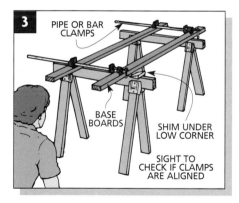

3 — PIPE OR BAR CLAMPS — BASE BOARDS — SHIM UNDER LOW CORNER — SIGHT TO CHECK IF CLAMPS ARE ALIGNED

POSITION THE CLAMPS. After aligning the end clamps, place clamps across the base boards every 16". Then set the workpieces in position on top of the clamps. Now place more clamps on top of the workpieces, so they're between the ones on the bottom.

CLAMPING BLOCK. To keep even pressure on the assembly and avoid denting the edges, place ³/₄"-wide clamping blocks centered on the outside edges of the assembly (see photo above).

Note: To help keep the clamping blocks in position when clamping up, I stick them to the edge boards with double-sided carpet tape.

GLUING

It's a good idea to go through this clamping procedure in a dry test assembly before actually applying the glue. It helps you see where problems might arise and make sure all the boards can be pulled together tight.

GLUE. To glue up the slab, I used yellow woodworker's glue in a glue roller bottle. You could also use a small paint roller. Either lets you get a uniform film of glue.

Now, tip up all the pieces on their sides so the gluing surfaces are exposed. Because of the time involved in spreading the glue and clamping up the assembly, it's easy to get a dry joint. For that reason, be generous with the glue and don't worry so much about squeeze-out. I usually apply a thick uniform coat to one side only. (It's always a good idea to have a friend around at this stage to help prevent panic.)

TIGHTEN THE CLAMPS. After the pieces are tipped into position, start tightening the clamps. Don't overtighten. The clamps should be tight enough so there's a uniform "squeeze-out" along the joints, but you should be able to loosen the clamp with one hand.

There's one last step. Check to be sure that all the pieces are seated down against the bottom row of clamps. To get all the pieces down flat, place a wood block on top of any high points and pound them with a hammer.

REMOVE EXCESS GLUE. Once the slab dries overnight, you can remove all the clamps. I usually scrape off the beads of dried glue with a paint scraper. But on this workbench slab, I used a slightly different procedure.

Since the workbench slab was made of hard maple, and maple usually has a

tendency to chip, I was afraid that if I hooked the scraper on a bead of glue, it might pull out a small fiber or chip along with it. Instead, I started by paring off all of the larger beads of glue with a sharp chisel. Then I attacked the rest with a belt sander.

Luckily, I keep old 80-grit belts around the shop just for this purpose. To remove the glue, sand *across* the grain, working just down to the wood on the joints. (Don't sand all the way to the edges of the slab.)

SANDING THE SURFACE FLAT

Now the real work begins — making the surface flat and true. Traditionally, this would be a job for a plane. And if the slab were oak, I'd consider it. But with hard maple, the grain can switch directions a couple times over the length of each board. Somewhere along the way, a plane is likely to start lifting chips.

BELT SANDER. Instead, I reached for my belt sander. Something should be said here about belt sanders. I don't think there's a tool in the shop that can destroy a project quicker. Out of control, a belt sander can bite and gouge wood like a shark in a feeding frenzy.

Most of the time when I work with a belt sander I'm consciously thinking about holding it back as it's cutting. I use my hands and arms only to hold it back and guide it — not to press down.

SAND ACROSS THE GRAIN. Most books warn to *never* sand across the grain. But that's exactly what I do when I start leveling off a slab since a belt sander will generally cut faster across the grain than with the grain. Since the slab requires a great deal of sanding to get it flat, sanding in both directions (first across, then with the grain) lessens the chance of deep gouges.

Also, by first sanding across the grain, and then finishing up with the grain, you end up with a flatter surface.

To start sanding, load a fresh 80-grit belt on the sander. When rough sanding, work in an elliptical pattern and never make a total sideways movement *(Fig. 4)*. Always move the sander forward (or backward) and slightly sideways at the same time.

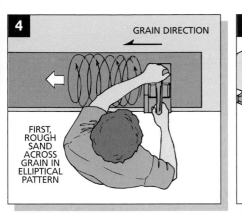

4 GRAIN DIRECTION

FIRST, ROUGH SAND ACROSS GRAIN IN ELLIPTICAL PATTERN

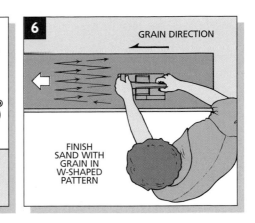

5 STOP SANDING ½" FROM EACH EDGE OF THE SLAB

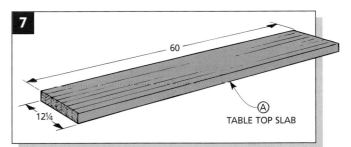

6 GRAIN DIRECTION

FINISH SAND WITH GRAIN IN W-SHAPED PATTERN

Concentrate on an area of about one square foot and try to remove all the ridges in that area. Don't oversand. As soon as the ridges are gone, move on to the next square foot.

The biggest problem is sanding the outside edges. If you allow the pad of the belt sander to work all the way out to the edges, the edges are likely to taper off or even round over. To prevent this I try to stop my sanding strokes about ½" from each edge *(Fig. 5)*.

SAND WITH THE GRAIN. Once all the sharp ridges are removed, switch and sand *with* the grain using a new 80-grit belt. When sanding with the grain, work slightly larger areas, but only as far as your arms will move.

The basic movement of the sander with the grain is a little different than the elliptical pattern followed when sanding across the grain. It's more of an angled up and back movement — like a long, tall "W" shape *(Fig. 6)*. (Note: Still keep ½" away from the edges.)

The goal now is to eliminate all of the cross grain scratches. Watch carefully what you've just completed and once all the scratches are gone, stop sanding.

Once the top is flat, switch to a 120-grit sanding belt and continue working *with* the grain. Follow the same basic tall "W" pattern as before. Your goal is to remove all of the scratches left by the 80-grit belt, and just leave fine scratches that can be removed with a pad sander (with 150-grit paper) or a hand block sander.

SAND THE BOTTOM. I didn't finish sand the bottom face. Just remove the glue and sand across the grain until it's fairly flat.

Note: It's a good idea, though, to apply finish later to the bottom face to slow down any moisture imbalances in the slab.

CUT TO LENGTH. Once the slab is smooth and flat, it can be cut to length *(Fig. 7* and the box below).

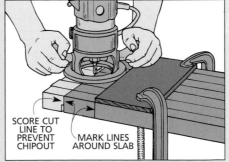

7 60

12¼

Ⓐ TABLE TOP SLAB

SHOP TIP .... Cutting a Slab to Length

After the workbench slab was flat, the next step was to cut it to length. At this point, it was so long and heavy that it was awkward to work with.

There was no way I would ever be able to cut it on the table saw, even with a panel cutting jig.

That left the portable circular saw. To be honest my circular saw and I have never gotten along very well on finish work. It can leave a rough cut, saw marks, and burns.

But if you want to try, concentrate on pushing the saw all the way

through. Don't slow down. Just feed the saw as fast as it will cut.

Using the router is a

little more time consuming, but will give a much smoother end.

Since the slab is so thick,

you will probably have to cut from both faces. I made a series of four passes from each face.

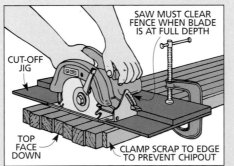

SAW MUST CLEAR FENCE WHEN BLADE IS AT FULL DEPTH

CUT-OFF JIG

TOP FACE DOWN

CLAMP SCRAP TO EDGE TO PREVENT CHIPOUT

CIRCULAR SAW. *To minimize chipout on the face side, cut with the good surface down. Use a fence or cut-off jig and clamp a piece of scrap at end of the cut.*

SCORE CUT LINE TO PREVENT CHIPOUT

MARK LINES AROUND SLAB

ROUTER. *Lay out cut and fence lines around workpiece. Make a series of cuts on one face, then flip slab and clamp fence on the opposite face to finish cut.*

Once the slab was cut to length, I built a dog block assembly for the front of the bench. Begin work by cutting three pieces (B) of ¾" stock to rough dimensions of 3⅝" wide by 60" long *(Fig. 8)*. Note: Later, these pieces will form a long fixed dog block and a short sliding dog block (refer to *Fig. 14*).

DOG HOLES. Before gluing the three pieces together, I laid out and cut angled dadoes across the *middle* board to form dog holes. The body of the dogs I used was ⅝" thick by ¾" wide, so I cut the dadoes ¹⁄₁₆" deeper and wider to allow some clearance *(Fig. 10a)*.

Note: It's best to buy or make the dogs first, and then cut a sample dado in scrap to check for fit. For more on making dogs, see the Shop Tip on page 33.

Before laying out the angled dadoes, you have to determine the location of the waste section between the fixed and sliding blocks *(Fig. 9)*. (Note: The length of the sliding block may vary depending on the vise screw used.)

Then, to mark the location of the first dadoes on each block, measure 1¾" from the waste toward the end *(Fig. 9)*. Now, continue laying out the rest of the dadoes. (Note: The dadoes angle different directions on the two blocks.)

LAMINATE PIECES TOGETHER. Before cutting the dadoes, I laminated one of the dog block pieces (B) to the back of the piece to be dadoed to give it more strength *(Fig. 8)*. To do this, clamp the pieces together so the edges and ends are flush and drill holes for alignment screws. These screws keep the pieces from sliding when the glue is applied. (Note the location of the screw holes in the Detail in *Fig. 8*.) Then glue and screw the pieces together.

CUT THE DADOES. Next, add a long auxiliary fence to the table saw miter gauge and angle the gauge 4° clockwise. (This reads 86° on some gauges.) Then cut the eight dadoes on the fixed end of the block (First step in *Fig. 10*).

Now angle the miter gauge 4° counterclockwise and cut the two dadoes for the sliding end (Second step).

DOG HEAD HOLE. There's one more step before gluing the third piece onto the face of the block to complete the assembly. The angled dadoes will accept the bodies of the dogs, but the top of each hole has to be enlarged to accept the dog's head *(Fig. 11)*.

ROUTER GUIDE. For help in making this cut, I decided to build a special guide for the base of my router. This guide slides into the angled dadoes and has a stop pin that determines the length of the hole.

To make the guide, replace your original router base with one made from ¼" hardboard *(Fig. 12)*. Then cut a ½"-thick runner block just wide enough to slide into the angled dadoes. Before attaching the runner to the base,

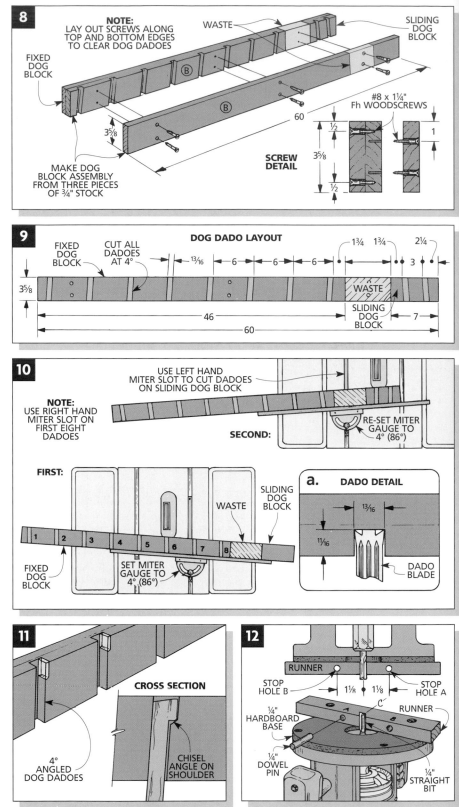

drill two $\frac{1}{4}$"-dia. stop pin holes in the edge of the runner. Locate the holes $1\frac{1}{8}$" from the center of the runner.

Next, mount a $\frac{1}{4}$" straight bit in the router and raise it so the height of the bit from the hardboard base is equal to the depth of the dadoes ($\frac{11}{16}$"). Now screw the runner to the hardboard so it just touches the bit and the bit is centered between the two stop holes.

ROUT HEAD AREAS. To enlarge the openings for the dog heads, set the router on the workpiece. The runner should be in the first dado in the long fixed dog block end, and the bit should be between the dado and the "waste" section (First step in *Fig. 13*).

Now insert a stop pin ($\frac{1}{4}$" dowel) into runner hole "A" and rout until the pin hits the edge of the workpiece. This should open up about a $1\frac{1}{8}$"-long slot for the dog head. Then rout the other slots.

To enlarge the slots in the short sliding block, turn the router completely around, switch the stop pin to the other hole ("B") in the runner, and rout using the same procedure (Second step in *Fig. 13*).

Note: The router bit will leave a little dished-out area. To prevent sawdust from building up here, I angled the shoulder with a chisel (*Fig. 11*).

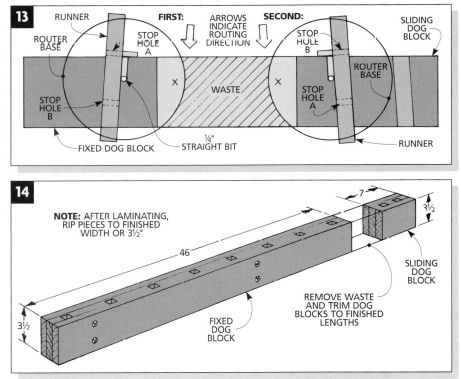

ADD FRONT PIECE. Now, screw and glue the third dog piece (B) to the front of the block (*Fig. 8*).

CUT TO SIZE. Next, skim cut enough off the top edge of the assembled block to clean up any chipout and make the pieces flush. Then rip off the bottom edge so the block is $3\frac{1}{2}$" wide (*Fig. 14*).

CUT BLOCK APART. Finally, cut out the waste section (*Fig. 14*). (The final length of the sliding dog is dependent on the vise screw you use.)

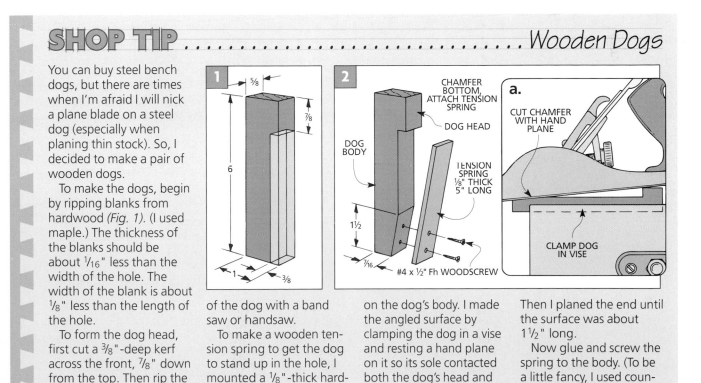

SHOP TIP .... Wooden Dogs

You can buy steel bench dogs, but there are times when I'm afraid I will nick a plane blade on a steel dog (especially when planing thin stock). So, I decided to make a pair of wooden dogs.

To make the dogs, begin by ripping blanks from hardwood (*Fig. 1*). (I used maple.) The thickness of the blanks should be about $\frac{1}{16}$" less than the width of the hole. The width of the blank is about $\frac{1}{8}$" less than the length of the hole.

To form the dog head, first cut a $\frac{3}{8}$"-deep kerf across the front, $\frac{7}{8}$" down from the top. Then rip the waste piece from the front of the dog with a band saw or handsaw.

To make a wooden tension spring to get the dog to stand up in the hole, I mounted a $\frac{1}{8}$"-thick hardwood strip to a chamfer on the dog's body. I made the angled surface by clamping the dog in a vise and resting a hand plane on it so its sole contacted both the dog's head and end of the body (*Fig. 2a*).

Then I planed the end until the surface was about $1\frac{1}{2}$" long.

Now glue and screw the spring to the body. (To be a little fancy, I used countersunk brass screws.)

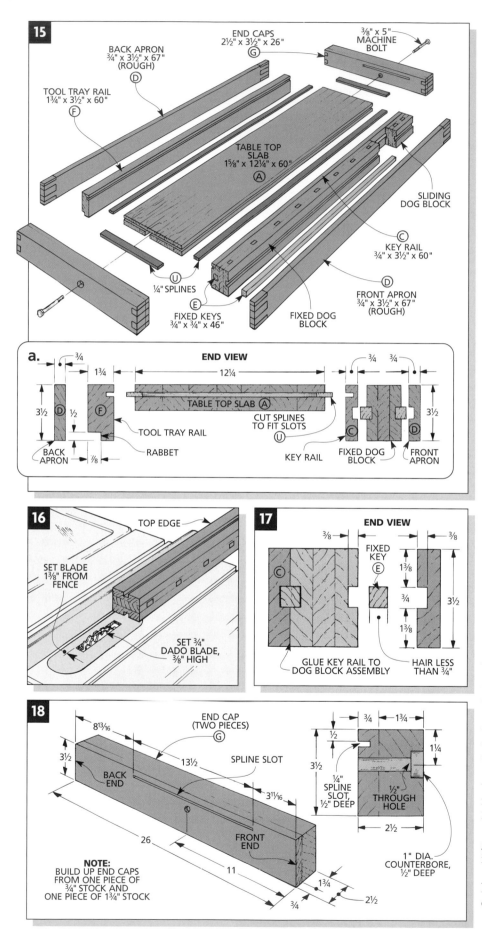

APRONS AND RAILS

After the dog block is cut apart, rails and aprons are added to the front and back edges of the top *(Fig. 15)*.

CUT TO SIZE. First, cut two aprons (D) for the front and back from $3/4$" stock to a rough length of 67". Then cut a tool tray rail (F) from $13/4$" stock and a key rail (C) from $3/4$" stock to match the length of the slab (60").

Now cut all four pieces to a width of $31/2$" *(Fig. 15a)*.

TOOL TRAY RAIL. After the pieces are cut to size, cut a $1/2$"-deep rabbet on the tool tray rail (F) to accept the $1/2$"-thick tool tray bottom *(Fig. 15a)*.

ALIGNMENT KEYS. The key rail (C) and the apron (D) for the front of the bench are mounted to the fixed dog block using two alignment keys (E). So I cut $3/4$"-wide grooves in these pieces to accept the alignment keys *(Fig. 17)*. (These same grooves will also act as guides for the keys that hold in the sliding dog block.)

Note: To keep all the pieces flush across the top when they're assembled, cut the grooves on each piece (the key rail, the fixed and sliding dogs, and the front apron) with a common top edge against the fence *(Fig. 16)*.

After the grooves are cut, cut two fixed keys (E) to fit the grooves and to length to match the length of the fixed dog block (46").

Now glue the key rail (C) to the back of the fixed dog block with one of the keys between the pieces *(Fig. 17)*. (The other key and the front apron will be added later.)

END CAPS

Before the rails and aprons were attached to the slab, I made end caps (G) for each end of the bench top. Each end cap is made by face-gluing a piece of $3/4$"-thick stock to a piece of $13/4$"-thick stock *(Fig. 18)*.

When the blanks have dried, cut them to width to match the aprons and rails ($31/2$") and to a finished length of 26" *(Fig. 18)*.

BOLT HOLE. The end caps are not glued to the end of the slab. They're held in place with a bolt and nut block system (refer to *Fig. 22a*). This system is made later, but now is a good time to drill a $1/2$" counterbored hole in each end cap (Detail in *Fig. 18*).

SPLINES

All the pieces that are joined to the four edges of the slab are held flush with the top face with $\frac{1}{4}$" splines (U) *(Fig. 15)*.

ROUT SLOTS. To cut slots for the splines, I used a $\frac{1}{4}$" slot cutter on the router *(Fig. 19)*. (Since it's a deep cut, I routed the slot in two passes.)

Begin by routing around the slab *(Fig. 19)*. Then rout stopped slots on the inside of the end caps *(Fig. 18)*.

Next, rout a slot on the tool tray rail (F). Be sure it's on the side opposite the rabbet (Detail in *Fig. 20*).

Finally, rout a slot on the fixed dog block assembly. To support the router, I temporarily clamped the sliding dog block to the key rail *(Fig. 20)*.

SPLINES. After the parts are slotted, cut $\frac{1}{4}$" hardboard splines (U) to match the slots (refer to *Fig. 15*). To allow glue space, cut the splines $\frac{1}{8}$" less than the combined depth of the slots.

BOLT/NUT BLOCK

When fastening the end caps to the slab, they need to be pulled up tight, but the slab still has to be able to expand and contract with changes in humidity. To allow this movement, I didn't glue the end caps on. Rather, I put together a bolt and nut block system that ties the end caps to the slab *(Fig. 22)*.

ROUT MORTISE. Start by laying out a "T-shaped" mortise at each end on the *bottom* of the slab *(Fig. 21)*. Then use a router and straight bit to freehand rout out the $\frac{3}{4}$"-deep mortise, and square up the corners with a chisel.

BLOCK. Next cut a small block (H) to fit loosely in the mortise. Then drill a $\frac{1}{2}$" hole through the center of the block to accept a $\frac{3}{8}$" machine bolt (Block Detail in *Fig. 21*). Finally, cut a notch in the back edge of the block that's exactly the same width as a $\frac{3}{8}$" nut.

ASSEMBLY

After the blocks are made and the nuts are in place, insert a spline between the slab and end cap and temporarily bolt each end cap on with a machine bolt.

Now the tool tray rail and fixed dog assembly can be glued and clamped to the front and back of the slab *(Fig. 22)*.

Note: Once the clamps are tight, remove the end caps so they don't get glued to the ends of the slab.

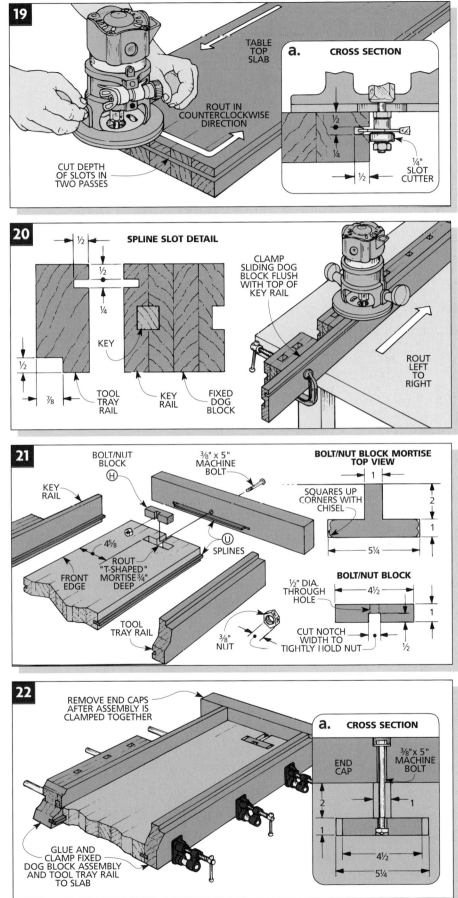

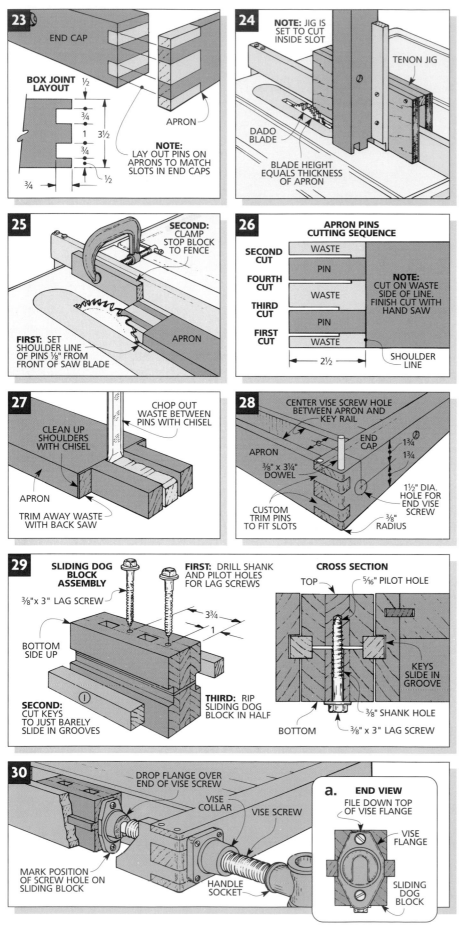

BOX JOINTS

The next step is to add the aprons. Start by cutting the front and back aprons (D) to length — the same length as the top (with end caps).

After the aprons are cut, they can be joined to the end caps with box joints — but these pieces are so long the joints can't be cut with a box joint jig.

CUT SLOTS IN END CAPS. To make the box joints, start by laying out the slots on the end caps (Detail in *Fig. 23*). To cut the slots, I used a dado blade and a tenon jig *(Fig. 24)*. Set the blade height to the thickness of the apron, and the fence so the jig is ½" from the blade.

Now stand the end cap on end and make one pass. Then turn the workpiece around and cut the other slot.

CUT PINS IN APRONS. After all the slots were cut, I laid out corresponding pins on the aprons. To cut the pins straight, start by mounting a combination blade on the saw. Next, clamp a stop block to the fence so the shoulder line on the apron is ⅛" in front of the blade *(Fig. 25)*.

Position the fence so the cut will be in the waste area (First Cut in *Fig. 26*). After the first cut, flip the piece over and make a second. Then move the fence and make the third and fourth cuts.

TRIM TO SHOULDER. Finish the cuts down to the shoulder with a hand saw. Then cut away the two outside waste pieces with a hand saw and clean up with a chisel. Next, chisel out the waste between the pins *(Fig. 27)* and custom-fit the pins to the slots *(Fig. 28)*.

VISE SCREW HOLE. Before gluing up the pieces, drill a hole for the vise screw in the *right* end cap *(Fig. 28)*.

ASSEMBLY. Now bolt (don't glue) the end caps to the slab and glue the aprons in place (including the box joint). After the glue dried, I rounded all the corners *(Fig. 28)* except the front left vise corner.

ADD DOWELS. To strengthen each of the box joints, I drilled two holes completely through each joint and glued in ⅜" dowels *(Fig. 28)*.

SLIDING DOG BLOCK

Now work can continue on the sliding dog block. Start by trimming a whisker off the block so it slides in the opening.

The block is held in the opening with two sliding keys (I), and it's removable (in case it ever needs replacing or trimming as the humidity changes). To make it removable, start by drilling two holes for lag screws *(Fig. 29)*.

Next, cut the keys (I) to fit in the grooves on the apron and key rail. Then cut the block in half, mount it in the opening, and screw it back together.

END VISE

Once the sliding dog block is in place, mount the vise collar so it's centered on the hole in the end cap *(Fig. 30)*. Now slide the flange onto the end of the vise screw and mark the position of the screw holes on the end of the dog block. Then remove the block from the bench, drill the holes, and replace the block.

Note: The top of the flange may extend above the top of the block. If so, file it down *(Fig. 30a)*.

TOOL TRAY

Next, I began work on the tool tray. To make the tool tray bottom (J), start by edge-gluing ¹⁄₂" stock to a rough width of 9" and a length of 62".

CUT TO WIDTH. To determine the final width, turn the bench over and measure the distance from the inside of the back apron to the inside of the rabbet on the tool tray rail *(Fig. 34)*. Then subtract ¹⁄₈" for expansion.

CUT INTO PIECES. After the bottom is cut to width, cut it into three pieces to make a cleanout door *(Fig. 31)*.

Since I wanted to add a tool holder, I had to cut two long notches on the back edge of the tray bottom *(Fig. 31)*.

TOOL HOLDER. Now cut the ³⁄₄"-thick tool holder (K) to a width of 2¹⁄₂" and to length so it fits inside the tray *(Fig. 32)*. Then cut slots to hold different tools.

After the slots are cut, chamfer the top edge (Detail in *Fig. 33*) and then glue it to the inside of the back apron.

SCREW ON BOTTOM. Now screw the tray bottom in place *(Fig. 34)*. (Slot the front holes to allow for expansion.)

SAWDUST DOOR. Next, add two ¹⁄₂"-thick cleats (T) to hold in the sawdust door *(Fig. 35)*.

Then cut a notch on the bottom of the tool tray rail so the door can slide into position *(Fig. 36)*. Finally, drill a finger hole in the door *(Fig. 36)*.

END BLOCKS. To keep sawdust from building up in the corners of the tool tray, I screwed beveled tray end blocks (L) at the ends *(Fig. 37)*.

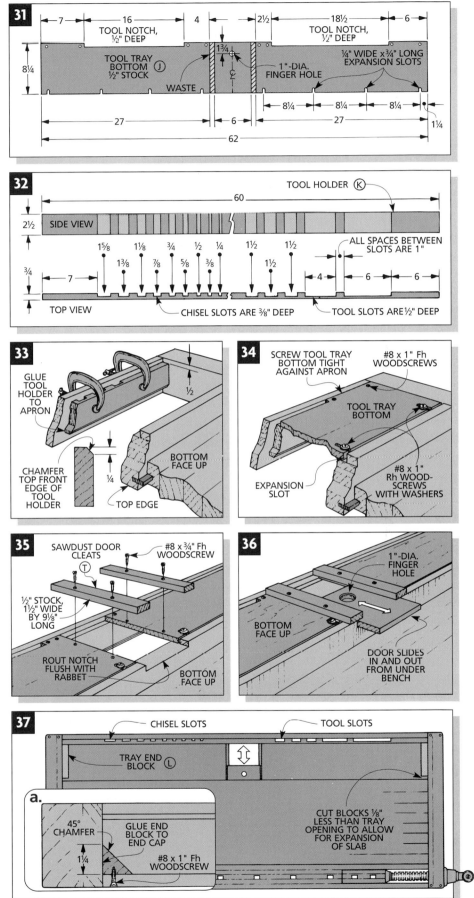

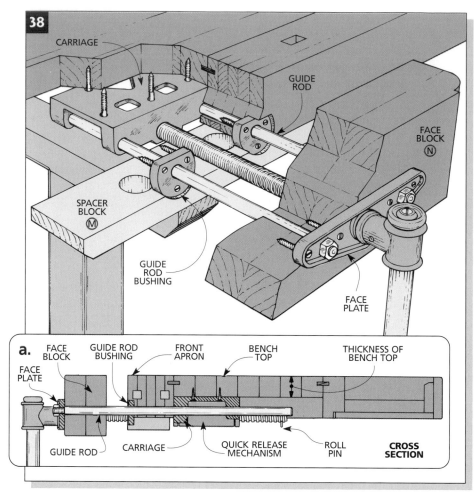

38

CARRIAGE

GUIDE ROD

FACE BLOCK Ⓝ

SPACER BLOCK Ⓜ

GUIDE ROD BUSHING

FACE PLATE

a.

FACE BLOCK

GUIDE ROD BUSHING

FRONT APRON

BENCH TOP

THICKNESS OF BENCH TOP

FACE PLATE

GUIDE ROD

CARRIAGE

QUICK RELEASE MECHANISM

ROLL PIN

CROSS SECTION

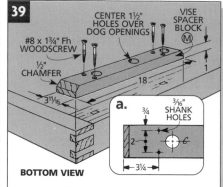

39

#8 x 1¾" Fh WOODSCREW

CENTER 1½" HOLES OVER DOG OPENINGS

VISE SPACER BLOCK Ⓜ

½" CHAMFER

18

3¹¹⁄₁₆

1

a.

¾

2

³⁄₁₆" SHANK HOLES

3¼

BOTTOM VIEW

FRONT VISE

When choosing the front vise for this bench, I had a couple of options. I could have chosen a metal vise (refer to page 42). But I decided on a "wooden vise." Actually, it only has wooden faces; the main parts are metal *(Fig. 38)*.

I liked the fact that there was no metal to mar the workpiece, knock the edge off a sharp tool, or rap knuckles. But I also felt that a wooden vise would look better on this bench. The vise becomes a part of the bench, not something that's fastened to it.

Note: The measurements and instructions given here are for the vise I used. Similar vises can be mounted the same way, but you may have to change dimensions. *Always* have the vise in hand before you start drilling holes. (For sources of vises, see page 126.)

To attach the vise hardware onto the bench, two wooden parts are needed: a spacer block and a face block.

SPACER BLOCK. The arm on the vise end of the base is notched to provide clearance for the vise assembly. To pro-

vide support for the front of the bench top, a 1"-thick vise spacer block (M) is needed *(Fig. 39)*.

After cutting the block to size, drill 1½" holes to provide clearance for the dogs. Then screw the block in place.

FACE BLOCK. To make the face block

(N) for the movable part of the vise, laminate two pieces of 1¾" hardwood together *(Fig. 40)*. When the glue dries, cut the block to size.

DRILL HOLES. Now holes can be drilled through the block for the guide rods and vise screw (refer to *Fig. 38*).

To locate the guide rod holes, measure the thickness of the table top slab and scribe a line this distance down from the top of the face block *(Fig. 40)*. Now, place the carriage centered on the block with its upper surface aligned with this line. Then slip a ¾" brad point bit through the carriage holes to mark the locations on the face of the block.

Next, the location for the vise screw hole is marked. To do this, trace the outline of the center hole of the carriage.

Now the holes can be drilled on the drill press *(Fig. 41)*. Since the holes for the guide rods have to be precise, I used a ¾" brad point bit (or whatever size is appropriate for your vise). The hole for the vise screw is oversized so I used a 1¼" spade bit.

SHOP TIP ... *Preventing Vise Rack*

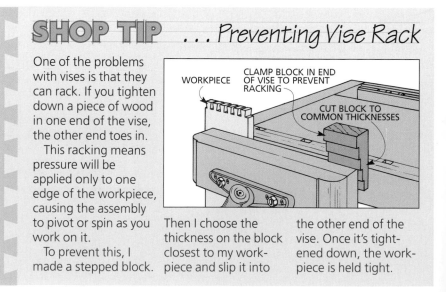

One of the problems with vises is that they can rack. If you tighten down a piece of wood in one end of the vise, the other end toes in.

This racking means pressure will be applied only to one edge of the workpiece, causing the assembly to pivot or spin as you work on it.

To prevent this, I made a stepped block.

WORKPIECE

CLAMP BLOCK IN END OF VISE TO PREVENT RACKING

CUT BLOCK TO COMMON THICKNESSES

Then I choose the thickness on the block closest to my workpiece and slip it into

the other end of the vise. Once it's tightened down, the workpiece is held tight.

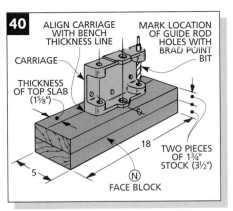

40 ALIGN CARRIAGE WITH BENCH THICKNESS LINE — MARK LOCATION OF GUIDE ROD HOLES WITH BRAD POINT BIT — CARRIAGE — THICKNESS OF TOP SLAB (1⅝") — THICKNESS OF TOP SLAB — 18 — 5 — TWO PIECES OF 1¾" STOCK (3½") — Ⓝ — FACE BLOCK

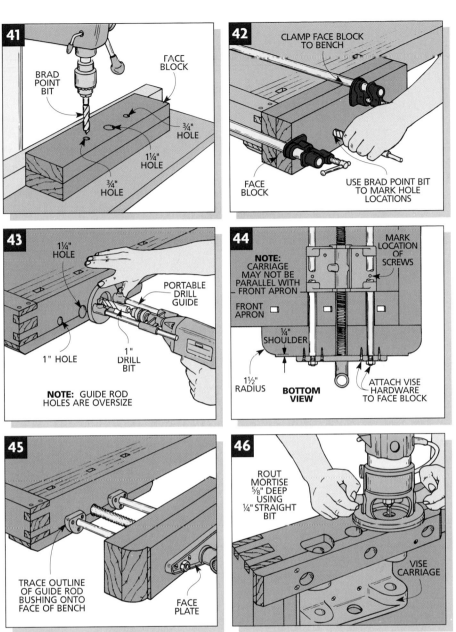

41 BRAD POINT BIT — FACE BLOCK — ¾" HOLE — 1¼" HOLE — ¾" HOLE

42 CLAMP FACE BLOCK TO BENCH — FACE BLOCK — USE BRAD POINT BIT TO MARK HOLE LOCATIONS

43 1¼" HOLE — PORTABLE DRILL GUIDE — 1" HOLE — 1" DRILL BIT — **NOTE:** GUIDE ROD HOLES ARE OVERSIZE

44 **NOTE:** CARRIAGE MAY NOT BE PARALLEL WITH FRONT APRON — FRONT APRON — ¼" SHOULDER — 1½" RADIUS — **BOTTOM VIEW** — MARK LOCATION OF SCREWS — ATTACH VISE HARDWARE TO FACE BLOCK

45 TRACE OUTLINE OF GUIDE ROD BUSHING ONTO FACE OF BENCH — FACE PLATE

46 ROUT MORTISE ⅝" DEEP USING ¼" STRAIGHT BIT — VISE CARRIAGE

LOCATE BENCH HOLES. Now matching holes can be drilled in the workbench. To do this, clamp the face block to the bench with its top and end flush with the top and end of the bench (*Fig. 42*). Then, use a brad point bit to mark the locations of the two outside holes for the guide rods and trace the middle hole for the vise screw.

To drill the holes, I used a portable drill guide (*Fig. 43*). (The guide rod holes are oversized in the bench, but *not* in the face block.)

At this point the outside edges and ends of the block (except the edge that's even with the top of the bench) can be chamfered. I also used a band saw to cut a rounded profile with a shoulder (*Fig. 44*).

ASSEMBLY. After the block is profiled, assembly can begin. First, the wooden face block is mounted to the metal face plate on the vise. To do this, fasten the guide rods to the metal plate with nuts. Then slide the face block onto the guide rods. Now drill pilot holes for screws, and screw the face block to the metal plate (*Fig. 44*).

MOUNT CARRIAGE. To mount the carriage to the bottom of the bench, turn the bench top upside down. Then, push the guide rods and vise screw through the holes in the bench and slide the carriage loosely onto the guide rods. Now clamp the wooden face block tight against the apron (*Fig. 44*).

With the wooden face block clamped in position, slide the carriage forward until the front of the carriage just touches the dog block assembly.

Note: If just one end of the carriage contacts the apron, don't try to force the other end flush. Even if the carriage itself is out of square, the holes for the guide rods are aligned with the front.

Then drill pilot holes and screw the carriage to the bottom of the bench.

GUIDE ROD BUSHINGS. To mortise the guide rod bushings into the front of the bench, begin by slipping the bushings onto the guide rods. Then insert the rods through the holes in the front of the bench, and trace the outline of the bushings on the apron (*Fig. 45*).

I used a router with a ¼" straight bit to rout the mortises (*Fig. 46*). Rout until the recess is ⅛" deeper than the thickness of the bushing. When the bushings fit the holes, drill pilot holes and screw the bushings in place.

ASSEMBLE VISE. To put the vise together, slide the guide rods and vise screw through the carriage. Then tap in the roll pin, near the end of the vise screw, to keep the assembly from pulling all the way out (refer to *Fig. 38a*).

HANDLE. Some vises don't come with handles. I made handles for both the front and end vises from 12"-long pieces of 1"-dia. dowel (*Fig. 47*).

For knobs on the ends of the handles, I used toy wooden wheels and counterbored the back face to accept the dowel. Then I screwed them on with brass woodscrews.

Finally, I used rubber 1" O-rings (from a plumbing supply house) to soften the blow on the knob when dropping the handle.

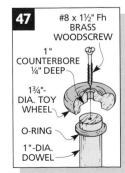

47 #8 x 1½" Fh BRASS WOODSCREW — 1" COUNTERBORE ¼" DEEP — 1¾"-DIA. TOY WHEEL — O-RING — 1"-DIA. DOWEL

The base of the workbench consists of end frames connected by stretchers. The two end frames are almost identical, but the arm at the left end is longer to support the vise *(Figs. 48 & 49).*

ARMS AND FEET. Each arm and foot is made from three pieces of $3/4$" stock laminated together *(Fig. 50).* Begin by cutting twelve pieces of stock to a rough width of $2^5/8$". Then cut nine of the pieces to a rough length of 23" and the other three pieces (for the long vise arm) to a rough length of 26".

Next, lay out $1^1/2$"-deep notches on the center board of each arm and foot *(Figs. 50 & 51).* (When the blanks are glued up, the notches form mortises.) After the notches are cut, glue up each blank with a notched board in the middle.

Once the blanks are dry, cut them to a final width (height) of $2^1/2$" *(Fig. 51).*

Now they can all be cut to length. To find the end points for cutting, measure out $1^3/4$" from the notches on the right arm and two feet *(Fig. 50a).* Since the vise arm is longer, the *front* end is $4^3/4$" from the notch *(Fig. 51).*

After the pieces are cut to length, cut a long notch on the top of the *vise* arm to make room for the vise *(Fig. 51).*

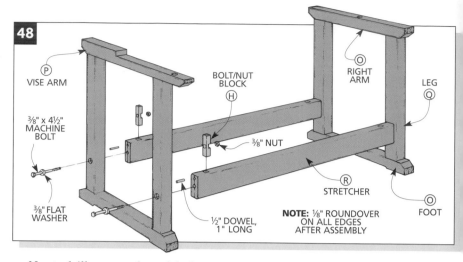

Next, drill counterbored holes on each arm to mount the top to the base *(Fig. 51).* Now cut 1" chamfers off the bottom ends of the arms and the top ends of the feet *(Figs. 51 & 52).*

The last step is to cut out an area on the bottom of each foot *(Fig. 52).* To do this, I temporarily clamped the two feet together and drilled a 1"-dia. hole so there would be a $1/2$" arc in each leg *(Fig. 53).* Then cut a straight line between the arcs.

LEGS. After the arms and feet were complete, I began work on the legs (Q). Start by cutting twelve pieces of $3/4$" stock to a rough width of $2^5/8$" and a rough length of 30". Then laminate the pieces together in sets of three.

After the glue dries, trim the leg blanks to a finished width of $2^1/2$" and length of $28^1/2$" *(Fig. 54).* (This measurement can be increased or decreased for a higher or lower bench.)

Next, cut tenons on the ends of each leg to fit into the mortises in the arms and feet *(Fig. 54).*

To attach the stretchers to the legs, drill a counterbored hole from the outside face *(Fig. 54).* Then drill a $1/2$"-deep hole for a dowel pin on the inside face.

Finally glue the legs to the arms and feet, checking for square *(Fig. 49).*

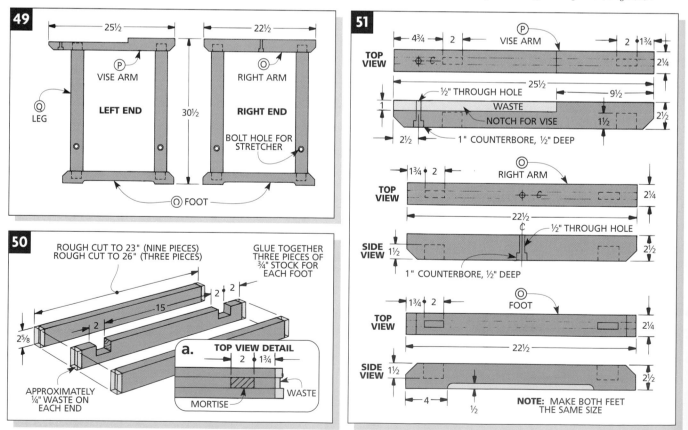

STRETCHERS. To make the two stretchers (R), cut four pieces of $3/4$" stock to a rough width of $4^5/8$" and finished length of $48^1/2$" *(Fig. 55)*.

Before laminating the pieces into pairs, I cut 1"-wide dadoes on the inside face of each piece *(Fig. 55)*. When the pieces are laminated, these dadoes form mortises for bolt/nut blocks (H).

BOLT/NUT BLOCKS. Now cut two 9"-long bolt/nut blocks (H) to fit in the mortises. Then glue the pairs together to form the stretchers *(Fig. 56)*.

Note: Remove the bolt/nut blocks before the glue sets.

Once the glue dries, trim the stretcher to $4^1/2$" wide. Then put the bolt/nut block back into place and drill a $1/2$"-dia. bolt hole in from the end of the stretcher through the bolt/nut block *(Fig. 57)*.

Next, insert a $3/8$" bolt into the hole, mark the block with a pencil, and cut it off flush with the top and bottom of the stretcher. Then, cut a notch in the back to tightly hold a $3/8$" nut.

DOWEL PIN. To prevent the stretchers from twisting as the bolts are tightened, I added a $1/2$" x 1" dowel pin to the ends of the stretcher *(Figs. 48 & 57)*.

ASSEMBLY. Before assembling the base, I rounded over all the edges with a $1/8$" roundover bit. Then fit a nut into the notch in each bolt/nut block and insert the blocks into the mortises. Then, push a bolt through the leg and into the stretcher and tighten the bolt *(Fig. 48)*.

MOUNTING THE TOP

I found it easiest to turn the top upside down to position the base *(Fig. 58)*. There are a couple of things to look for here. First, the vise arm and the right arm should be the same distance from the back edge ($1/4$"). Then check that the vise arm is *between* the dog holes.

Now use a $1/2$" brad point bit to mark through the hole in each arm into the bottom of the bench top.

MOUNTING BLOCK. Also, while the base is in position, I measured the distance from the bottom of the slab to the top of the right arm ($1^7/8$".) Then I cut a mounting block (S) to fill this space.

Now drill a $1/2$" hole through the center of the mounting block.

Note: To allow for expansion, I drilled $1/2$" holes, but used $5/16$" bolts.

Next, remove the base from the top and drill holes for threaded inserts. Then mount the top to the base. ∎

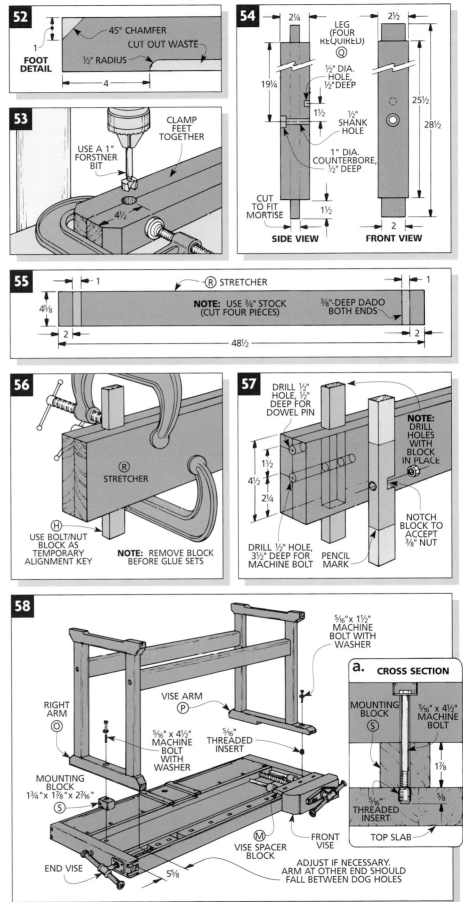

DESIGNER'S NOTEBOOK

Here's an alternate top for the Maple Workbench that's easier to build and less expensive. It's built up from layers of high density particleboard and hardboard.

CONSTRUCTION NOTES:

■ Start building the top by cutting a core layer (V) of ¾"-thick high density particleboard 23½ wide and 63½" long *(Fig. 1)*. (Or, you could use plywood or MDF.)

■ Cut a second core layer and a ¼" hardboard cover (W) slightly larger than the first layer (24" x 64").

■ Glue the second layer and cover on top of the first layer with contact cement. They should extend beyond the first layer on each side.

■ Use a flush trim bit to trim the overhang so all three layers are the same size. (For more on this technique, see page 16.)

■ To get the desired thickness (2½"), glue ¾"-thick particleboard spacers (X, Z) around the bottom perimeter of the benchtop *(Fig. 1)*. If any of the spacers are not flush with the edges of the benchtop, trim the excess with the flush trim bit.

Note: It may seem easier to add another full-size layer instead of using the spacers. But using spacers limits the amount of ¾" particleboard needed to one 4' x 8' sheet.

■ Lay out a large notch on the edge at the left front corner of the top *(Fig. 2)*. This will form a pocket for the rear face of the vise (refer to *Fig. 5*).

Note: The size of this notch will depend on the vise you use. Always have your vise in hand before you start laying out the notch.

Though the depth and length of the notch is not critical (lay it out slightly oversize for your vise), the height of the notch needs to be more precise. Leave ⅜" covering the top edge of the vise.

■ Rout out the notch using a router and a straight bit *(Fig. 3)*. Clamping an extra block to the side of the benchtop helps support the router. Rout close to the layout lines and then finish it up with a chisel. Since the notch will not be visible, it doesn't have to be precise.

■ Cut end aprons (AA) from ¾"-thick stock to width (height) to match the

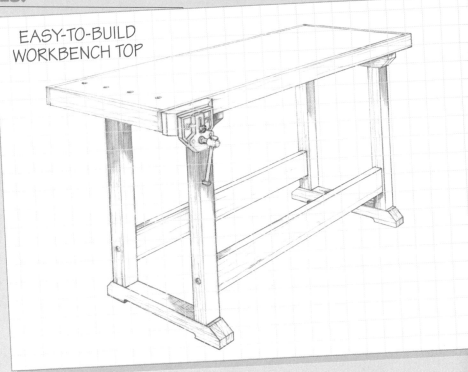

EASY-TO-BUILD WORKBENCH TOP

thickness of the benchtop (2½"), and the same length as the benchtop's width (23½") *(Fig. 4)*. Then glue and nail the end aprons in place.

■ Cut front and back aprons (BB) the same width (2½") and to length to cover the side aprons (65") *(Fig. 4)*. Then glue

and nail them in place.

■ Drill four "dog" holes in line with what will be the center of the vise *(Fig. 4)*. The size of these holes should match the dogs you will be using. I used a ¾" cut-off hex head bolt as a dog *(Fig. 4a)*. To make it easier to

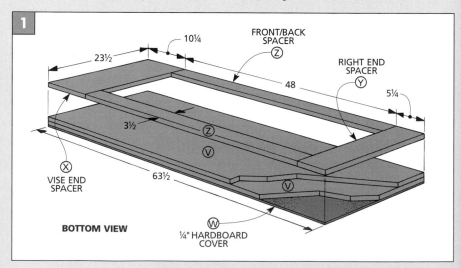

1

23½

10¼

FRONT/BACK SPACER
Z

RIGHT END SPACER
Y

48

5¼

3½

Z

V

X
VISE END SPACER

63½

V

W
¼" HARDBOARD COVER

BOTTOM VIEW

insert the dog, rout $\frac{1}{8}$" chamfers around the top edges of these holes.

■ With the benchtop turned upside down, set the vise in the vise pocket *(Fig. 5)*. The top edge of the vise should bottom out in the pocket. If there's space between the benchtop and the mounting platform on the vise, cut a spacer (M) to fill this space. (I used $\frac{1}{4}$" hardboard as a spacer.)

■ Tighten the vise to the apron to keep it in position and drill and bolt the vise (and the spacer) down with $2\frac{1}{2}$" lag screws and washers *(Fig. 5)*.

■ Glue two layers of $\frac{3}{4}$" stock face-to-face to make a vise face block (N) *(Fig. 6)*. Cut to finished size (3" x 9") and trim a 45° bevel off each end. Open the vise, position the block flush with the top of the bench, and screw it in place.

■ The only difference in the base of the workbench is that you do *not* need a special vise arm (P) for this alternate top. The left arm is now the same as the right arm (O) (refer to *Fig. 7*).

■ Before gluing the legs (Q) and arms (O) together, drill *two* counterbored holes in each arm to mount the benchtop to the base *(Fig. 7)*.

■ Turn the benchtop upside down and center the base (front to back) on top of it *(Fig. 8)*. But *offset* the benchtop (right to left) so there's $8\frac{3}{4}$" from the left (vise) end of the bench to the left arm of the base.

■ Mark through the holes in the arms into the bottom of the benchtop. Then install $\frac{5}{16}$" threaded inserts at each mark *(Fig. 7)*. Finally, attach the base to the benchtop with machine bolts.

CHANGES TO MATERIALS

EASY-TO-BUILD WORKBENCH TOP

M	Vise Spacer (1)	$\frac{1}{4}$ hdbd. - 4 x 7$\frac{1}{2}$
N	Face Block (1)	1$\frac{1}{2}$ x 3 - 9
V	Cores (2)	$\frac{3}{4}$ ptbd. - 23$\frac{1}{2}$ x 63$\frac{1}{2}$
W	Cover (1)	$\frac{1}{4}$ hdbd. - 23$\frac{1}{2}$ x 63$\frac{1}{2}$
X	Vise End Spcr. (1)	$\frac{3}{4}$ ptbd. - 10$\frac{1}{4}$ x 23$\frac{1}{2}$
Y	Rt. End Spcr. (1)	$\frac{3}{4}$ ptbd. - 5$\frac{1}{4}$ x 23$\frac{1}{2}$
Z	Fr./Bk. Spcrs. (2)	$\frac{3}{4}$ ptbd. - 3$\frac{1}{2}$ x 48
AA	End Aprons (2)	$\frac{3}{4}$ x 2$\frac{1}{2}$ - 23$\frac{1}{2}$
BB	Fr./Bk. Aprons (2)	$\frac{3}{4}$ x 2$\frac{1}{2}$ - 65

Note: Only need (4) parts H. Need (4) parts O. Do not need A, B, C, D, E, F, G, I, J, K, L, P, S, T, U

HARDWARE

(28) 6d (2") finish nails
(4) $\frac{5}{16}$" I.D. threaded inserts
(4) $\frac{5}{16}$" x 2$\frac{1}{2}$" machine bolts w/washers
(4) $\frac{3}{8}$" x 2$\frac{1}{2}$" lag screws w/washers
(2) No. 12 x 1$\frac{1}{2}$" Rh woodscrews
(1) $\frac{3}{4}$" x 4" hex head bolt (cut off for dog)
(1) Record 42ED vise

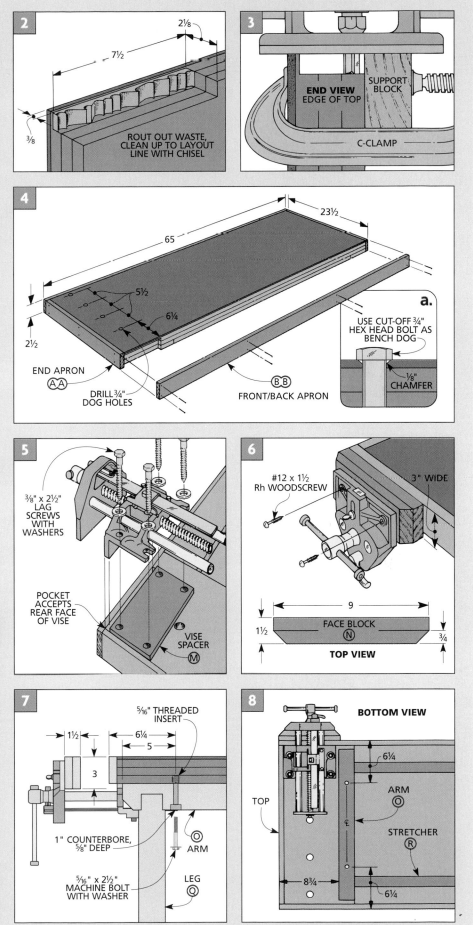

2
2$\frac{1}{8}$
7$\frac{1}{2}$
$\frac{3}{8}$
ROUT OUT WASTE, CLEAN UP TO LAYOUT LINE WITH CHISEL

3
END VIEW
EDGE OF TOP
SUPPORT BLOCK
C-CLAMP

4
23$\frac{1}{2}$
65
5$\frac{1}{2}$
6$\frac{1}{4}$
2$\frac{1}{2}$
END APRON
AA
DRILL $\frac{3}{4}$" DOG HOLES
FRONT/BACK APRON
BB
a.
USE CUT-OFF $\frac{3}{4}$" HEX HEAD BOLT AS BENCH DOG
$\frac{1}{8}$" CHAMFER

5
$\frac{3}{8}$" x 2$\frac{1}{2}$" LAG SCREWS WITH WASHERS
POCKET ACCEPTS REAR FACE OF VISE
VISE SPACER
M

6
#12 x 1$\frac{1}{2}$ Rh WOODSCREW
3" WIDE
9
1$\frac{1}{2}$
FACE BLOCK
N
$\frac{3}{4}$
TOP VIEW

7
$\frac{5}{16}$" THREADED INSERT
1$\frac{1}{2}$
6$\frac{1}{4}$
5
3
1" COUNTERBORE, $\frac{5}{8}$" DEEP
$\frac{5}{16}$" x 2$\frac{1}{2}$" MACHINE BOLT WITH WASHER
ARM
O
LEG
Q

8
BOTTOM VIEW
6$\frac{1}{4}$
TOP
ARM
O
STRETCHER
R
8$\frac{3}{4}$
6$\frac{1}{4}$

Workbench Cabinet

This space-saving underbench cabinet not only increases your storage capacity, but when full of tools its weight also adds extra strength and stability to the workbench.

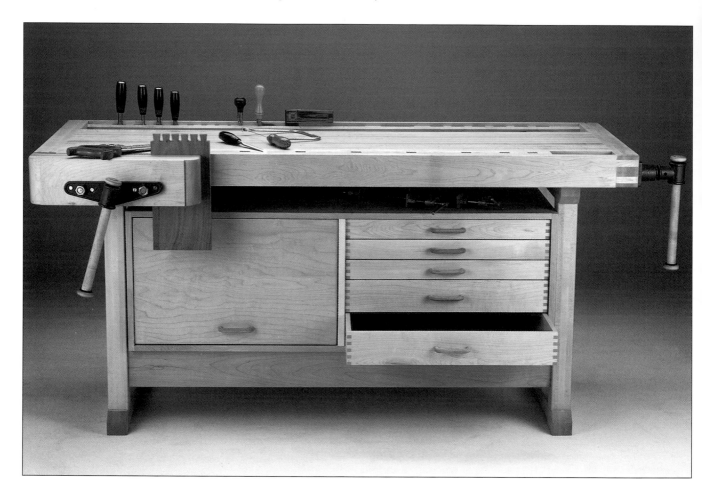

O nce the last coat of tung oil was dry on the Maple Workbench shown on page 27, I started building my first project on it: a storage cabinet that could fit underneath.

This underbench cabinet actually serves two purposes. Of course it keeps tools within reach and easy to put away. The other benefit is sort of a windfall. When the cabinet is filled with tools, it adds weight and stability to the bench.

PLYWOOD BOX. The cabinet is an open-front plywood box that's divided into two compartments. The left compartment is for storing bulky items like portable power tools. These are con-cealed behind a flip-up door. The right compartment has five drawers for hand tools or hardware.

BOX JOINTS. One of my favorite parts of this cabinet is the box joints on these drawers. First of all, they just plain look good. They complement the larger box joints on the corners of the bench top as well as "show off" a little bit of my wood-working skill.

But they're also strong joints. And for a cabinet that's designed to hold heavy tools, that's important. When you're opening and closing the drawers all the time, the tools are constantly banging into the fronts and backs of the drawers. A strong interlocking joint with a lot of glue surface (such as a box joint) is what I'd recommend.

But there's something to keep in mind with these box joints: since they're built in increments (you don't want half a finger), the overall height of each drawer is set. So we had to design the final height of the cabinet by starting with the drawers and working out.

ANOTHER OPTION. If you're not interested in drawers, and want larger storage areas, take a look at the Designer's Notebook on page 49. There you'll see a simpler door system that takes on a completely different look.

EXPLODED VIEW

OVERALL DIMENSIONS:
48³/₈W x 21D x 16¹/₈H

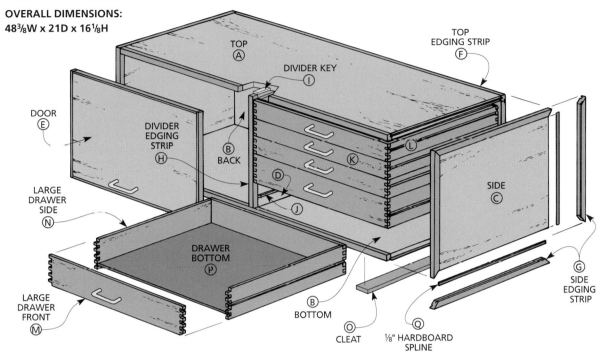

TOP ⒶA

TOP EDGING STRIP Ⓕ

DIVIDER KEY Ⓘ

DOOR Ⓔ

DIVIDER EDGING STRIP Ⓗ

BACK Ⓑ

SIDE Ⓒ

LARGE DRAWER SIDE Ⓝ

Ⓚ

Ⓛ

Ⓓ

Ⓙ

DRAWER BOTTOM Ⓟ

LARGE DRAWER FRONT Ⓜ

BOTTOM Ⓑ

CLEAT Ⓞ

¹/₈" HARDBOARD SPLINE Ⓠ

SIDE EDGING STRIP Ⓖ

MATERIALS LIST

WOOD

A	Top/Bottom (2)	³/₄ ply - 19¹/₂ x 46⁷/₈
B	Back (1)	³/₄ ply - 14⁵/₈ x 46⁷/₈
C	Sides (2)	³/₄ ply - 14⁵/₈ x 19¹/₂
D	Divider (1)	³/₄ ply - 14⁵/₈ x 19¹/₂
E	Door (1)	³/₄ ply - 13¹⁵/₁₆ x 22¹/₂
F	Top/Btm. Edging (4)	³/₄ x ³/₄ - 46⁷/₈
G	Side Edging (8)	³/₄ x ³/₄ - 21 rough
H	Divider Edging (1)	³/₄ x ³/₄ - 16 rough
I	Divider Keys (3)	¹/₄ x ³/₄ - 21 rough
J	Drw. Runners (10)	³/₈ x ¹/₂ - 19¹/₂
K	Sm. Drw. Fr./Bk. (6)	¹/₂ x 2¹/₄ - 22¹⁵/₁₆
L	Sm. Drw. Sides (6)	¹/₂ x 2¹/₄ - 19³/₄
M	Lg. Drw. Fr./Bk. (4)	¹/₂ x 3³/₄ - 22¹⁵/₁₆
N	Lg. Drw. Sides (4)	¹/₂ x 3³/₄ - 19³/₄
O	Cleats (2)	¹/₂ x 2 - 15³/₈
P	Drw. Bottoms (5)	¹/₄ hbd. - 19³/₁₆ x 22³/₈
Q	Splines*	¹/₈ hbd. - ⁷/₁₆ wide

* Approximately 30 ft. of ¹/₈" hardboard is needed for the splines.

HARDWARE SUPPLIES

(2) No. 8 x 1" Fh woodscrews
(2) ¹/₂"-dia x ¹/₂"-long dowels
(2) ¹/₄"-dia. x ³/₄"-long dowels
(6) ⁷/₁₆"-dia. x 3³/₄"-bore wood pulls

CUTTING DIAGRAM

³/₄ x 5¹/₂ - 72 (2.7 Bd. Ft.)

G | F | G | G
H

¹/₂ x 7¹/₄ - 72 (Two Boards @ 3.6 Sq. Ft. Each)

K | K | K
M | M | O

¹/₂ x 7¹/₄ - 72 (Two Boards @ 3.6 Sq. Ft. Each)

L | L | L
N | N | J

³/₄" PLYWOOD   48 x 96

A
A
B
C
D
C
E

NOTE: ALSO NEED 4"x 8' SHEET OF ¹/₄" HARDBOARD FOR DRAWER BOTTOMS (P) AND ¹/₈" HARDBOARD SCRAPS FOR ⁷/₁₆"-WIDE SPLINES (Q) (APPROX. 30 FT. NEEDED)

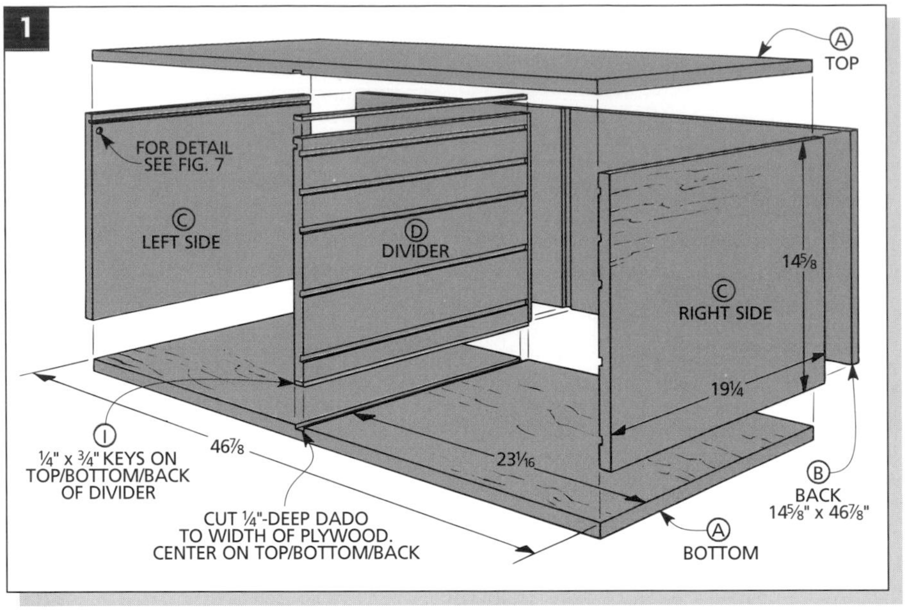
1
A TOP
FOR DETAIL SEE FIG. 7
C LEFT SIDE
D DIVIDER
14 5/8
C RIGHT SIDE
19 1/4
I
1/4" x 3/4" KEYS ON TOP/BOTTOM/BACK OF DIVIDER
46 7/8
23 1/16
B BACK 14 5/8" x 46 7/8"
CUT 1/4"-DEEP DADO TO WIDTH OF PLYWOOD. CENTER ON TOP/BOTTOM/BACK
A BOTTOM

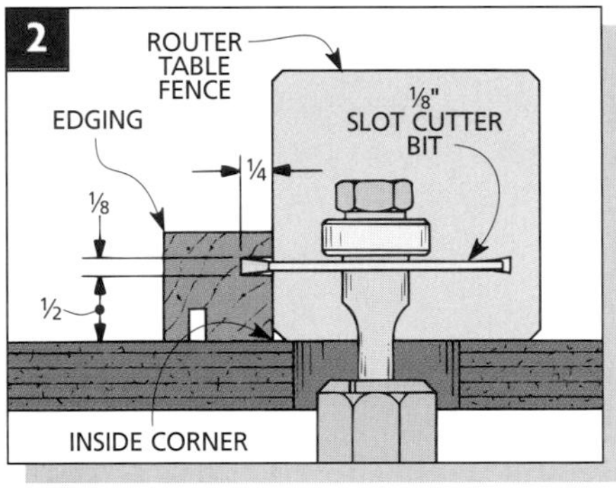
2
ROUTER TABLE FENCE
EDGING
1/8" SLOT CUTTER BIT
1/4
1/8
1/2
INSIDE CORNER

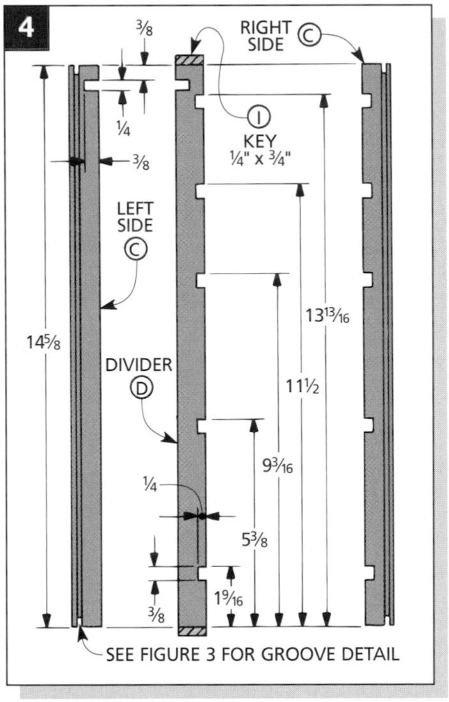
4
3/8
RIGHT SIDE C
1/4
3/8
I KEY 1/4" x 3/4"
LEFT SIDE C
13 13/16
14 5/8
DIVIDER D
11 1/2
9 3/16
1/4
5 3/8
1 9/16
3/8
SEE FIGURE 3 FOR GROOVE DETAIL

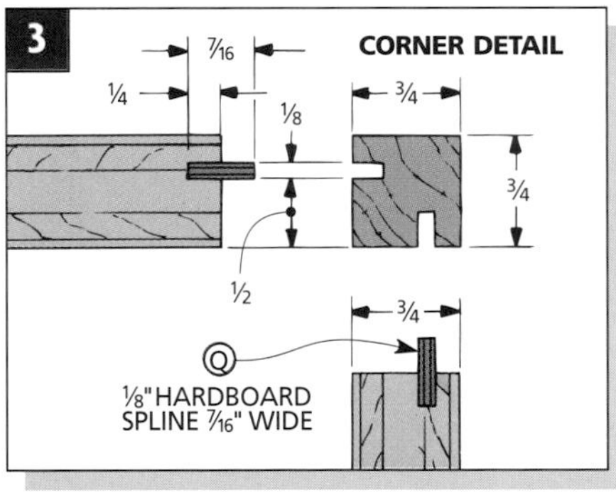
3
7/16
CORNER DETAIL
1/4
3/4
1/8
3/4
1/2
3/4
Q
1/8" HARDBOARD SPLINE 7/16" WIDE

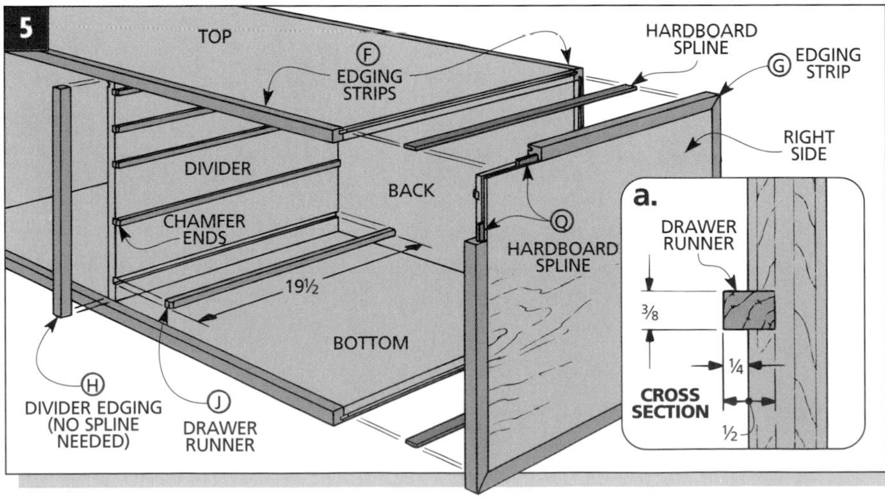
5
TOP
F EDGING STRIPS
HARDBOARD SPLINE
G EDGING STRIP
RIGHT SIDE
DIVIDER
BACK
CHAMFER ENDS
Q HARDBOARD SPLINE
19 1/2
BOTTOM
H DIVIDER EDGING (NO SPLINE NEEDED)
J DRAWER RUNNER
a.
DRAWER RUNNER
3/8
1/4
CROSS SECTION
1/2

CABINET

To build the cabinet, start by cutting all the plywood pieces to size *(Fig. 1)*. (I used 3/4" maple plywood, but birch plywood would work just as well.) The top/bottom (A) and back (B) are cut 1 5/8" less than the distance between the legs of the bench (to allow for edging strips and clearance).

The divider (D) is cut to the same size as the sides (C) to begin with to make it easier to match the spacing of the dadoes for the drawer guides. Then later, special "keys" are added to make up for the difference *(Fig. 1)*.

EDGING STRIPS. Next, 3/4" x 3/4" edging strips (F, G, H) are ripped to rough length. These strips hide the edges of the plywood and join the corners of the cabinet (refer to *Fig. 5*).

GROOVES. To help align the edging strips and the plywood, I used 1/8" hardboard splines (refer to *Fig. 3*). The splines fit into grooves routed into both the edging strips and all four edges of all the plywood pieces (except the divider). To rout the grooves, I used a slot cutter in the router table *(Fig. 2)*. All the edging strips, except those on the front, are grooved on two sides.

DADOES. Before the case can be assembled, dadoes have to be cut in the plywood. The first dadoes join the divider to the other panels *(Fig. 1)*.

The next dadoes are channels for 1/4" dowels (glide pins) that are part of the flip-up door assembly. These dadoes are positioned 3/8" down from the top of the divider and left side panel *(Fig. 4)*.

And finally, five pairs of dadoes are cut for the drawer runners on the right side panel and divider *(Fig. 4)*.

RUNNERS. When the dadoes are finished, rip ten drawer runners (J) to fit in the dadoes and glue them in place before the plywood warps *(Fig. 5a)*.

APPLY EDGING STRIPS. Now the edging strips can be applied to the edges of the plywood panels.

Begin by ripping 1/8" hardboard splines (Q) 7/16" wide. (This is 1/16" less than needed, to provide glue relief.) Then cut all the splines 1/2" shorter than the plywood edges they'll be joined to. (This allows 1/4" at each end so the splines won't interfere with one another.)

I glued the edging strips (G) to the side panels first *(Fig. 5)*. They're mitered to length to fit around the plywood.

Next glue the edging (F, H) to the

top and bottom panels and the front of the divider. (The top and bottom use splines; the divider doesn't.) Then saw the ends flush with the ends of the plywood.

DIVIDER KEYS. Finally, keys (I) are needed to fasten the divider into the other panels *(Figs. 1 & 6)*. Glue them to the top, bottom, and back of the divider.

DOOR PREPARATION. Before the cabinet can be glued together, the left side and the divider have to be prepared to install the door. The first step is to locate and bore holes for the $1/2$" dowels that hold the door up when it's open *(Fig. 7)*.

The door actually hangs on two glide pins ($1/4$" dowels) that slide in the grooves already routed on the inside of the panels *(Fig. 6)*. These grooves have to be extended into the front edging strip by notching out a small section with a chisel *(Fig. 7)*.

ASSEMBLE CASE. Now the cabinet can be assembled by joining the corners with the edging strips and splines.

DOOR

After the cabinet is assembled, measure the opening to get the dimensions needed to make the door *(Fig. 8)*. For the door to swing freely, allow for a $1/8$" gap at the top, a $1/16$" gap at the bottom, and a $1/32$" gap on each side. Then, subtract an additional $1/2$" from the width and height for $1/4$"-thick trim strips that will be on the edges of the door.

TRIM STRIPS. After cutting the plywood door to size, rip the trim strips and glue them onto the edges *(Fig. 9)*.

GLIDE PINS. The door rides on pins that slide in the routed grooves. These pins are $1/4$" dowels mounted in the side edges of the door *(Fig. 9)*. (Don't glue in the dowels — they might have to be removed if the door needs trimming.)

INSTALL DOOR. To hang the door, begin by chamfering the front upper corner *(Fig. 9)*. Then install the pull.

While holding the door in the compartment at an angle *(Fig. 10)*, align the pins with the grooves and twist the door parallel with the front of the case.

SUPPORT DOWELS. The last step in installing the door is putting in the dowels that hold it horizontal when it's open *(Fig. 11)*. Begin by cutting two $1/2$" dowels $1/2$" long. Next drill a shank hole through the center. Then swing the door up and screw the dowels in place. (Note: Don't glue in the support dowels. You may want to replace the glide pins.)

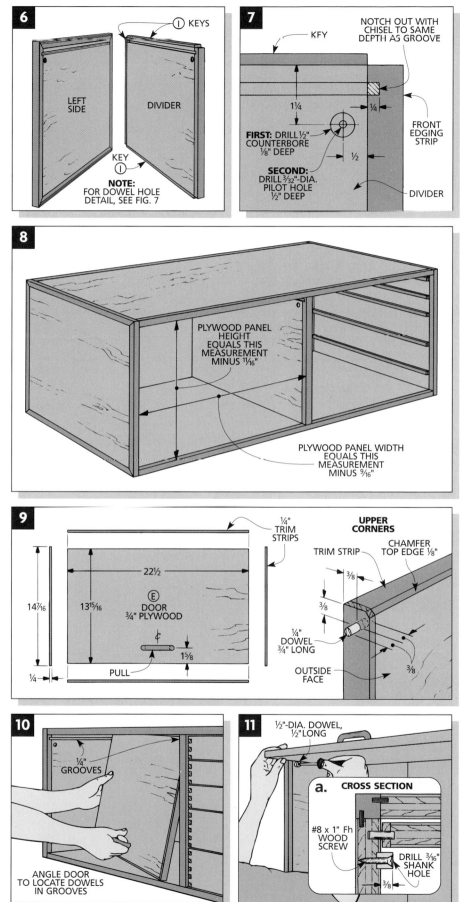

After the door is installed, the five drawers can be made. First, rip the drawer pieces (K, L, M, N) to width from ½" stock *(Fig. 12)*. Then cut them to length. The front/back pieces are ⅛" less than the width of the opening.

BOX JOINTS. Now cut the box joint fingers on each piece *(Fig. 13)*. (For more on box joints, see pages 90 to 93.)

GROOVES. Once the box joints are complete, grooves need to be cut in the drawer parts for the runners and bottoms. The critical part of positioning these grooves is making sure they remain invisible from the front.

Start by cutting ⅜"-wide grooves on the outside of the drawer's *side* pieces (L, N) to fit over the runners. These grooves should align with the second box joint slot from the bottom *(Fig. 13)*.

The second set of grooves are cut on the inside of *all* the pieces for the ¼" hardboard bottom (P). To make sure these grooves are not visible from the front, align the dado blade with the bottom edge of the bottom slot *(Fig. 13)*.

ASSEMBLY. Now, the drawers can be assembled (see Shop Tip below). Then chisel out the finger that blocks the rear of the runner groove *(Fig. 14)*. And fill the void in the sides (created by the bottom groove) with wood putty.

CLEATS. The last step is to screw two cleats to the bottom of the cabinet. These prevent the cabinet from sliding off the stretchers *(Fig. 17)*. ■

SHOP TIP
Clamping Blocks

To apply pressure only on the fingers of a box joint, make special clamping blocks. I use the box joint jig to make these blocks.

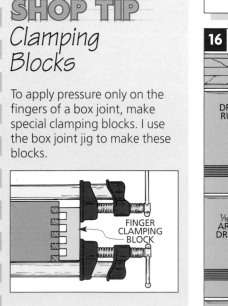

FINGER CLAMPING BLOCK

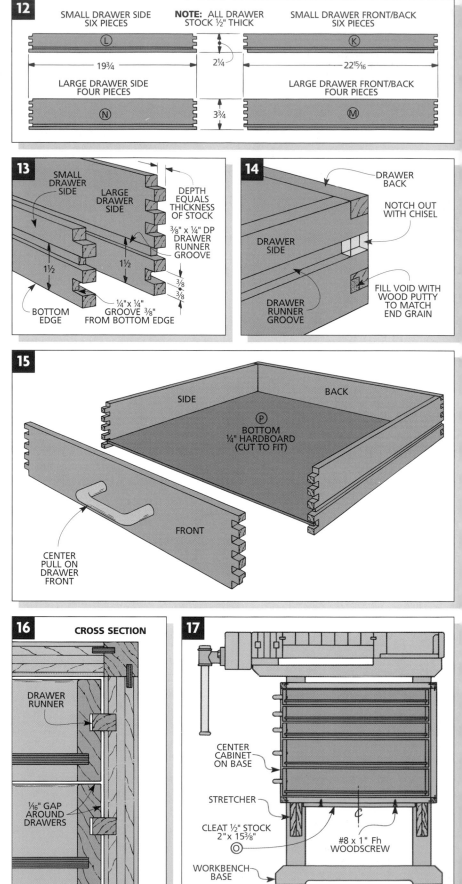

12 SMALL DRAWER SIDE SIX PIECES — L — 19¾ — **NOTE:** ALL DRAWER STOCK ½" THICK 2¼ — SMALL DRAWER FRONT/BACK SIX PIECES — K — 22¹⁵⁄₁₆

LARGE DRAWER SIDE FOUR PIECES — N — 3¾ — LARGE DRAWER FRONT/BACK FOUR PIECES — M

13 SMALL DRAWER SIDE / LARGE DRAWER SIDE / DEPTH EQUALS THICKNESS OF STOCK / ⅜" x ¼" DP DRAWER RUNNER GROOVE / 1½ / 1½ / ⅜ / ⅜ / BOTTOM EDGE / ¼" x ¼" GROOVE ⅜" FROM BOTTOM EDGE

14 DRAWER BACK / NOTCH OUT WITH CHISEL / DRAWER SIDE / DRAWER RUNNER GROOVE / FILL VOID WITH WOOD PUTTY TO MATCH END GRAIN

15 SIDE / BACK / P / BOTTOM ¼" HARDBOARD (CUT TO FIT) / FRONT / CENTER PULL ON DRAWER FRONT

16 CROSS SECTION / DRAWER RUNNER / ¹⁄₁₆" GAP AROUND DRAWERS

17 CENTER CABINET ON BASE / STRETCHER / CLEAT ½" STOCK 2" x 15⅜" / WORKBENCH BASE / #8 x 1" Fh WOODSCREW

DESIGNER'S NOTEBOOK

Adding sliding doors and shelves actually makes this version of the cabinet simpler to build. It also provides more storage space for larger objects or portable tools.

CONSTRUCTION NOTES:

■ The joinery for this version of the cabinet is similar to the original, but to allow for sliding doors, some of the measurements change.

■ Cut the top and bottom plywood panels (A) $3/4$" narrower ($18^3/4$") than in the original.

■ The top/bottom edging (F) at the front of the original cabinet is replaced by upper (R) and lower (S) door tracks. Cut these tracks $1^1/2$" wide *(Fig. 2)*.

■ Cut two $5/16$"-wide grooves in each of the tracks for the doors *(Fig. 2)*. The grooves in the upper track are deeper ($7/16$") than those in the lower ($3/16$").

■ Glue the tracks with splines (G) to the top and bottom panels.

■ Cut the divider (D) to size. You won't need the divider keys (I).

■ If you want to add shelves, drill $1/4$" shelf support holes in the sides (C) and divider (D).

■ Glue and assemble the case.

■ Add a $1/4$"-thick edging strip (H) to the front edge of the divider *(Fig. 2)*.

■ Cut $3/4$" plywood shelves (T) and edge with $1/4$"-thick edging (U).

■ Glue small $2^1/2$"-long door stops (V) into the back groove at the left end of the lower door track and the front groove at the right end *(Fig. 1)*.

■ Cut two overlapping sliding doors (W) from $1/4$" hardboard $3/8$" higher than the cabinet opening (15") *(Fig. 2)*.

■ Screw a wood pull onto each door.

■ Slip each door into position by raising it all of the way up into the groove in the upper track and then lowering it into the lower track.

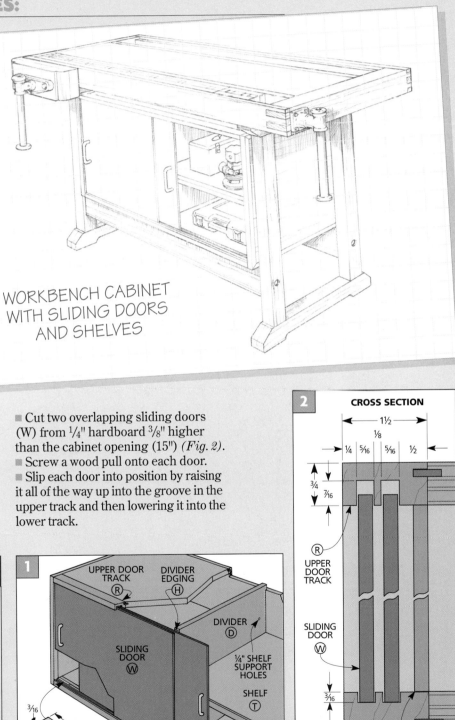

WORKBENCH CABINET WITH SLIDING DOORS AND SHELVES

CHANGES TO MATERIALS

CABINET WITH SLIDING DOORS

A	Top/Bottom (2)	$3/4$ ply. - $18^3/4$ x $46^7/8$
D	Divider (1)	$3/4$ ply. - $15^1/8$ x 19
F	Top/Btm. Edging	Only Need Two
H	Divider Edging (1)	$1/4$ x $3/4$ - 16 rough
R	Upr. Door Track (1)	$3/4$ x $1^1/2$ - $46^7/8$
S	Lwr. Door Track (1)	$3/4$ x $1^1/2$ - $46^7/8$
T	Shelves (2)	$3/4$ ply. - $18^1/2$ x $22^{15}/16$
U	Shelf Edging (2)	$1/4$ x $3/4$ - $22^{15}/16$
V	Door Stops (2)	$3/16$ x $5/16$ - $2^1/2$
W	Sliding Doors (2)	$1/4$ hdbd. - 15 x $23^3/4$

Do not need parts E, I, J, K, L, M, N, P

HARDWARE

(8) $1/4$" shelf supports
(2) $7/16$"-dia. x $3^3/4$"-bore wood pulls

TOOL STANDS

When it comes to machine tools, it seems as though there is always room for improvement. Whether it's adding storage space, dust collection, or efficiency, there is really no end to the customizing and updating you can do for your tools. Take the table saw cabinet shown in this section as an example. It allows you to rip long boards, without throwing a lot of dust in the air, and roll the stand out of the way when you're done.

The router table also comes with features designed for efficiency, including a miter gauge slot. You could also choose just to make the fence to fit your existing router table. Several optional accessories are included.

The mobile miter saw station with fold-down wings offers perhaps the greatest convenience: the ability to cut long pieces to length without measuring or marking.

Table Saw Cabinet — 52

Shop Tip: Leg Levelers 55
Shop Tip: Dust Collector Hook-up 56
Shop Tip: Making and Using a Push Stick 58
Designer's Notebook: Outfeed Support 59

Router Table — 60

Shop Tip: Pattern Bit. 63
Shop Tip: Adding a Miter Gauge Slot 65
Shop Tip: Installing Threaded Inserts. 67
Accessories: Fence Add-Ons 70

Miter Saw Station — 72

Shop Tip: Cutting Plywood Without Chipout 74
Shop Tip: Routing Chamfers on Edges 76
Shop Tip: Customizing To Your Saw. 79
Setup: Miter Saw Station. 81

Table Saw Cabinet

This sturdy but mobile cabinet will improve your table-saw setup with storage space, two different options for dust collection, and an outfeed support for long workpieces.

The stand that came with my table saw always struck me as a bit of an afterthought — a "bare bones" metal frame that supported the saw. But by replacing it with this shop-built cabinet, I was able to make a number of worthwhile improvements.

STORAGE. First, there's a large drawer for storing jigs, accessories, and saw blades. And the miter gauge, rip fence, and push stick are held in place with simple holders when not in use.

DUST COLLECTION. Besides adding storage, the cabinet also provides a way to control dust. A pullout bin collects the dust (see photo at right). Or, as an option, you could hook a dust collector up to the bin (refer to page 56).

STABILITY. Another thing I like about this cabinet is that it's much more stable than my old metal stand. The reason is simple — it's heavier. Made from medium-density fiberboard (MDF) and Douglas fir, there's enough mass to damp the saw's vibration.

But regardless of its weight, casters make the stand easy to roll wherever you need it. And once it's in place, spe-

cial levelers raise it off the casters for rock solid support.

OPTIONAL OUTFEED SUPPORT. Once I finished the cabinet, I decided to add an outfeed support. It attaches to the back of the cabinet with a couple of knobs. For more on the outfeed support, see the Designer's Notebook on page 59.

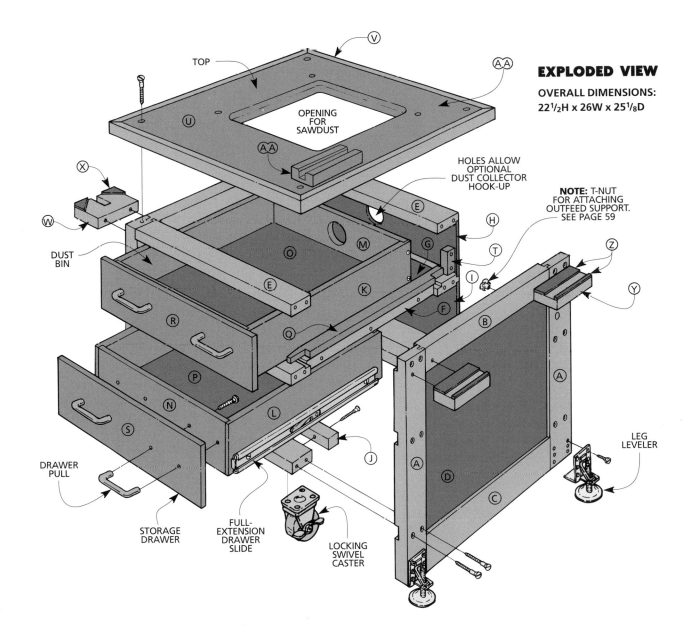

TOP

OPENING FOR SAWDUST

EXPLODED VIEW

OVERALL DIMENSIONS:
22½H x 26W x 25⅛D

HOLES ALLOW OPTIONAL DUST COLLECTOR HOOK-UP

NOTE: T-NUT FOR ATTACHING OUTFEED SUPPORT. SEE PAGE 59

DUST BIN

DRAWER PULL

STORAGE DRAWER

FULL-EXTENSION DRAWER SLIDE

LOCKING SWIVEL CASTER

LEG LEVELER

MATERIALS LIST

BASE

A	Stiles (4)	1½ x 3 - 21
B	Upr. Side Rails (2)	1½ x 3 - 19
C	Lwr. Side Rails (2)	1½ x 4¾ - 19
D	Sides (2)	¾ MDF - 14¼ x 19
E	Frt./Back Rails (6)	1½ x 3 - 21½
F	Cleats (2)	1½ x 1½ - 18
G	Dust Shelf (1)	¼ hdbd. - 19 x 19¾
H	Upr. Bk. Panel (1)	¼ hdbd. - 6¼ x 21¾
I	Lwr. Bk. Panel (1)	¼ hdbd. - 8½ x 21¾
J	Support Strips (2)	1½ x 2 - 21

DUST BIN & STORAGE DRAWER

K	Bin Sides (2)	¾ MDF - 5 x 22
L	Drawer Sides (2)	¾ MDF - 7¼ x 22
M	Bin Front/Back (2)	¾ MDF - 5 x 19¼
N	Drwr. Frt./Bk. (2)	¾ MDF - 7¼ x 19¼
O	Bin Bottom (1)	¼ hdbd. - 19¼ x 21¼
P	Drwr. Bottom (1)	¼ hdbd. - 19¼ x 21¼

Q	Guides (2)	¾ MDF - ⅞ x 21½
R	False Bin Front (1)	¾ MDF - 5⅜ x 20⅞
S	False Drwr. Frt. (1)	¾ MDF - 7⅝ x 20⅞
T	Stops (2)	¾ MDF - 1 x 3

TOP

U	Top Pieces (2)	¾ MDF - 23⅝ x 24½
V	Trim Strips (4)	1½ x ¾ - 27 rough

ACCESSORIES

W	Miter Gge. Blk. (1)	1½ x 3 - 7
X	Corner Trim (2)	¼ hdbd. - 1⅜ x 1⅜
Y	Rip Fence Blks. (2)	1½ x 3 - 6
Z	Hdbd. Strips (4)	¼ hdbd. - 1¼ rgh. x 6
AA	Pushstk. Hlster. (1)	1½ x 3 - 8½

HARDWARE SUPPLIES

(24) No. 6 x ¾" Fh woodscrews
(4) No. 8 x 1½" Fh woodscrews
(1) No. 8 x 3" Fh woodscrews

(6) No. 10 x 4" Fh woodscrews
(24) No. 8 x ¾" Rh woodscrews
(16) No. 14 x ⅝" panhead screws
(10) No. 8 x 1¼" Fh sheet metal screws*
(20) No. 8 x 1½" Fh sheet metal screws*
(6) No. 8 x 2" Fh sheet metal screws*
(8) 8-32 x 1¾" machine screws
(4) 3¾" drawer pulls
(4) ⁵⁄₁₆" T-nuts
(4) ⁵⁄₁₆" x 1½" hex bolts
(16) ¼" flat washers
(4) ⁵⁄₁₆" flat washers
(2) 3" locking swivel casters
(2) 3" fixed casters
(4) Heavy-duty leg levelers
(1 pr.) 22" full-extension drawer slides
* To avoid splitting MDF, use flathead sheet metal screws with a straight shank.

CUTTING DIAGRAM

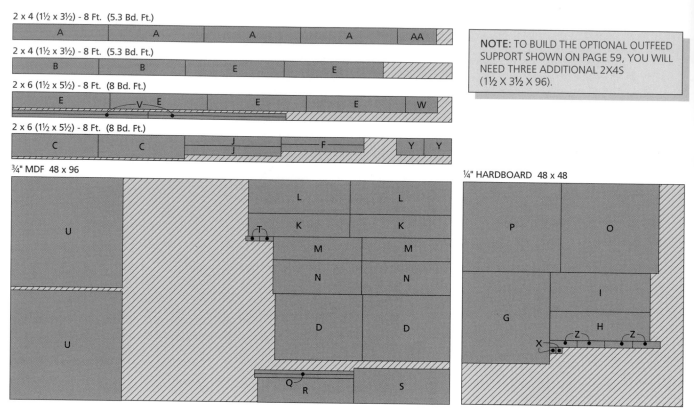

2 x 4 (1½ x 3½) - 8 Ft. (5.3 Bd. Ft.)

2 x 4 (1½ x 3½) - 8 Ft. (5.3 Bd. Ft.)

2 x 6 (1½ x 5½) - 8 Ft. (8 Bd. Ft.)

2 x 6 (1½ x 5½) - 8 Ft. (8 Bd. Ft.)

¾" MDF 48 x 96

¼" HARDBOARD 48 x 48

NOTE: TO BUILD THE OPTIONAL OUTFEED SUPPORT SHOWN ON PAGE 59, YOU WILL NEED THREE ADDITIONAL 2X4S (1½ X 3½ X 96).

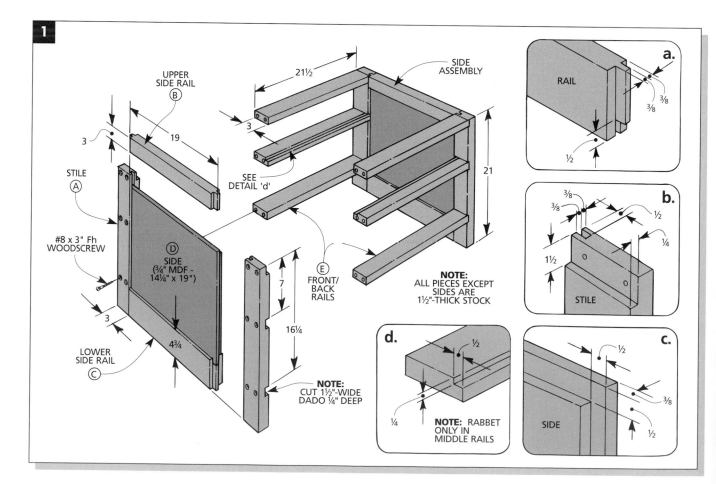

1

UPPER SIDE RAIL (B)

21½

SIDE ASSEMBLY

3

19

STILE (A)

SEE DETAIL 'd'

#8 x 3" Fh WOODSCREW

(D) SIDE (¾" MDF - 14¼" x 19")

3

4¾

LOWER SIDE RAIL (C)

7

16¼

(E) FRONT/ BACK RAILS

21

NOTE: ALL PIECES EXCEPT SIDES ARE 1½"-THICK STOCK

NOTE: CUT 1½"-WIDE DADO ¼" DEEP

a. RAIL — ⅜ · ⅜ · ½

b. STILE — ⅜ · ⅜ · ½ · ¼ · 1½

d. **NOTE:** RABBET ONLY IN MIDDLE RAILS — ½ · ¼

c. SIDE — ½ · ⅜ · ½

BASE

The first thing to build is the base of the cabinet. It houses the dust bin and storage drawer and supports the top.

SIDE ASSEMBLIES. The base starts out as two side assemblies. These are "two-by" wood frames with ³⁄₄"-thick MDF panels that are held together with stub tenon and groove joints *(Fig. 1)*.

Each frame consists of two stiles (A), an upper side rail (B), and a lower side rail (C). To accept the stub tenons on the rails and a tongue on the panel (to be cut later), there's a groove cut in each piece *(Fig. 1b)*. What's unusual here is the fact that these grooves are cut off-center.

That's because the panels that form the sides (D) of the cabinet are rabbeted on all four edges to form tongues *(Fig. 1c)*. Fitting these tongues into the grooves centers the sides in the frames.

Before gluing up the side assemblies, you'll need to cut stub tenons on the ends of the side rails *(Fig. 1a)*. And two dadoes and a rabbet cut in each stile will accept a set of rails that will hold the side assemblies together.

RAILS. Besides adding rigidity, the front/back rails (E) form the openings for the dust bin and storage drawer. Although they're identical in size, the top inside edge of each middle rail is rabbeted for a dust shelf *(Fig. 1d)*. Then the rails are screwed in place.

DUST SHELF. The dust shelf keeps dust from falling into the storage drawer. In addition to the middle rails, it's supported on the sides by two cleats (F) that are also rabbeted on the top inside edge *(Figs. 2 and 2a)*. After gluing and screwing the cleats in place, cut a ¹⁄₄" hardboard dust shelf (G) to fit. Then glue this shelf into the rabbets.

BACK. The back of the cabinet is also enclosed with pieces of hardboard. After routing a rabbet around each opening in back, just cut an upper back panel (H) and a lower back panel (I) to fit those openings. Then each of the panels can be glued and screwed in place *(Figs. 3 and 3a)*.

CASTERS. To make the cabinet easy to roll around the shop, I added a set of heavy-duty casters. But first, to provide a large mounting surface, a support strip (J) is glued and screwed to each bottom rail. Then install a pair of locking swivel casters in front and fixed casters in back *(Fig. 3b)*.

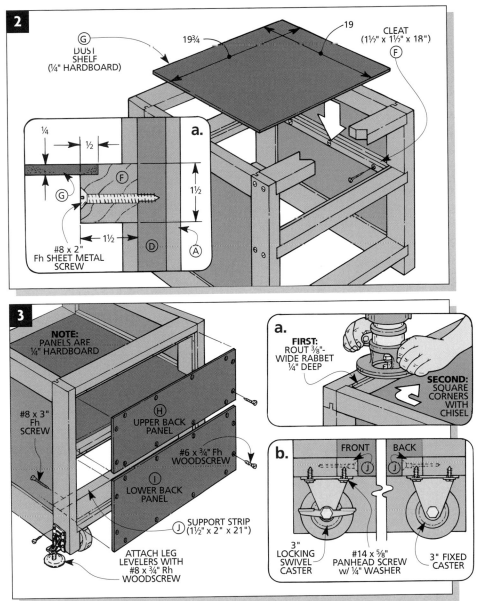

SHOP TIP .... Leg Levelers

Even with the locking casters, I was still a bit concerned that the cabinet might "creep" when the saw was running. I needed a way to increase stability without sacrificing mobility.

So I decided to install four heavy-duty leg levelers to raise the table saw cabinet off the casters when the saw is in use (see photo at right).

An Allen wrench is all that's needed to adjust these levelers and give your cabinet some added stability.

Now with the base completed, you can begin building the dust bin and drawer to fit their openings.

The lengths of the bin and drawer are the same (22") *(Fig. 4)*. And so are their widths (20"). This allows for guides for the bin and for the drawer slides. But their heights are different. To allow for false fronts (to be added later), they're $\frac{1}{2}$" shorter than their openings (5" and $7\frac{1}{4}$").

To build the bin and drawer, start by cutting the sides (K, L) to finished size *(Fig. 4)*. Rabbet the ends of each side to accept front/back pieces (M, N) *(Fig. 4a)* and cut grooves for the bottoms (O, P) *(Fig. 4b)*. To keep the MDF from splitting, drill pilot holes. Then assemble the pieces with glue and screws.

SLIDES AND GUIDES. To provide easy access to the storage drawer, full-extension slides are installed on the storage drawer. But I decided to take a different approach with the dust bin.

To eliminate the hassle of releasing a slide to pull out the dust bin, I made two guides (Q) *(Fig. 5)*. These are just strips of MDF that are notched to fit around the stiles. To help guide the bin into the opening, the front ends are tapered *(Fig. 5a)*.

FALSE FRONTS. With the guides glued in place, I installed the bin and drawer and added false fronts (R, S) *(Fig. 4)*. They're cut to allow a $\frac{1}{16}$" gap all the way around, and then attached with screws *(Fig. 4b)*.

Finally, after installing pulls, I screwed in stops (T) to keep the bin and drawer flush with the front of the cabinet *(Fig. 5a)*.

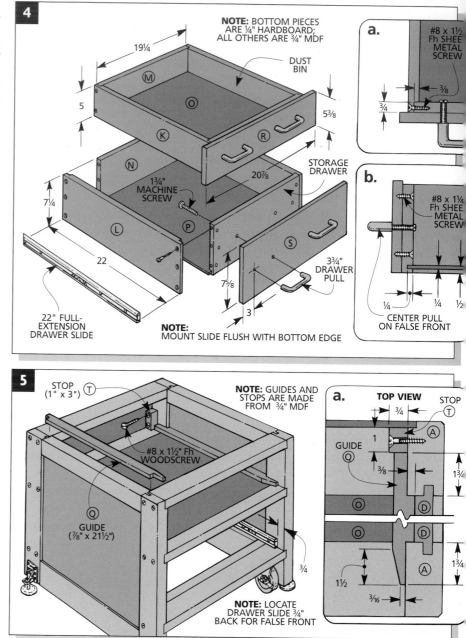

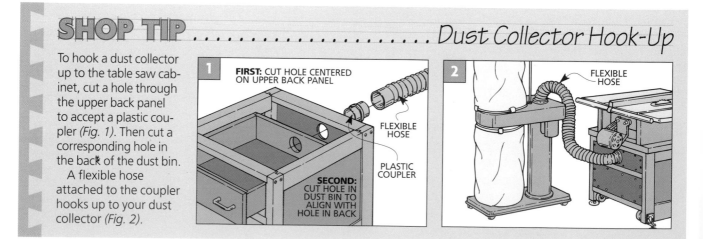

SHOP TIP .... *Dust Collector Hook-Up*

To hook a dust collector up to the table saw cabinet, cut a hole through the upper back panel to accept a plastic coupler *(Fig. 1)*. Then cut a corresponding hole in the back of the dust bin.

A flexible hose attached to the coupler hooks up to your dust collector *(Fig. 2)*.

TOP

The top of the cabinet acts as a mounting platform for the table saw. So I wanted a thick, heavy slab to help damp any vibration.

Note: If you're planning to hook up a dust collector, it's easiest to do it before making the top (refer to the Shop Tip at the bottom of the opposite page).

The top is built up from two pieces of $3/4$"-thick MDF *(Fig. 6)*. What I found worked best here was to cut one top piece (U) to size first. Then glue on a second (slightly oversized) piece with contact cement and rout the edges with a flush trim bit. (This is similar to the technique for building a top for the cabinets shown on page 16).

TRIM. To cover the exposed edges, the top is "wrapped" with trim strips (V) *(Fig. 6)*. These are just pieces of $1\frac{1}{2}$"-thick stock that are ripped to a width of $3/4$". After mitering the strips to length to fit the table top, they can simply be glued in place.

OPENING. At this point you can screw the top to the base, and then lay out an opening for dust to fall through *(Fig. 7)*. The location of this opening is determined by the position of your metal saw cabinet.

If it's a contractor-type saw where the motor hangs off the back, there's one thing to be aware of. Since the motor swings to the side when you tilt the blade, you'll have to allow for clearance to keep it from hitting the top of the cabinet.

To allow this clearance, position the metal saw cabinet so it's flush with the *back* edge of the cabinet top and centered between the sides *(Figs. 7 and 7a)*. Next, mark an outline around the saw cabinet with a pencil. Then remove the saw and set it on the floor.

Now, to lay out the actual opening, measure $3\frac{1}{8}$" in from the back of the cabinet and $2\frac{1}{4}$" in from the pencil lines, and draw the shape of the opening. Finally, drill out each corner of the opening, and then cut between the holes with a sabre (jig) saw.

ATTACH SAW. Once the opening is cut, you can attach the saw. It's held in place with bolts that are threaded into T-nuts installed in the top from underneath *(Figs. 7 and 7a)*.

Note: For clearance, you may need to drill additional holes in the metal flange of the saw.

A built-up top with a large opening allows sawdust to fall into the dust bin below. It also provides a sturdy platform for mounting the table saw.

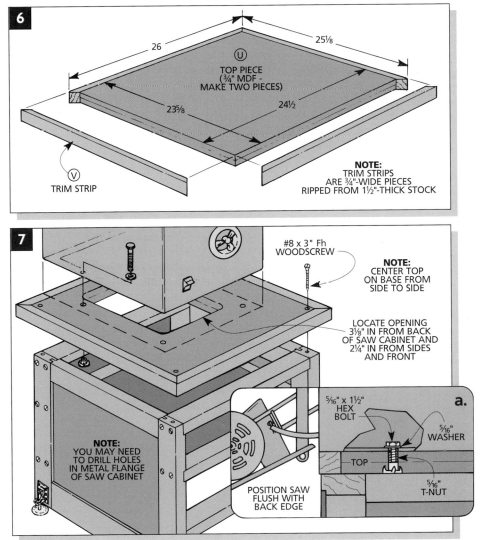

6

26

$25\frac{1}{8}$

U

TOP PIECE
($3/4$" MDF - MAKE TWO PIECES)

$23\frac{5}{8}$

$24\frac{1}{2}$

NOTE:
TRIM STRIPS ARE $3/4$"-WIDE PIECES RIPPED FROM $1\frac{1}{2}$"-THICK STOCK

V

TRIM STRIP

7

#8 x 3" Fh
WOODSCREW

NOTE:
CENTER TOP ON BASE FROM SIDE TO SIDE

LOCATE OPENING $3\frac{1}{8}$" IN FROM BACK OF SAW CABINET AND $2\frac{1}{4}$" IN FROM SIDES AND FRONT

NOTE:
YOU MAY NEED TO DRILL HOLES IN METAL FLANGE OF SAW CABINET

POSITION SAW FLUSH WITH BACK EDGE

a.

$5/16$" x $1\frac{1}{2}$"
HEX BOLT

$5/16$"
WASHER

TOP

$5/16$"
T-NUT

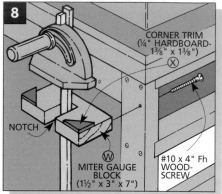

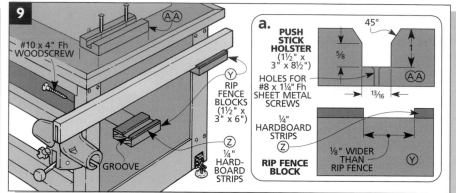

ACCESSORIES

When I'm working on the table saw, it seems like I'm constantly switching between ripping and crosscutting. And that means I'm always reaching for the miter gauge, rip fence, and push stick.

The problem is that I've never had a really convenient and safe place to set these accessories when they're not in use. So I decided to add a "home" for each of these on the table saw cabinet.

MITER GAUGE BRACKET. I started making a miter gauge bracket by cutting a block (W) out of 1½"-thick stock (*Fig. 8*). Then I cut a notch in it, big enough to easily accept the bar on my miter gauge. Next, glue a triangular-shaped trim piece (X) at each corner. These hold the miter gauge and keep it from slipping off.

Then I screwed the bracket to the left side of the cabinet (*Fig. 8*).

RIP FENCE BRACKETS. A rip fence needs a couple of brackets to support it (*Fig. 9*). Again, I used 1½" stock for the blocks (Y). But this time I created a groove on the top of each block with a pair of hardboard strips (Z). To make it easy to position the fence on the blocks, glue the strips down so the groove is ⅛" wider than the fence (*Fig. 9a*).

Then screw the brackets to the stiles on the right side of the cabinet (*Fig. 9*).

PUSH STICK HOLSTER. After making a push stick (see Shop Tip box below), I wanted to make a "holster" for it that would make it convenient to grab.

The holster is just a piece of 2x4 with a groove cut in it that's slightly wider than the thickness of the push stick (*Fig. 9a*). To make it easier to insert the push stick, bevel the edges of the groove. Then screw the holster down to the top of the cabinet (*Fig. 9*). ∎

SHOP TIP . . . . Making and Using a Push Stick

Every table saw should come with a good push stick. Most don't — so you have to make your own.

The one shown here is big enough to keep your hands away from the blade. And it can easily be made (or repaired if it gets chewed up). But most important, it allows you to hold the workpiece *down* tight against the table as well as push straight ahead.

I made my push stick out of ¾" medium density fiberboard (MDF) but you could use plywood. First cut it to the shape shown in the grid drawing (*Fig. 1*). The base area is wide so that you can recut it and create a new bottom and heel if it gets chewed up (*Fig. 2*).

To make it easier on the hand, I rounded the handle with a ¼" roundover bit.

To prevent kickback when cutting thin strips, be sure that the heel of the push stick hooks over the strip *between* the blade and the fence (*Fig.3*).

When ripping wider pieces, *center* the push stick between the blade and the fence (*Fig. 4*).

DESIGNER'S NOTEBOOK

This optional outfeed support system is a great way to "catch" a long workpiece when completing a cut. And it's simple enough to easily be added to the basic Table Saw Cabinet design.

CONSTRUCTION NOTES:

■ Start by making a crossbar. Glue a cover (BB) on top of a $1\frac{1}{2}$"-thick arm (CC). Then cut a wide bevel in the cover *(Detail 'a')*. This will help direct thin, sagging workpieces onto and over the crossbar.

■ The top of the crossbar must be at the same height as the saw table. So measure from the bottom of the cabinet to the top of the saw table and subtract the thickness of the crossbar ($1\frac{3}{4}$"). Then cut the uprights (DD) to length.

■ Cut a rabbet at the top and a dado near the bottom of each upright.

■ Cut two rails (EE) to fit between the uprights and screw them in place.

■ Screw the crossbar to the top rail.

■ Cut two 20"-long connecting arms (FF) to attach the outfeed support to the cabinet. Rabbet both ends of each arm to fit over the uprights (DD) and the stiles (A) of the cabinet *(Detail 'b')*.

■ Drill a $\frac{5}{16}$" hole near one end and a $\frac{5}{16}$"-wide height adjustment slot near the other end of each arm.

■ Drill corresponding holes into the uprights and cabinet stiles, and install $\frac{5}{16}$" T-nuts *(Detail 'b')*. These accept threaded knobs that will lock the outfeed support in place.

■ Install a leg leveler at the bottom of each upright.

■ To allow for storage, add two T-nuts to the *outside* of each upright. Then the arms can be stored vertically on the inside faces of the uprights.

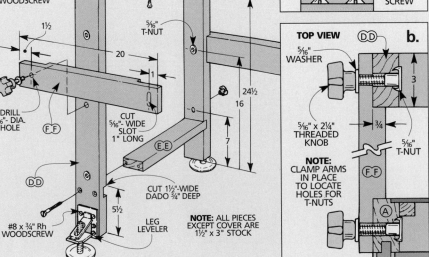

OUTFEED SUPPORT

MATERIALS LIST

OUTFEED SUPPORT
BB Crossbar Cover (1) $\frac{1}{4}$ hdbd. - 3 x 40
CC Crossbar Arm (1) $1\frac{1}{2}$ x 3 - 40
DD Uprights (2) $1\frac{1}{2}$ x 3 - $33\frac{3}{4}$
EE Rails (2) $1\frac{1}{2}$ x 3 - $22\frac{1}{2}$
FF Connect. Arms (2) $1\frac{1}{2}$ x 3 - 20

HARDWARE
(12) No. 8 x 3" Fh woodscrews
(12) No 8 x $\frac{3}{4}$" Rh woodscrews
(8) $\frac{5}{16}$" T-nuts
(4) $\frac{5}{16}$" x $2\frac{1}{4}$" threaded knobs
(4) $\frac{5}{16}$" flat washers
(2) Heavy-duty leg levelers

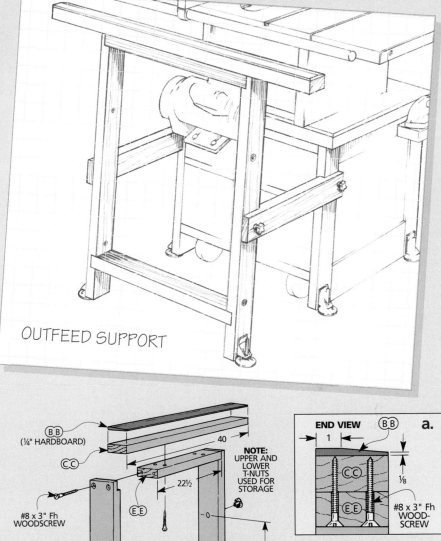

Router Table

This sturdy router table can be built as shown, with a solid base made entirely from 2x4s. But you can also build just the fence system with a number of tailor-made accessories to fit an existing router table.

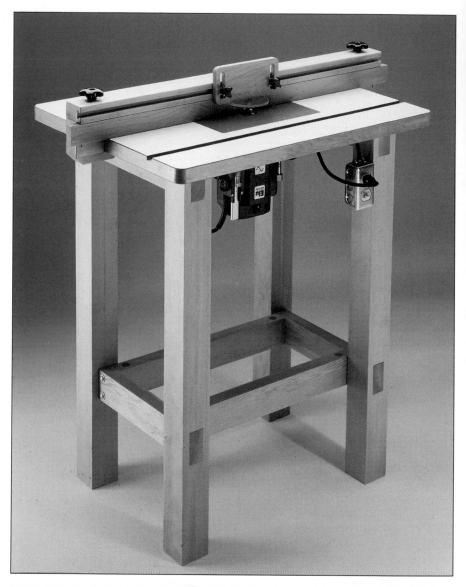

Over the years I've kept a list of all the features that should be on a router table. This table is designed with those features, but also with flexibility, so you can use only the parts you want — the base, the top with an insert plate, or the fence with a T-slot for accessories.

BASE. Sturdy and easy to build, the base is made entirely out of 2x4s. (I used Douglas fir.) Rails and stretchers provide solid support with simple joinery techniques.

TOP. I thought three features were essential for the top. First, I wanted a removable insert plate to hold the router. I also wanted a heavy top (to damp the vibration) and a miter slot.

The insert plate, which fits in a recessed opening in the table, can be made from $1/4$"-thick hardboard or durable phenolic plastic. By screwing the router to the bottom of this plate, you can simply lift the router out to change bits or to do freehand routing.

Routing out this recess can be tricky, so I used a special technique (refer to pages 64 and 65).

The top is a sandwiched core of plywood and hardboard, edged with hardwood and covered with plastic laminate on the top and bottom. This damps vibration and provides smooth, hard-wearing edges when the recess and miter gauge slot are routed in the surface.

FENCE. Even if you already have a router table, consider building just the fence. It has a T-slot that's designed to accept a variety of accessories (refer to pages 70 and 71). And the system used to clamp the fence to the table is easy to adapt to *any* size table.

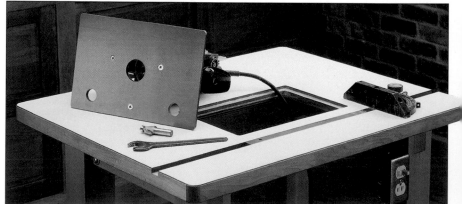

MATERIALS LIST

BASE
A Leg Pieces (8) $1\frac{1}{2}$ x 3 - 36
B Rails (4) $1\frac{1}{2}$ x 3 - 18
C Stretchers (3) $1\frac{1}{2}$ x 3 - $20\frac{1}{2}$

TABLE TOP
D Base (1) $\frac{3}{4}$ ply. - $21\frac{1}{2}$ x $28\frac{1}{2}$
E Covers (2) $\frac{1}{4}$ hdbd. - $21\frac{1}{2}$ x $28\frac{1}{2}$
F Side Edging (2) $\frac{3}{4}$ x $1\frac{1}{4}$ - $21\frac{1}{2}$
G Fr./Bk Edging (2) $\frac{3}{4}$ x $1\frac{1}{4}$ - 30
H Insert Plate (1) $\frac{1}{4}$ hdbd.* - $7\frac{3}{4}$ x $11\frac{3}{4}$

FENCE**
I Base Top (1) $1\frac{1}{16}$ x $1\frac{3}{4}$ - 36
J Base Bottom (1) $\frac{3}{4}$ x $1\frac{3}{4}$ - 36
K Sliding Faces (2) $\frac{3}{4}$ x $1\frac{3}{4}$ - 18
L Top Bars (2) $\frac{3}{4}$ x $2\frac{1}{2}$ - 36
M Arm Blank (1) $\frac{3}{4}$ x $1\frac{3}{4}$ - 8
N Spacers (2) $1\frac{1}{4}$ x $1\frac{3}{4}$ - $2\frac{7}{8}$
O Splines (2) $\frac{1}{8}$ hdbd. - $\frac{7}{8}$ x $1\frac{3}{4}$

*Or phenolic plastic
**Use hardwood for frame and accessories

HARDWARE SUPPLIES
(8) No. 8 x $\frac{7}{8}$" Fh woodscrews
(12) $\frac{1}{4}$" x $3\frac{1}{4}$" lag screws & washers
(1) $\frac{3}{4}$" x 24" hardwood dowel
(2 pcs.) $23\frac{1}{2}$" x $30\frac{1}{2}$" plastic laminate
(4) L-shaped mounting brackets
(4) $\frac{5}{16}$" inside dia. threaded inserts
(4) $\frac{5}{16}$" x $2\frac{1}{4}$" threaded knobs & washers
(2) $\frac{3}{8}$" x 6" carriage bolts
(2) $\frac{3}{8}$" plastic knobs (or wing nuts) & washers
T-slot nuts (for accessories, see pages 70-71)

EXPLODED VIEW

OVERALL DIMENSIONS (with fence).
$41\frac{1}{2}$H x 36W x 23D

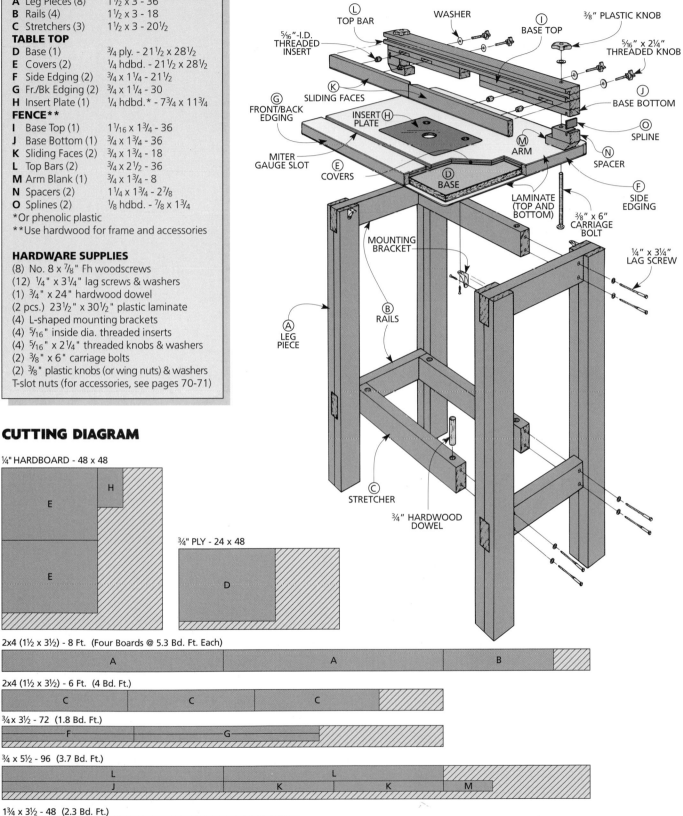

CUTTING DIAGRAM

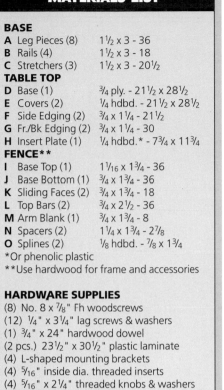

$\frac{1}{4}$" HARDBOARD - 48 x 48

$\frac{3}{4}$" PLY - 24 x 48

2x4 ($1\frac{1}{2}$ x $3\frac{1}{2}$) - 8 Ft. (Four Boards @ 5.3 Bd. Ft. Each)

2x4 ($1\frac{1}{2}$ x $3\frac{1}{2}$) - 6 Ft. (4 Bd. Ft.)

$\frac{3}{4}$ x $3\frac{1}{2}$ - 72 (1.8 Bd. Ft.)

$\frac{3}{4}$ x $5\frac{1}{2}$ - 96 (3.7 Bd. Ft.)

$1\frac{3}{4}$ x $3\frac{1}{2}$ - 48 (2.3 Bd. Ft.)

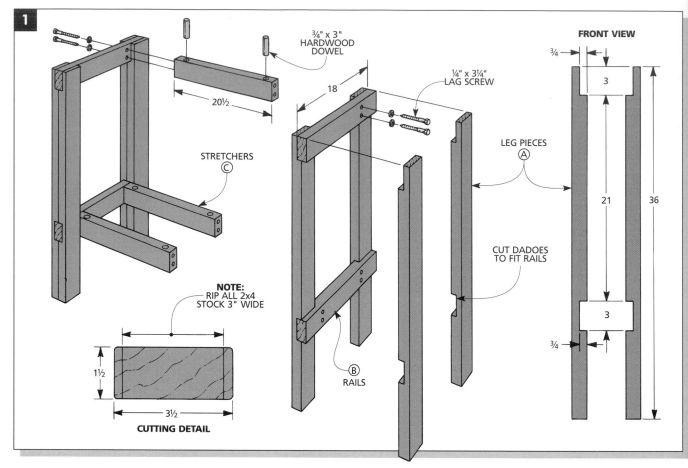

1

¾" x 3" HARDWOOD DOWEL

20½

STRETCHERS ©C

18

¼" x 3¼" LAG SCREW

LEG PIECES Ⓐ

CUT DADOES TO FIT RAILS

Ⓑ RAILS

NOTE: RIP ALL 2x4 STOCK 3" WIDE

1½

3½

CUTTING DETAIL

FRONT VIEW

¾

3

21

36

3

¾

BASE

All you need to build the base is four 8 ft. 2x4s and a 6 ft. 2x4. But before I started, I cleaned up the 2x4s a little by ripping ¼" off each edge, reducing the width to 3" (see Cutting Detail in *Fig. 1*).

END FRAMES. The base has two end frames, each consisting of two legs and two rails. Each leg is made from two 2x4s. These leg pieces (A) are cut to length and then sandwiched together in pairs *(Fig. 1)*.

To simplify the joinery and provide mortises for the rails (B), I pre-cut 3"-wide dadoes and rabbets in each leg piece before gluing them together.

After these cuts are made in the leg pieces, glue the legs and rails together to complete the two end frames *(Fig. 2)*.

STRETCHERS. Next, the end frames are joined together with three stretchers (C), also made from 2x4s.

Note: To provide access to the router, there isn't a top stretcher between the front legs.

The stretchers are fastened to the frames with lag screws. But since these lag screws are being threaded into end grain, there's a trick I decided to use to help strengthen this joint.

I drilled a ¾" hole, 1⅛" from the end of each stretcher and glued a dowel into each hole *(Fig. 3)*. The cross grain of the dowel holds the screw firmly.

ASSEMBLY. Finally, assemble the base by joining the end frames and the stretchers with ¼" x 3¼" lag screws (refer to *Figs. 1 and 3*).

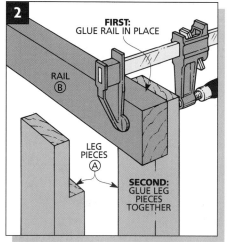

2

FIRST: GLUE RAIL IN PLACE

RAIL Ⓑ

LEG PIECES Ⓐ

SECOND: GLUE LEG PIECES TOGETHER

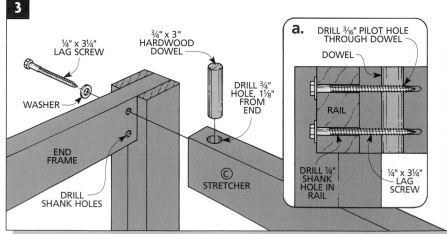

3

¼" x 3¼" LAG SCREW

¾" x 3" HARDWOOD DOWEL

DRILL ¾" HOLE, 1⅛" FROM END

WASHER

END FRAME

DRILL SHANK HOLES

STRETCHER ©C

a. DRILL 3/16" PILOT HOLE THROUGH DOWEL

DOWEL

RAIL

DRILL ¼" SHANK HOLE IN RAIL

¼" x 3¼" LAG SCREW

TABLE TOP

I began making the table top by cutting a base (D) to size ($21^1/_2$" x $28^1/_2$") from $^3/_4$"-thick plywood (*Fig. 4*).

The next step is to cut two slightly oversize covers (E) from $^1/_4$" hardboard and glue them on top of the plywood base with contact cement. Then use a flush trim bit (as shown on page 16) or a pattern bit (as shown in the Shop Tip below) to trim the hardboard flush with the plywood.

EDGING. Now the the whole core section can be edged with hardwood. I used $^3/_4$"-thick maple edging (F, G).

First, rip the edging to match the thickness of the top (*Fig. 5a*). Then cut it to length (*Fig. 5*).

Now, glue and clamp the edging pieces so they're flush with the edges of the top. When the glue is dry, sand or file a radius onto each corner (*Fig. 5b*).

LAMINATE. The last step is to glue plastic laminate to both the top and bottom faces of the table top (*Fig. 6*).

Note: It's important to glue laminate to *both* faces. This will help prevent the top from warping.

Here again, I cut the laminate oversize, then trimmed it — but this time with a chamfer bit to chamfer the edge of the top at the same time (*Fig. 6a*).

FINISH. Before going any further, I finished the base and edging with a tung-oil finish.

SHOP TIP

Pattern Bit

A pattern bit is like a flush trim bit, but the bearing is *above* the cutter on the shaft. You can use a pattern bit to trim pieces flush as shown below, or to rout openings as shown on page 65.

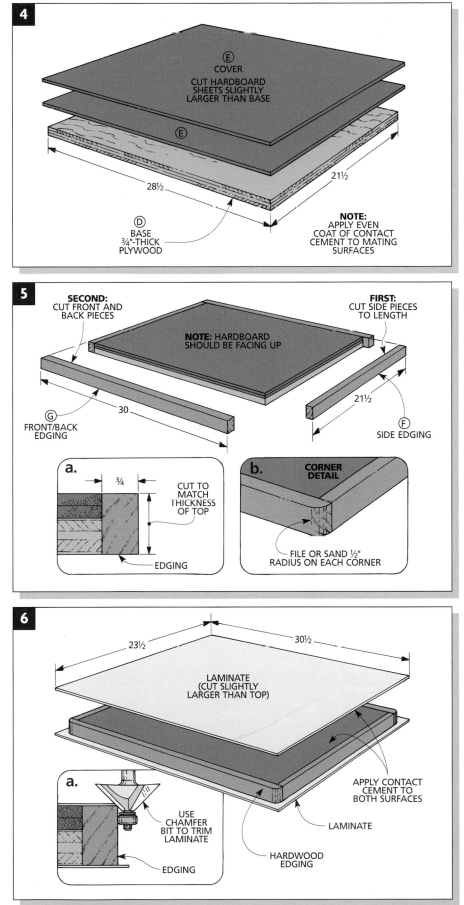

Before continuing, I found it easiest to work if I permanently mounted the table top onto the base with four L-shaped brackets (refer to the Exploded View on page 61 and the Shop Tip on page 16).

Once the top is fastened down, the next step is to make the removable insert plate. I used a piece of $1/4$"-thick phenolic plastic, but $1/4$" hardboard would also work just fine.

CUT TO SIZE. First, cut the insert plate (H) to finished size *(Fig. 7)*. If you plan to use a large router, you'll need to make the insert plate about 1" wider than the handles on the router.

Now use the base from your router as a template to locate and drill the mounting holes and the center hole. Also drill two finger holes *(Fig. 7)*.

Next, sand or file a $1/4$" radius on each corner of the insert. (This equals the radius of the pattern bit used to rout the recess later, refer to *Fig. 12*.) Finally, chamfer all the edges *(Fig. 7a)*.

LAY OUT OPENING. After the insert plate is complete, I used it as a template for laying out the opening in the top.

To do this, first position the plate 6" in from the front edge of the top, making sure it's centered side-to-side *(Fig. 8)*. Then you can simply trace around it with a pencil.

But *don't* cut out the opening yet. First you need to lay out a lip to hold up the plate. To do this, start by drawing cut lines for the lip, $3/8$" *in* from the outline *(Fig. 9)*. Next, drill a hole in each corner that's formed by those cut lines.

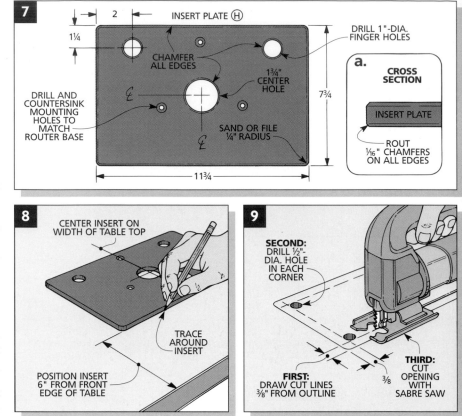

Then, finally, use a sabre saw to cut out the opening.

ROUT THE LIP. The next step is to rout the lip for the insert plate to sit on. There's a trick to getting the outline of the lip to perfectly match the insert plate. I used the plate itself as a setup guide for positioning four guide strips. These strips were then used to guide a pattern bit to rout out the lipped recess. By using the plate itself I was assured

that the opening I routed would be the exact same size as the insert plate.

To do this, first place the insert plate over the opening so it aligns with the outline previously drawn on the table top.

The pattern bit I used has a cutter length of 1". So, in order to provide a surface for the bearing to ride against, the guide strips also needed to be 1" thick. I made these by gluing up $1/4$" hardboard and $3/4$" plywood. *(Fig. 10a)*.

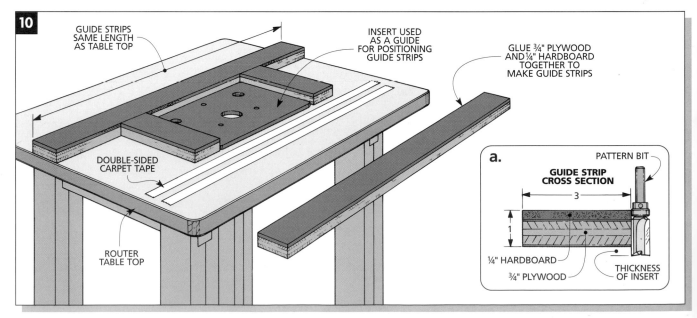

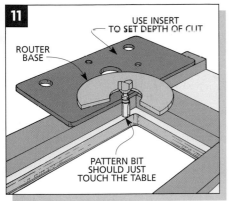

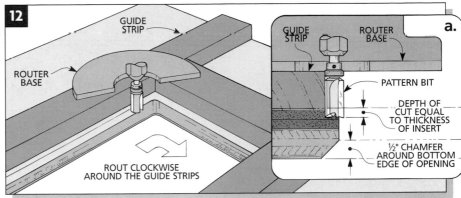

11
ROUTER
BASE
USE INSERT
TO SET DEPTH OF CUT
PATTERN BIT
SHOULD JUST
TOUCH THE TABLE

12
GUIDE
STRIP
ROUTER
BASE
ROUT CLOCKWISE
AROUND THE GUIDE STRIPS

a.
GUIDE
STRIP
ROUTER
BASE
PATTERN BIT
DEPTH OF
CUT EQUAL
TO THICKNESS
OF INSERT
½" CHAMFER
AROUND BOTTOM
EDGE OF OPENING

All the guide strips should be 3" wide, to support the base of the router.

Note: Cut two of these strips long enough to match the total width of the table top (30"). These longer strips will be used again later for routing out the miter slot (refer to the Shop Tip below).

After fastening the guide strips to the table top with double-sided carpet tape *(Fig. 10)*, the insert plate can then be lifted out.

DEPTH OF CUT. Before routing the lip, you need to set the bit depth so it matches the exact thickness of the insert plate.

To do this, first mount the pattern bit in the router. Next, place the insert plate on top of a guide strip *(Fig. 11)*. Set the router on top of the insert plate, and lower the bit until it just *barely* touches the table top. Now remove the insert plate and rout out the recess lip in a clockwise direction *(Fig. 12)*.

Finally, to improve the air flow to the router, I routed a ½" chamfer on the bottom of the opening *(Fig. 12a)*.

SHOP TIP . . . . *Adding a Miter Gauge Slot*

If you cut a slot in the top of your router table, you can use a miter gauge when you're routing

To do this, use double-sided carpet tape to position a 1"-thick guide strip 4" from the front edge of the table top. This guide strip will form the inside edge of the miter gauge slot *(Fig. 1a)*.

Now, to position the other guide strip, hold the miter gauge snugly between the two strips and stick down the second strip *(Fig. 1)*.

To set the depth of a pattern bit, place the miter gauge bar on top of a guide strip, and the router on top of the bar.

Then lower the bit to barely touch the table top. Now remove the miter gauge and rout the slot *(Fig. 2)*.

Note: You can use this same method for routing miter gauge slots in other wood table tops and jigs.

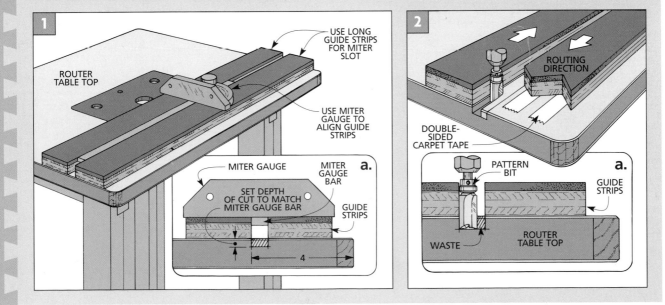

1
ROUTER
TABLE TOP
USE LONG
GUIDE STRIPS
FOR MITER
SLOT
USE MITER
GAUGE TO
ALIGN GUIDE
STRIPS

a.
MITER GAUGE
MITER
GAUGE
BAR
SET DEPTH
OF CUT TO MATCH
MITER GAUGE BAR
GUIDE
STRIPS
4

2
ROUTING
DIRECTION
DOUBLE-
SIDED
CARPET TAPE

a.
PATTERN
BIT
GUIDE
STRIPS
WASTE
ROUTER
TABLE TOP

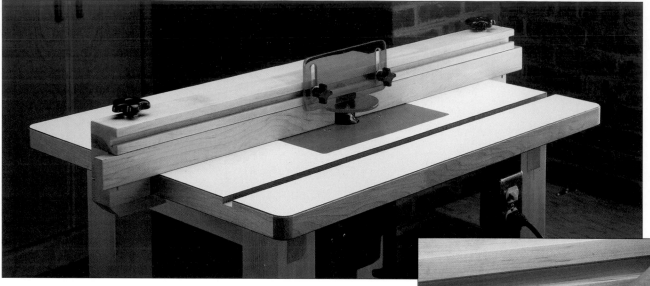

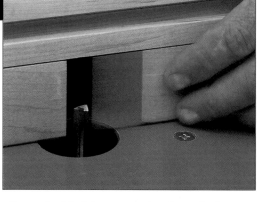

ROUTER TABLE FENCE

Whether or not you build any other part of this router table, the hardwood fence is definitely worthy of consideration. It has three useful features: a T-slot for accessories, a pair of sliding faces, and a special clamping system.

T-SLOT. The T-slot is designed to accept T-shaped nuts. These nuts slide in and let you add a variety of accessories, including a guard and a featherboard. (For more on accessories, see pages 70 and 71. For sources of hardware for the fence, see page 126.)

SLIDING FACES. The faces on the front of the fence are made to slide open. This flexibility allows you to adjust the opening so it fits whatever router bit you're using.

CLAMPING SYSTEM. The fence is also designed so it can be adapted to fit any router table (even one you may already own). The built-in clamp heads on each end that secure the fence to the table can easily be adjusted to match almost any table top.

BASE

The fence is made up of four sections: a split base, a top bar (with the T-slot), sliding faces, and the clamp heads.

TOP & BOTTOM. The base is eventually cut in half to fit around the router bit. But it starts out as a long strip that consists of two pieces. One is a $1^{1}/_{16}$"-thick top piece (I) with four dadoes cut in it. And the other is a $^{3}/_{4}$"-thick bottom piece (J) (Fig. 13).

The idea is to sandwich these two

pieces together to form one base with four slots. Knobs will eventually be able to pass through these slots to hold the sliding faces in place (refer to the Exploded View on page 61).

To determine the length of these base pieces, first measure the total length of the router table top (30" for the table shown here), and then add 6". This will allow 3" on each end for the clamp heads.

After the two base pieces are cut to length, cut the four dadoes (slots) in the top piece (I). Space one $^{3}/_{8}$"-deep dado $3^{3}/_{4}$" from each end (Fig. 13). Then move in another $3^{3}/_{4}$" and cut another set of identical dadoes.

ASSEMBLY. Now you can glue these two base pieces together.

Note: Since glued surfaces tend to slide around as they're clamped, I

decided to use a simple technique to keep the two base pieces aligned. Before applying any glue, align the edges of the two pieces so they're flush, and dry-clamp them together. Then screw the pieces together with a couple of countersunk woodscrews (Fig. 13).

Now remove the clamps, apply glue, and screw the pieces back together. The screws will automatically realign the pieces and keep them from sliding as the clamps are tightened.

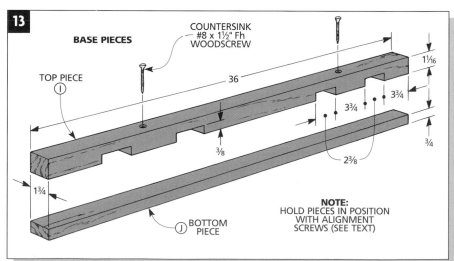

13

BASE PIECES

COUNTERSINK
#8 x 1½" Fh
WOODSCREW

TOP PIECE
(I)

36

1¹⁄₁₆

3¾

3¾

3¾

¾

⅜

2⅜

1¾

BOTTOM
PIECE
(J)

NOTE:
HOLD PIECES IN POSITION
WITH ALIGNMENT
SCREWS (SEE TEXT)

SLIDING FACES

Later, the base will be cut into two sections to create an opening for the router bit (see inset photo at left). But for now, leave it as one piece, and begin working on the sliding faces (K).

Each sliding face is half the length of the base (18"). And the width (height) of each face is $1/16$" less than the height of the base (*Fig. 14*). This creates clearance so the sliding faces won't bind against the top bar (added later).

To allow the sliding faces to get as close as possible to the router bit, I beveled one end of each piece (*Fig. 14*). I also routed a small chamfer along the bottom edge of each face. This chamfer serves as a relief for sawdust.

THREADED INSERTS. After the chamfers are routed, the sliding faces are almost complete — all that's left to do now is install the threaded inserts.

The problem here is making sure the threaded inserts are aligned properly with the slots in the base. To do this, hold the sliding faces in the closed position and flush with the bottom of the base. Then use an awl to scribe the positions of the slots on the backs of the faces (*Fig. 15*).

With the slots located, you can drill holes for the threaded inserts. Center these holes on the scribed lines and near the end of each slot closest to the bevel (*Fig. 16*).

Note: The hole needed to fit most $5/16$"-inside diameter threaded inserts is $5/8$" deep. Just drill to fit the insert; don't drill too deep (*Fig. 16a*).

Finally, install the threaded inserts in the faces (see Shop Tip below).

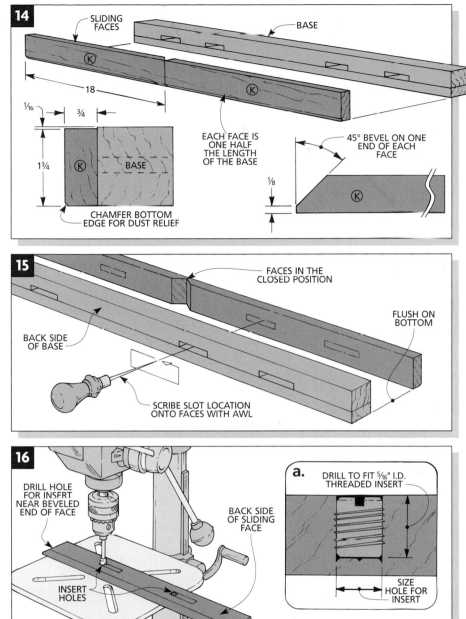

SHOP TIP .... Installing Threaded Inserts

Whenever possible, I like to use my drill press to install threaded inserts to make sure they are straight and square in the workpiece.

To use the drill press for installation, start by sawing off the head of a bolt that fits the insert. Next, thread two nuts and the insert onto the bolt and tighten the nuts against the insert.

The next step is to mount the bolt in the chuck. Finally, with the drill press turned off, you can install the insert. Using the control arm for pressure, screw the insert into the hole, turning the chuck clockwise by hand until the insert is flush with or slightly below the surface of the workpiece.

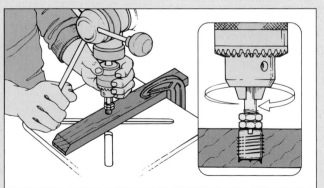

5/16" Insert Drill Hole 15/32"
(maple)

TOP BAR

The base of the fence serves as a platform so you can add the top bar (and the clamps). This top bar (L) will include a T-slot, which is actually a convenient system for adding different accessories (refer to pages 70 and 71).

CUT THE PIECES. The first step is to cut two $3/4$"-thick pieces of stock (L) to size to make the bar *(Fig. 17)*. The length of each piece is the same length as the base (36"). And the width of each piece ($2^1/2$") equals the width of the base plus the width of the sliding face pieces (refer to *Fig. 18a*).

CUT THE SLOT. After cutting the pieces to size, the next step is to make the T-slot. This is a two-step operation.

Start out by cutting a $3/8$"-wide groove $3/8$" deep into the face of each of the pieces *(Step 1 in Fig. 17)*. Then turn each piece on its edge and trim $1/4$" off the end of the "tongue" formed by the groove *(Step 2 in Fig. 17)*.

GLUE-UP. By gluing these two pieces together, a T-slot is formed in the top bar *(Fig. 18a)*.

Here again, I used the screw and glue technique (mentioned on page 66) to keep these pieces aligned while gluing them together. But this time, to keep the heads of the screws from showing, you can screw them in from the *bottom* face of the top bar *(Fig. 17)*.

GLUE TOP BAR TO BASE. When the glue is dry on the top bar, the next step is to glue the top bar to the base.

To help align these two pieces, I temporarily attached the sliding face pieces to the base with threaded knobs (you could also use bolts) *(Fig. 18a)*.

Then, to make sure that the top bar and the base are flush and square with each other, clamp them together (no glue yet) on a flat surface (I used my saw table) *(Fig. 18)*.

Once again, use the screw and glue technique, this time screwing from the bottom of the base into the top bar.

After the glue has completely dried, remove the screws and the sliding face pieces that you had temporarily attached to the base.

CUT BIT OPENING. Now that the top bar has been attached to the base, the next step is to cut out the opening for the router bit. This opening is 4" wide,

and centered on the length of the fence. I cut this opening with a dado blade on the table saw *(Fig. 19)*.

To do this, start by setting the dado

blade slightly shorter than the height of the base *(Fig. 19a)*. Then, you can make repeated passes to waste out the stock for the bit opening.

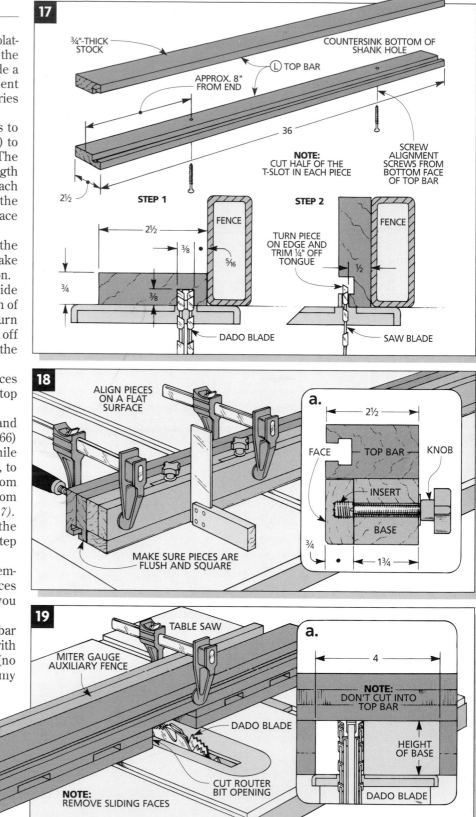

When the bit opening has been cut, the fence is almost complete — the only thing that's left to be worked on is the clamp system.

HOW IT WORKS. What makes this clamp system work is a simple carriage bolt. This carriage bolt passes through the clamp head and up through the bottom of the fence. By tightening a knob (or wing nut) onto this bolt, the clamp head pinches against the bottom of the table top, holding the fence in place *(Fig. 20a)*.

Each of the clamp heads consists of two pieces — a spacer that's slightly ($^{1}/_{8}$") thinner than the table top, and an arm that extends under the table top.

The clamp heads are then "hinged" to the fence with $^{1}/_{8}$" hardboard splines *(Fig. 20)*. The important thing is that the kerfs that accept the splines in the clamp head and the fence align.

ARM BLANK. I started by making a long $^{3}/_{4}$"-thick blank for the two arms (M) *(Fig. 21)*. It's cut to the same width as the router fence base ($1^{3}/_{4}$").

Note: Since you're working with small pieces, the safest way to make the arms is to cut one long (8") arm blank and cut it into two pieces later.

SPACERS. Before cutting the arm blank apart, glue a spacer (N) on each end of it *(Fig. 21)*. To determine the thickness of the spacers, start by measuring the total thickness of your router table top ($1^{3}/_{8}$" in my case). Then, for clearance, subtract $^{1}/_{8}$". This creates enough space so the arm can pinch against the table top *(Fig. 20a)*.

To determine the length of each spacer, first center the fence from side to side on the table top. Next, measure the amount of overhang on each side (3"), and finally subtract $^{1}/_{8}$" for clearance ($2^{7}/_{8}$").

Now cut the two spacers to these dimensions, and glue them to the arm blank *(Fig. 21)*.

SPLINES. The next step is to cut matching $^{3}/_{8}$"-deep kerfs for the $^{1}/_{8}$" hardboard splines in both the spacers *(Fig. 21a)* and the bottom of the fence. The easiest way I found to do this was to use the miter gauge on my table saw with the rip fence as a stop at the end of the workpiece. Make the kerf cuts in *both* pieces without changing the setup.

Now, cut hardboard splines that are $^{1}/_{8}$" wider than the combined depth of

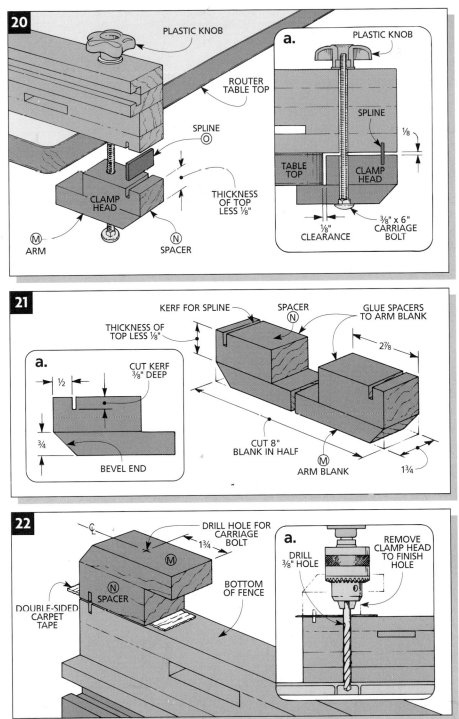

the two kerfs ($^{7}/_{8}$"). And finally, before cutting the blank in half, I cut bevels on the ends of the arm blank (for appearance) *(Fig. 21)*.

CARRIAGE BOLTS. As mentioned earlier, each clamp head is attached to the fence with a $^{3}/_{8}$" x 6" carriage bolt and a knob or wing nut *(Fig. 20a)*.

Note: There is an easy way to get the holes to align in these two pieces. Just start by fastening the clamp heads to the fence with double-sided carpet

tape *(Fig. 22)*. Then you can simply drill through both pieces at once. This ensures they will be aligned properly.

If your drill bit isn't quite long enough, just drill as deeply as you can into the bottom of the fence. Then remove the clamp heads, and complete the hole *(Fig. 22a)*.

FINISH. To keep the wood parts from getting soiled or stained, I applied two coats of tung-oil finish to all the parts before I assembled the fence. ∎

ACCESSORIES .... Fence Add-Ons

Once the router table was built, I decided to spend some time making a group of accessories. The first thing to consider, of course, is safety. The two guards shown below should be the first two accessories you build for your new router table. And before long you'll probably want to add both a featherboard and a vacuum attachment.

ROUTER BIT GUARD

For safety, include a bit guard on the router table. This is made of two pieces: a $1/2$"-thick hardwood back with two long slots cut in it, and a $1/4$"-thick clear acrylic plastic shield.

The slots in the back allow for height adjustment. The guard assembly is held in the T-slot in the fence with threaded knobs and T-slot nuts.

MATERIALS LIST

(1 pc.) $1/2$" hardwood - $3^1/2$" - $7^1/2$"
(1 pc.) $1/4$" clear acrylic plastic - $2^1/2$" x 4"
(2) No. 8 x $3/4$" Fh woodscrews
(2) 1" threaded knobs
(2) Washers (to fit knobs)
(2) T-slot nuts

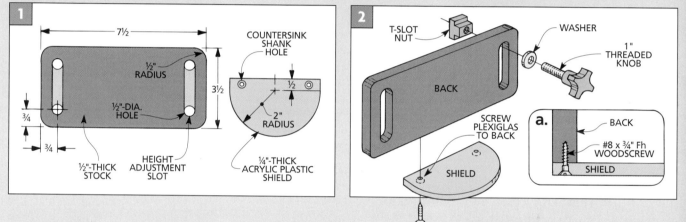

GUARD FOR FREEHAND ROUTING

To make a guard for freehand routing, all you need is a single piece of $1/4$"-thick clear acrylic plastic.

Two straight slots are cut on the back edge to accept mounting screws, and two 45° notches are cut in the sides to fit over the sliding faces of the fence.

To install the guard, turn the fence over and pinch the sliding faces against the guard. Then tighten sheet metal screws in the slots.

MATERIALS LIST

(1 pc.) $1/4$" clear acrylic plastic - 4" x 10"
(2) No. 6 x $3/4$" Ph sheet metal screws
(2) Washers (to fit screws)

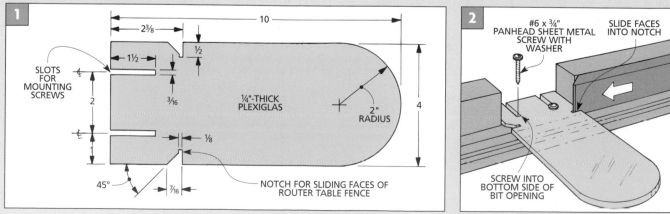

FEATHERBOARD

A featherboard keeps boards tight against the table for consistent cuts.

For this one, cut a workpiece from ½" stock with ends cut at 30° (*Fig. 1*).

To cut the fingers, attach a tall auxiliary fence to the miter gauge of your table saw (*Fig. 2*). Now, tilt the saw blade to 30° and raise it to make a 1½"-high cut (*Fig. 2a*).

With the blade height set, make equally spaced cuts to leave identical fingers.

Finally, make two slots for attaching the featherboard to the fence. To do this, drill ⅜" holes, centered 2¾" up from the bottom edge of the featherboard (*Fig. 3*). Then, cut out the slots with a sabre saw or band saw.

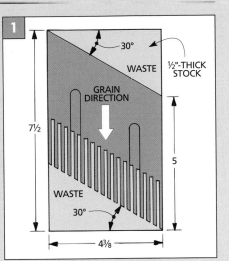

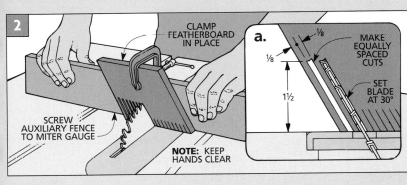

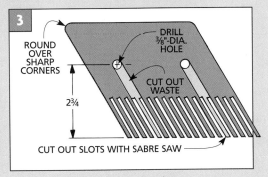

VACUUM ATTACHMENT

Here's an easy-to-build dust collection system that screws to the back of the fence (over the router bit opening) and connects to your shop vacuum.

To build the attachment, cut two triangular-shaped side pieces from ½"-thick stock (*Fig. 1*).

Next, make a face plate from ¼" hardboard. It's 5" wide and beveled on the top and bottom edges to match the side pieces (*Fig. 2*). The bevels allow the attachment to fit tight against the fence and the table.

Drill a hole in the face plate so your vacuum hose fits snugly into it (*Fig. 2*). Glue the pieces together and screw the attachment to the back of the fence.

Note: As you're driving in the screws, the bottom of the vacuum attachment is forced down and tends to lift the fence. To get around this, put pennies under the side pieces before starting the screws (*Fig. 2*). After they're started, remove the pennies and finish tightening the screws.

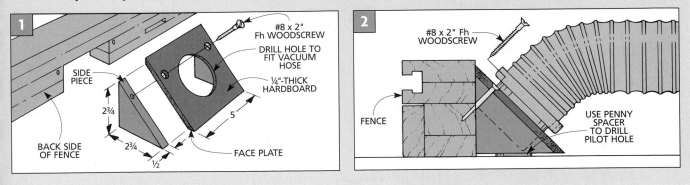

Miter Saw Station

Fold-out tables extend the usefulness of your miter saw, and a stop block saves you the trouble of measuring and marking the workpiece. There's also a convenient storage space for cutoffs.

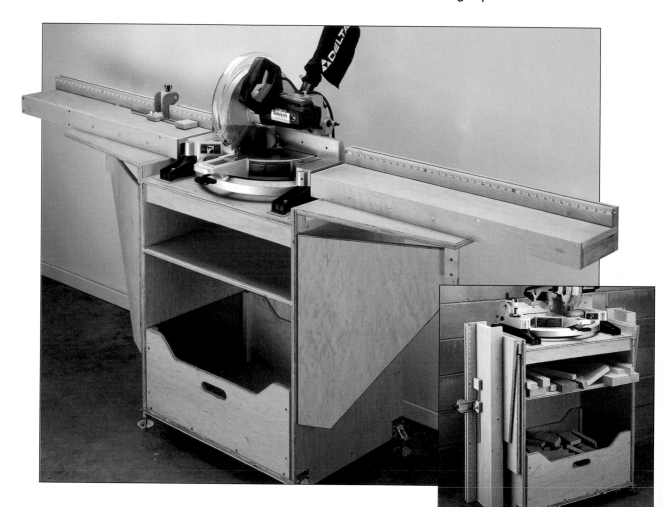

Wings up. Flaps out. Levelers down. No, this isn't a lesson on flying airplanes. It's just one way of explaining how this miter saw station works.

The "wings" are really the underpinnings for two long extension tables. With the miter saw mounted to a center cabinet, the tables provide sturdy support on each side when you're cutting long workpieces to length.

FENCE & STOP BLOCK. But there's more to these tables than holding up a workpiece. Each extension has a fence

that will accept an adjustable stop block. A tape measure on each fence then lets you cut workpieces to length without measuring or marking them beforehand.

FOLD-DOWN EXTENSIONS. Regardless of the speed and accuracy this provides, the long extension tables would be in the way when you're not using the the miter saw. Especially when you consider that they have an overall "wingspan" of nearly eight feet.

So to save space when the saw is not in use, the extension tables fold down when you're done. This creates a com-

pact tool stand that can roll out of the way for storage or out to the driveway to tackle the next job.

BIN & SHELF. Wherever you happen to be working, there's bound to be a number of cutoffs. But you don't need to throw them on the floor. That's because there's a removable scrap bin on the bottom. And if you're working with several pieces, there's a simple shelf to hold them until you're ready to start cutting.

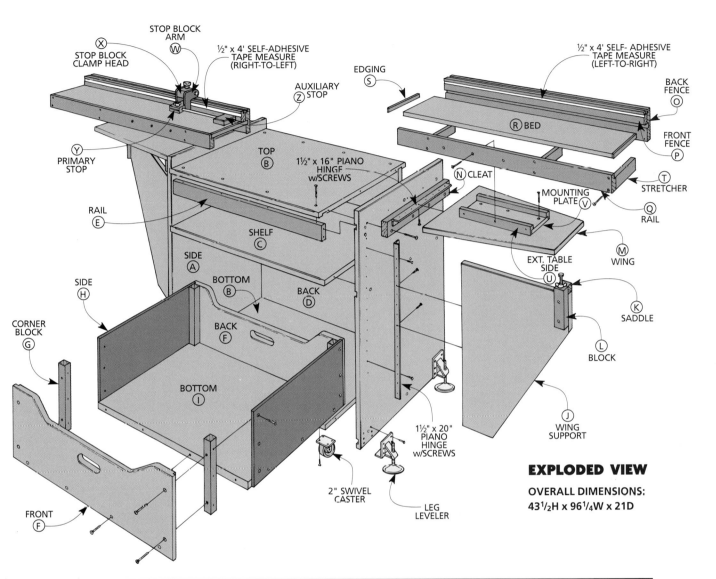

STOP BLOCK ARM
W

STOP BLOCK CLAMP HEAD
X

½" x 4' SELF-ADHESIVE TAPE MEASURE (RIGHT-TO-LEFT)

½" x 4' SELF- ADHESIVE TAPE MEASURE (LEFT-TO-RIGHT)

EDGING
S

BACK FENCE
O

AUXILIARY STOP
Z

R BED

FRONT FENCE
P

PRIMARY STOP
Y

TOP
B

1½" x 16" PIANO HINGE w/SCREWS

N CLEAT

T STRETCHER

MOUNTING PLATE
V

Q RAIL

RAIL
E

SHELF
C

EXT. TABLE SIDE
U

M WING

SIDE
A

SIDE
H

BOTTOM
B

BACK
D

K SADDLE

CORNER BLOCK
G

BACK
F

L BLOCK

BOTTOM
I

1½" x 20" PIANO HINGE w/SCREWS

J WING SUPPORT

FRONT
F

2" SWIVEL CASTER

LEG LEVELER

EXPLODED VIEW

OVERALL DIMENSIONS:
43½"H x 96¼"W x 21D

MATERIALS LIST

CASE
A Sides (2)   ¾ ply. - 21 x 34¾
B Top/Bottom (2)   ¾ ply. - 21 x 27
C Shelf (1)   ¾ ply. - 19⅝ x 27
D Back (1)   ¾ ply. - 26¼ x 31½
E Rail (1)   ¾ ply. - 3 x 26¼

SCRAP BIN
F Front/Back (2)   ¾ ply. - 11 x 26
G Corner Blocks (4) ¾ x ¾ - 10¼
H Sides (2)   ¼ hdbd. - 11 x 18⅞
I Bottom (1)   ¾ ply. - 18⅞ x 25½

TABLE SUPPORTS
J Wing Suppts. (2)   ¾ ply. - 19 x 23
K Saddles (2)   ¾ x 1½ - 1
L Blocks (2)   ¾ x 1½ - 4
M Wings (2)   ¾ ply. - 17½ x 20½ rgh.
N Cleats (2)   ¾ x 2 - 17¼

EXTENSION TABLES
O Back Fences (2)   ¾ x 4¾ - 36
P Front Fences (2)   ¾ x 2 - 36
Q Rails (2)   ¾ x 2¾ - 36
R Beds (2)   ¾ ply. - 7¼ x 35½
S Edging (4)   ¼ x ¾ - 7¼
T Stretchers (6)   ¾ x 2 - 6½
U Sides (4)   ¾ x 1¾ - 14½
V Mount. Plates (2) ¾ ply. - 5¾ x 14½

STOP BLOCK
W Arms (2)   ¼ hdbd. - 3 x 3⅝
X Clamp Head (1)   1½ x 1½ - 2
Y Primary Stop (1)   ¾ x 2 - 2½
Z Auxiliary Stop (1) ¾ x 2 - 2½

HARDWARE SUPPLIES
(18) No. 8 x ¾" Fh woodscrews
(98) No. 8 x 1¼" Fh woodscrews
(8) No. 8 x 2" Fh woodscrews

(12) No. 8 x 1¼" Ph sheet metal screws
(40) No. 10 x ¾" Ph sheet metal screws
(12) No. 8 flat washers
(5) ¼" flat washers
(16) ¼" lock washers
(2) ¼" x 2" full-thread hex bolts
(1) ¼" x 2½" hex bolt
(1) ¼" x 3½" toilet bolt
(1) ¼" x 1" carriage bolt
(2) ¼" inside diameter threaded inserts
(1) ¼" lock nut
(3) ¼" wing nuts
(1) ¼" plastic knob
(1) 4' tape measure (left-to-right)
(1) 4' tape measure (right-to-left)
(1) ⅜" x 11⅞" steel rod
(2) 1½" x 36" piano hinges w/screws
(4) 2" swivel casters
(4) Heavy-duty leg levelers

CUTTING DIAGRAM

¾" x 5¼"- 96 (3.5 Bd. Ft.)

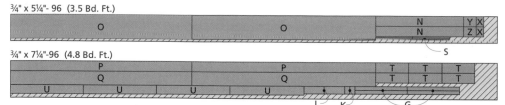

¾" x 7¼"-96 (4.8 Bd. Ft.)

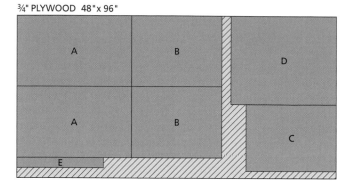

¾" PLYWOOD 48"x 96"

¾" PLYWOOD 48"x 96"

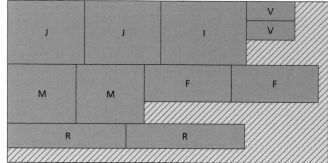

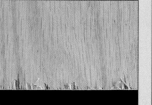

¼" HARDBOARD 24"x 48"

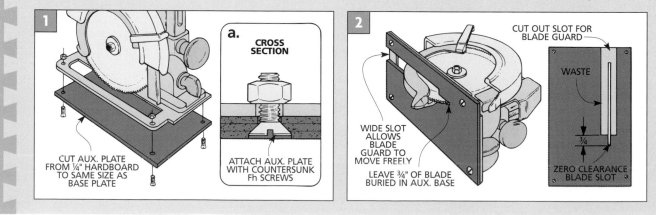

SHOP TIP .... *Cutting Plywood Without Chipout*

There are a lot of large pieces of plywood to cut for the miter saw station. You'll probably want to start by cutting them from a 4x8 sheet with a circular saw (see Cutting Diagram).

When cutting plywood with a circular saw, I always face the good surface of the plywood *down* since the blade causes chipout on the top ("up") side. But sometimes I want a clean cut on *both* sides of the plywood.

To prevent chipout on the top side, I attach an auxiliary plate to the saw's base plate *(Fig. 1)*. The plate has a "zero clearance" blade slot cut in it. This backs up the wood fibers along the cut line and prevents chipout (see photos at right).

The idea is pretty simple. Screw a piece of ¼" hardboard to the saw's base plate *(Fig. 1)*. Then plunge the blade through it. Now you've got a plate with a zero clearance blade slot.

The only problem is that now the blade guard

Blades on circular saws chip out fibers on the top side of the plywood.

Attaching a "zero clearance" auxiliary base plate prevents chipout.

won't work. It's held back by the auxiliary plate, so the blade is left exposed.

To solve this problem, cut a wide second slot centered on the first one

(Fig. 2). Cut it wide enough to allow the guard to move freely, but stop it ¾" back from the forward end of the blade slot (Detail in *Fig. 2*).

1 CUT AUX. PLATE FROM ¼" HARDBOARD TO SAME SIZE AS BASE PLATE

a. CROSS SECTION

ATTACH AUX. PLATE WITH COUNTERSUNK Fh SCREWS

2 WIDE SLOT ALLOWS BLADE GUARD TO MOVE FREELY

LEAVE ¾" OF BLADE BURIED IN AUX. BASE

CUT OUT SLOT FOR BLADE GUARD

WASTE

¾

ZERO CLEARANCE BLADE SLOT

CASE

I started building the miter saw station by making the case. Basically, it's just a simple open plywood box (I used $\frac{3}{4}$" maple plywood) with a recessed top that will support the miter saw *(Fig. 1)*.

But the case has other features. An opening in the bottom is designed to hold a convenient scrap bin (refer to page 77). And a shelf below the top of the case provides a handy storage space to hold workpieces that you're not ready to use yet.

SIDES. I began working on the case by making the two sides (A) *(Fig. 1)*. They're held together with a top (B), a bottom (B), and a shelf (C) that fit into dadoes cut in the sides *(Figs. 1a and 1d)*.

The shelf, top, and bottom are all cut to the same length (27"). But the back (which will be added later) will be set in just a bit, so the shelf has to be narrower than the top and bottom to allow room for it *(Fig. 1)*.

Note: The final width of the shelf is easier to determine *after* the case has been assembled. So for now, just rough cut it a little oversize. Then set it aside until later.

Then rip the top and bottom to final width (21").

GROOVES. Before assembling the case, you'll need to cut a groove for a rail (E) (which will be added later) on the underside of the top *only*. It's located near the front edge *(Fig. 1c)*.

Then there's another groove cut near the back edge of both the top and the bottom. This groove accepts the back (D) of the case *(Fig. 1b)*.

BACK. To determine the size of the back (D), it's easiest to dry assemble the case *(Fig. 1)*. While the back is cut so it fits between the grooves in the top and bottom, it will simply butt against the sides.

ASSEMBLY. Because of this design, the easiest process I found for assembling the case is to first glue up a U-shaped assembly. This assembly consists of one side (A) along with the top (B) and the bottom (B). Then you can slide the back (D) into place, and add the other side *(Fig. 2)*.

Note: I found the easiest way to assemble the case is on its side *(Fig. 2)*.

Finally, to strengthen the whole plywood case, reinforce each of the glue joints with No. 8 x $1\frac{1}{4}$" flathead woodscrews *(Fig. 2)*.

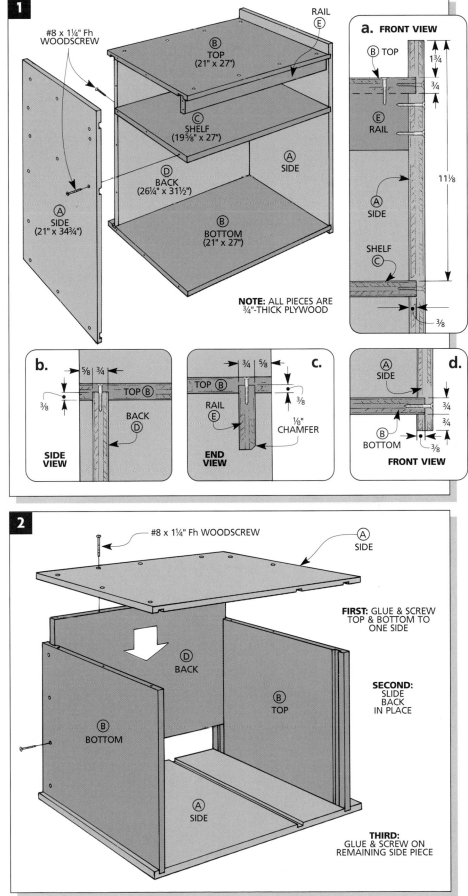

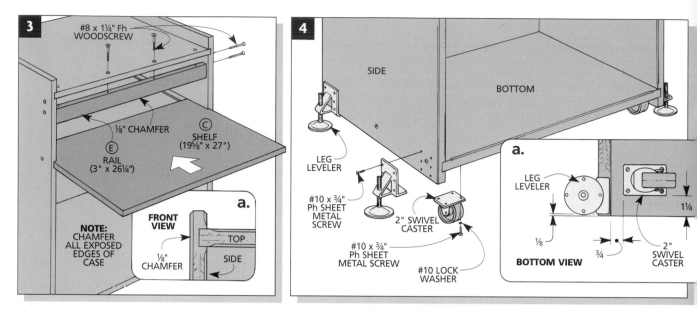

SHELF. Once the cabinet is assembled, you can measure the inside distance from the back panel to the front edge and trim the shelf (C) to this final width. Then apply glue in the dadoes and slide the shelf in place *(Fig. 3)*. To secure the shelf, screw it tight from the outside with No. 8 x 1¼" woodscrews.

RAIL. To add rigidity to the top, I added a rail (E) *(Fig. 3)*. After chamfering the bottom edge, it's glued and screwed into the groove in the underside of the top (refer to *Fig. 1c*, page 75).

CHAMFER ALL EDGES. With the case parts assembled, I routed ⅛" chamfers on all of the exposed edges (see *Fig. 3a*

and the Shop Tip box below).

CASTERS & LEVELERS. Finally, to make it easy to roll the miter saw station around, I mounted four casters to the bottom *(Fig. 4)*. But I didn't want it to move around when making a cut. So I added four leg levelers to raise the casters off the floor (refer to page 55).

SHOP TIP . . . . *Routing Chamfers on Edges*

Routing a chamfer on the edge of a project after it's assembled can be a challenge. Especially if there's

only a thin edge to support the base of the router. In this case, it's all too easy to tip the router and gouge the workpiece.

So when routing the chamfers on the miter saw station, I used a couple of different methods to hold the router steady.

One of the simplest ways is to use the insert

plate from the router table as a support. To make this work, the plate needs to straddle at least two edges of the cabinet (see photo and left drawing below). This works best when chamfering the edges around the opening at the top of the case.

But using the insert plate for the lower part of the

case doesn't work. The plate is simply too small to span the opening.

So here, it's best to build up the thickness of the edge by clamping a scrap to the case (see right drawing). This provides a wide support for the base of the router so it won't tip as you rout the chamfer.

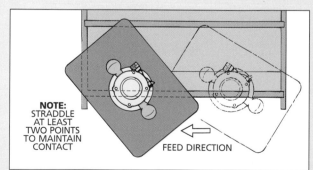

INSERT PLATE. *By spanning the opening at the top of the case, the insert plate that's used to mount a router in a table provides a large, stable support.*

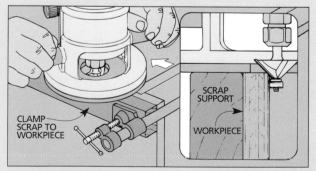

SCRAP SUPPORT. *To add extra support that keeps the router from tipping on a narrow edge, clamp a scrap board to the side of the case.*

To help keep my work area clear of cut-offs, I decided to add a removable scrap bin (see photo at right).

I wanted this bin to be sturdy, but also light enough so it wouldn't be a chore to empty. So it's made up of a combination of plywood, hardwood, and hardboard.

FRONT & BACK. Begin working on the bin by cutting the front and back pieces (F) from ³/₄"-thick plywood. To determine their lengths, measure the opening and subtract ¹/₄" (26"). This allows a ¹/₈" gap at either side so the bin can easily be removed. After cutting them to length, cut both pieces 11" wide (high).

The sides of the bin are joined to the front and back with rabbet joints. So cut rabbets in each end of the front and back pieces to accept the ¹/₄"-thick sides (*Figs. 5b and 6*). Also cut a wide rabbet in the bottom edge of each piece for the ³/₄"-thick bottom (*Fig. 6*).

To improve my shooting percentage when I toss scraps into the bin, I cut away the top edges of both the front and the back pieces (*Fig. 5a*).

Also, I cut handholds in both the front and back pieces to make it easier to carry the bin out to the firewood pile. To cut the handholds, I started by drilling two 1¹/₄"-dia. holes 3" apart (*Fig. 5a*). Then I cut out between the holes with a sabre saw.

With all of the work completed on the front and back pieces, rout ¹/₈" chamfers on all of the exposed edges.

CORNER BLOCKS. In order to help strengthen the corners, I added four ³/₄" x ³/₄" hardwood corner blocks (G) (*Fig. 6*). They're glued and screwed to the front and back flush with the rabbets.

SIDES. When the corner blocks are in place, you can add the bin sides (H) (*Fig. 5*). To reduce the weight of the bin, the sides are made from pieces of ¹/₄" hardboard. They can simply be glued and screwed to the corner blocks.

BOTTOM. Finally, a ³/₄"-thick plywood bottom (I) is cut to fit the rabbets you cut earlier. Then it can be glued and screwed in place on the bottom of the bin (*Fig. 5*).

The removable scrap bin is big enough to hold lots of cut-offs. But the handles make it easy to lift out and empty.

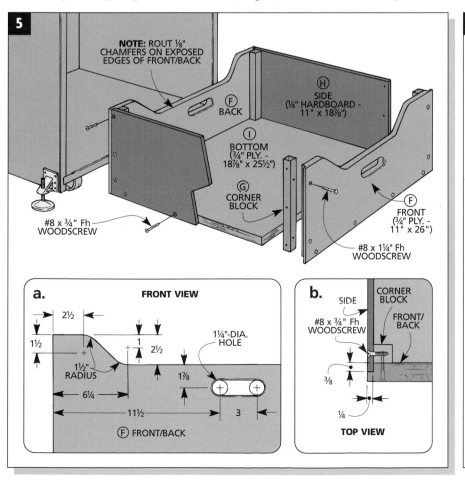

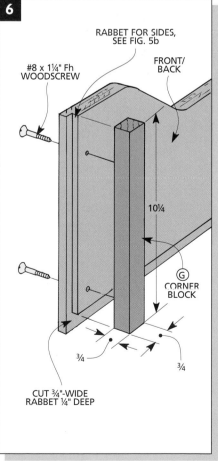

When the case was completed, I added two plywood supports to each side. A wedge-shaped wing (M) serves as a platform for the extension table (refer to *Figs. 7 and 11*). And a triangular-shaped support (J) props up the wing.

WING SUPPORTS. Start by cutting the wing supports (J) to shape from $\frac{3}{4}$"-thick plywood *(Fig. 8)*.

Each wing support (J) is attached to the side of the case with a piano hinge *(Fig. 8)*. This way, you can swing it out to hold up the wing, or fold it flat for storage. The easiest method I found for attaching the hinge is to first screw one leaf to the wing support. Then mount the assembly to the case. To provide clearance for a cleat (added later), the wing support is $2\frac{7}{8}$" from the top. And it's flush at the front when it's fully opened *(Fig. 8a)*.

LEVELERS. Next, I added two levelers to adjust the height of the wings. Each one consists of two glued-up blocks: a saddle (K) that fits over the support and a block (L) that houses an adjustment mechanism *(Fig. 9)*.

The key to this mechanism is a bolt. As you thread it in (or out) of an insert

in the end of the block, the head of the bolt lowers (or raises) the wing. Tightening a wing nut locks it down.

WINGS. Now you can cut out the two wings (M) *(Fig. 10)*. A shallow hole in the bottom of each wing creates a pocket for the bolt in the leveler. This keeps the wing support from acciden-

tally getting knocked out from under the wing.

To fold the wings up or down, they're attached with a piano hinge. Again, it's easiest to screw one leaf to the wing first. Then attach the other leaf to a hardwood cleat (N) that's glued and screwed to the case *(Fig. 10a)*.

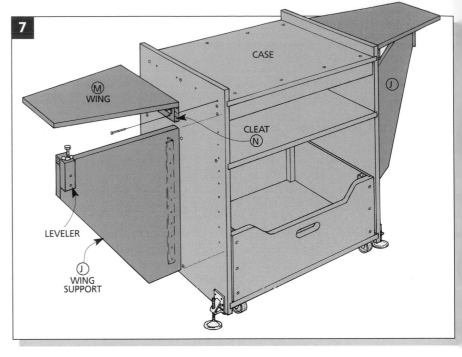

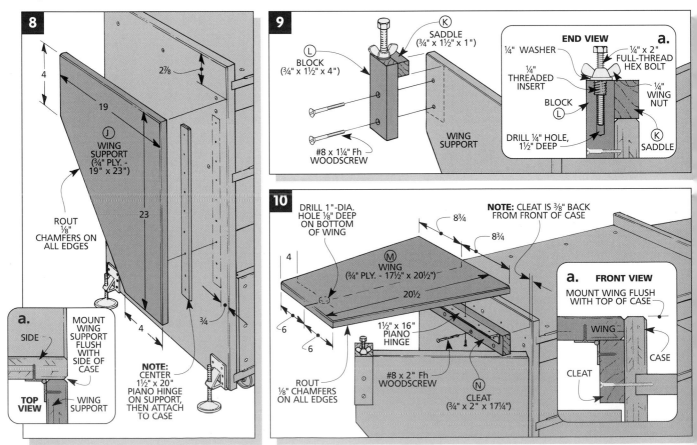

EXTENSION TABLES

Now you can begin work on the extension tables *(Fig. 11)*.

FENCE. I started by making the fences. Each fence consists of a tall back fence (O) and a short front fence (P) *(Fig. 12)*. (I used maple.) Both pieces are cut to finished length first (36").

Next, form a T-slot with two cuts in each piece. First, to accept the head of a toilet bolt, cut a $^3/_{16}$" groove near the top edge. Then cut a rabbet on the *inside* edge bolt's shank.

Now cut a shallow groove in the front face of each front fence (P) to provide a recess for a tape measure. And chamfer the bottom edge for dust relief.

RAIL & BED. Next cut a rail (Q) from $^3/_4$" stock and a bed (R) from $^3/_4$" plywood for each extension table *(Fig. 12)*. The bed fits in another groove cut in the

back fence and a corresponding rabbet cut in the rail. To end up with a flat bed, make sure the groove and rabbet align.

ASSEMBLY. Now all the pieces can be put together. After gluing $^1/_4$"-thick hardwood edging (S) to the ends of the bed, glue and clamp the bed between the back fence and rail *(Fig. 12)*. Then

glue the front fence piece (P) in place.

STRETCHERS. To complete each table, I added three hardwood stretchers (T) *(Fig. 12)*. They work together with a mounting platform (added next) to position the table on the wing.

One stretcher is flush with the table's outside end. But the stretcher nearest the saw is set in $3^1/_4$". With the middle (offset) stretcher, it controls the side-to-side adjustment of the table.

MOUNTING PLATFORMS. That's where the two mounting platforms come in. Each U-shaped platform consists of two hardwood sides (U) rabbeted to fit a plywood mounting plate (V) *(Fig. 13)*. When the platforms are attached to the wings later (page 81), the tables will fit down over them.

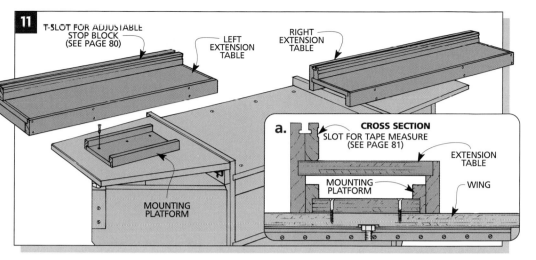

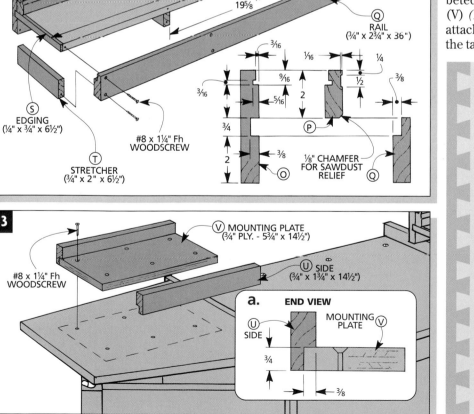

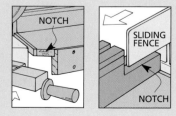

SHOP TIP

Customizing to Your Saw

Depending on your saw, you may need to notch the corner of the extension table to provide clearance for the miter lock handle (see left drawing). And if your saw has a tall sliding fence, also notch the wood fence on the left extension table (see right drawing).

One of the handiest things about this miter saw station is the flip-up stop block. It consists of four parts: a pair of L-shaped arms, a clamp head, and two stops, plus hardware *(Fig. 14)*.

ARMS. Start by cutting two identical L-shaped arms (W) from $1/4$" hardboard *(Fig. 15)*. A hole is drilled through each arm to accept a bolt that acts as a pivot when you flip up the stop.

CLAMP HEAD. The next step is to add the clamp head (X) *(Fig. 16)*. It's a hardwood block with a centered tongue on the bottom that fits in the T-slot.

Note: When cutting the tongue, it's safest to start with an extra-long blank. Cut rabbets on both faces and sneak up on the final thickness of the tongue until it just fits the T-slot.

After cutting the clamp head to length, drill a centered hole in it for the toilet bolt that slides in the T-slot. Tightening a knob onto the bolt will lock the stop block in place *(Fig. 14a)*.

STOP. Once you're finished with the clamp head, the next piece to make is the primary stop (Y) *(Fig. 17)*. It's nothing more than a $3/4$"-thick hardwood block with notches cut to fit between the two arms.

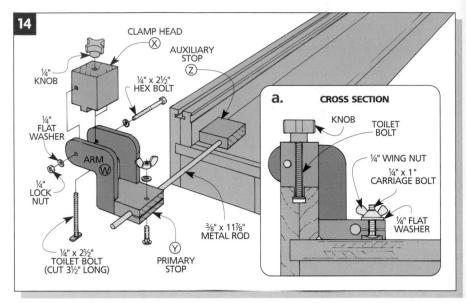

Also, make an auxiliary stop (Z) that's the same size but without the notches *(Fig. 17)*. It's used for cutting short pieces.

To accept a metal rod, there's a hole drilled completely through the primary stop and one halfway through the auxiliary stop. The rod is glued to the auxiliary stop with epoxy, but it must slide through the primary stop.

To allow the rod to lock into position, cut a saw kerf through the edge of the primary block. Then drill a counter-bored hole through the face. To pinch down on the rod, a carriage bolt fits through the hole and then a wing nut is tightened onto the bolt.

ASSEMBLY. To assemble the stop block, start by gluing the arms to the primary stop. Then cut $1/8$" chamfers on the bottom edges of the arms and both stops to allow for dust relief. Finally, drill a hole through the clamp head *(Fig. 18)* and insert a hex bolt as a pivot axle for the arms *(Fig. 14)*.

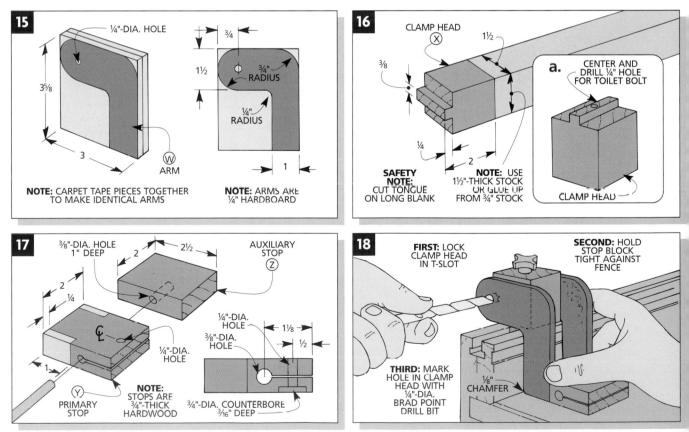

Before you can use the miter saw station, you'll need to take a few minutes to set it up.

To ensure the workpiece will lie flat, first level the wings *(Step 1)*.

Next, attach the mounting platforms *(Step 2)*. Since these determine the location of the fences, it's important that they are in line with each other and perpendicular to the sides of the case.

Next, install the extension tables. Fit the tables down over the mounting platforms and slide them toward the miter saw *(Step 3)*.

Note: To allow side-to-side adjustment, drill pilot holes through the mounting platforms and oversized holes through the table rails, and attach them with screws.

Now you can mount the miter saw to the top of the station *(Step 4)*.

The only step that's left is to apply a self-adhesive tape measure to each fence *(Steps 5 and 6)*. (One reads right-to-left, the other left-to-right.)

Once everything is set up, set the stop block on a whole number and cut a test piece. Then measure the piece. If you need to "fine tune" the setup, just loosen the screws that hold the table and nudge it one way or the other.

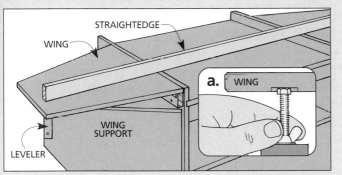

1 To level both of the wings, hold a straightedge across the top of the miter saw station. Then adjust the bolt in the leveler to raise or lower the wings so they're flush with the bottom of the straightedge.

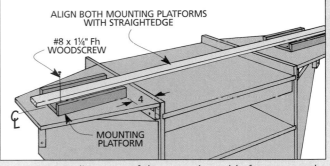

2 To ensure alignment of the extension table fences, use the straightedge to align the two mounting platforms. Then screw the mounting platforms to the wings with six No. 8 x 1¼" flathead woodscrews (refer to Fig. 13, page 79).

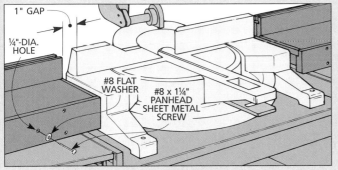

3 After fitting the extension tables down over the mounting platforms, slide them into position next to the miter saw. (I left 1" gaps between the saw and the tables). Then just screw the tables to the mounting platform through oversized holes.

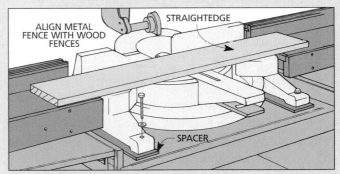

4 Before bolting the miter saw in place, use spacers (if needed) to raise the table flush with the bed of each extension table. Also, make sure that the metal fence aligns with both of the wood fences.

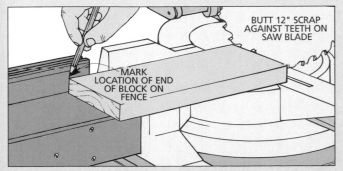

5 To position the tape measure, first measure and cut a piece of scrap exactly 12" long. Then butt the scrap tight against the blade and clearly mark the location of the end of the block on the wooden fence.

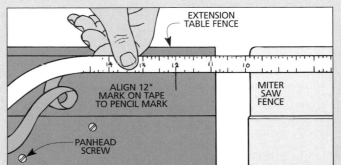

6 Finally, align the 12" increment on a self-adhesive tape measure with the mark and press it in place. Cut off any excess tape. If the fence needs any "fine tuning," loosen the panhead screws and tap the fence one way or the other.

SHOP STORAGE

These projects all have something in common: they use your shop's wall space to organize anything that doesn't have a home. The spacious tool cabinet, for example, protects all your power and hand tools. The pegboard system provides another option for hanging tools.

Meanwhile, those long boards, cutoffs and scraps will find a home in the lumber rack, and all your finishing supplies will stay together in one convenient station. Finally, the modular workshop gives you options for storing a variety of shop essentials, or for items in another room of the house.

Tool Cabinet 84

Accessories: Custom Tool Holders 88
Joinery: Box Joints. 90
Shop Tip: Pin Spacing 91

Pegboard System 94

Shop Tip: L-Hook System 97

Lumber Rack 100

Shop Tip: Angled Drilling Guide 102
Shop Tip: Using Stretch Cords 104
Designer's Notebook: Sheet Goods Bin 105

Finishing Cabinet 106

Shop Tip: Dowel Centers 110
Technique: Cleaning Brushes 111

Modular Workshop 112

Designer's Notebook: Kid's/Laundry Room 113
Shop Tip: Cleaning Up Conduit 115
Shop Tip: Installing the Grid. 115
Shop Tip: Slot-Cutting Jig 116
Shop Tip: Adding Bin Labels. 122
Designer's Notebook: Bulletin Board 123
Shop Tip: Preventing Stuck Bits 124

Tool Cabinet

With unique tool holders and adjustable shelves, you can customize this wall-mounted birch tool cabinet to organize and protect all of your special hand and power tools.

There's something reassuring about building your own tool cabinet. You know that each one of your tools has a "home" where it won't get knocked around or damaged. It also provides you with the opportunity to organize your tools so they're right at hand when you need them.

All those things were in the back of my mind when I decided to build this tool cabinet. In addition, I wanted a simple, straightforward design to provide different types of storage for hand tools, as well as power tools and accessories.

TOOL HOLDERS. Small hand tools hang on holders mounted on the insides of the cabinet doors. To keep the tools from banging around when you open and close the doors, each holder can be customized to fit one of your tools and "lock" it in place. (For more on the tool holders, see pages 88 and 89.)

ADJUSTABLE SHELVES. A set of adjustable shelves also provides storage for larger hand tools such as planes and portable power tools. But unlike some adjustable shelves that have a tendency to tip, a unique system

holds them in place when you remove a tool or put it away.

DRAWERS. Finally, two large drawers can be used to keep accessories or shop supplies handy. Tight-fitting box joints make these drawers as strong as they are good-looking.

WOOD AND FINISH. I used birch plywood, edged with solid birch, for the case, doors, and shelves. But for the drawers, I used solid 1/2" birch for more attractive box joints. And, for protection, I applied three coats of a tung oil and urethane combination finish.

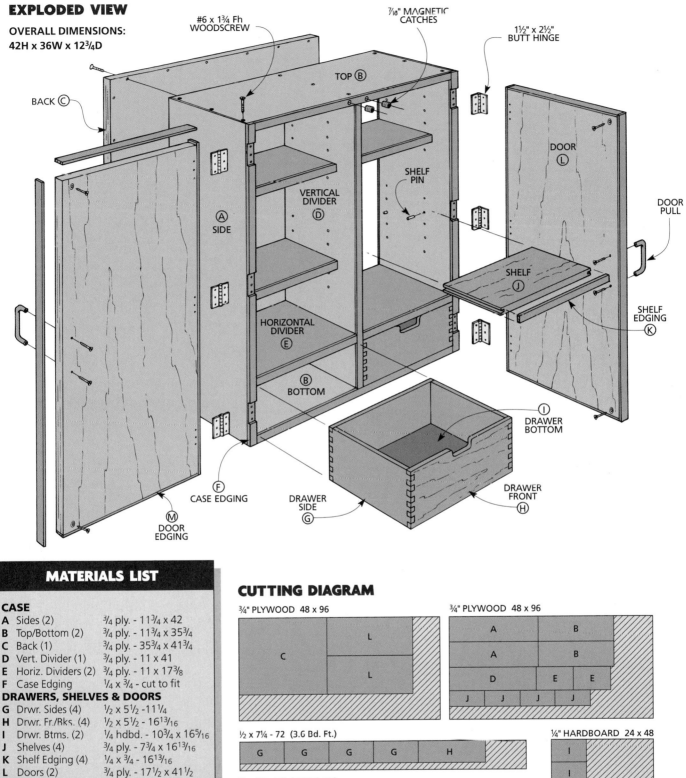

EXPLODED VIEW

OVERALL DIMENSIONS:
42H x 36W x 12¾D

#6 x 1¾ Fh WOODSCREW

⁷⁄₁₆" MAGNETIC CATCHES

1½" x 2½" BUTT HINGE

BACK Ⓒ

TOP Ⓑ

DOOR Ⓛ

DOOR PULL

SHELF PIN

Ⓐ SIDE

VERTICAL DIVIDER Ⓓ

SHELF Ⓙ

SHELF EDGING Ⓚ

HORIZONTAL DIVIDER Ⓔ

Ⓑ BOTTOM

DRAWER BOTTOM Ⓘ

Ⓕ CASE EDGING

DRAWER SIDE Ⓖ

DRAWER FRONT Ⓗ

Ⓜ DOOR EDGING

MATERIALS LIST

CASE
A	Sides (2)	¾ ply. - 11¾ x 42
B	Top/Bottom (2)	¾ ply. - 11¾ x 35¾
C	Back (1)	¾ ply. - 35¾ x 41¾
D	Vert. Divider (1)	¾ ply. - 11 x 41
E	Horiz. Dividers (2)	¾ ply. - 11 x 17⅜
F	Case Edging	¼ x ¾ - cut to fit

DRAWERS, SHELVES & DOORS
G	Drwr. Sides (4)	½ x 5½ - 11¼
H	Drwr. Fr./Bks. (4)	½ x 5½ - 16¹³⁄₁₆
I	Drwr. Btms. (2)	¼ hdbd. - 10¾ x 16⁵⁄₁₆
J	Shelves (4)	¾ ply. - 7¾ x 16¹³⁄₁₆
K	Shelf Edging (4)	¼ x ¾ - 16¹³⁄₁₆
L	Doors (2)	¾ ply. - 17½ x 41½
M	Door Edging	¼ x ¾ - cut to fit

HARDWARE SUPPLIES
(48) No. 6 x 1¾" Fh woodscrews
(2) 3¾" door pulls
(3 pr.) 1½" x 2½" butt hinges
(4) ⁷⁄₁₆"-dia. magnetic catches
(1) ¼" x 18" hardwood dowel

CUTTING DIAGRAM

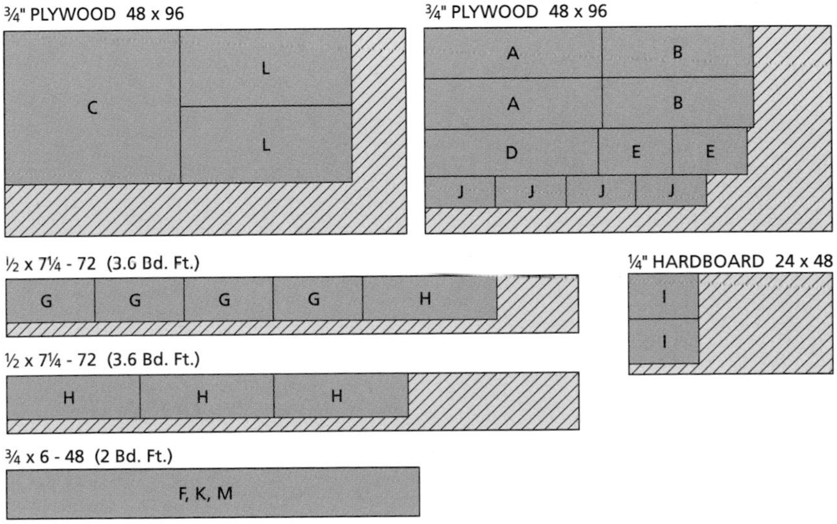

¾" PLYWOOD 48 x 96

C
L
L

¾" PLYWOOD 48 x 96

A	B
A	B
D	E	E
J	J	J	J

½ x 7¼ - 72 (3.6 Bd. Ft.)

| G | G | G | G | H |

¼" HARDBOARD 24 x 48

| I |
| I |

½ x 7¼ - 72 (3.6 Bd. Ft.)

| H | H | H |

¾ x 6 - 48 (2 Bd. Ft.)

| F, K, M |

CASE

I began work on the tool cabinet by making the plywood case. It's just an open box with dividers.

CUT PIECES TO SIZE. Start by cutting the sides (A), top and bottom (both B) for the case from ¾"-thick birch plywood *(Fig. 1).*

DADOES. To accept the dividers added later, a dado needs to be cut in each piece. There are dadoes centered on the length of the top and bottom pieces. And the side pieces are dadoed near the bottom.

RABBETS. The top and bottom pieces fit in a deep rabbet cut on each end of the sides *(Fig. 1a).* And the back inside edge of each piece is rabbeted for a ¾" plywood back (C) *(Figs. 1 and 1b).*

DIVIDERS. After assembling the case with glue and screws, you can add the dividers. A vertical divider (D) separates the case into two halves *(Fig. 2).* But before installing it, a dado is cut on each face to match the dadoes in the sides *(Fig. 2a).*

Note: This would be a good place to use a "story stick" (see the Shop Tip box on page 22).

Now just glue and screw the vertical divider in place. Then cut two horizontal dividers (E) to fit and attach them the same way.

EDGING. To complete the case, I covered the front of the plywood edges with ¼"-thick strips of hardwood edging (F) (see Exploded View, page 85).

DRAWERS

The next step is to build the two drawers to fit their openings.

BOX JOINTS. The sides (G), front and back (both H) of the drawers are held together with box joints *(Figs. 3 and 3a).*

Note: For information on cutting box joints, see pages 90 to 93.

FINGER PULL. After cutting the box joints, cut a recess in each drawer front to act as a finger pull *(Fig. 3b).*

BOTTOM GROOVE. Next, cut a groove in each piece for the ¼" hardboard bottom (I) *(Fig. 3).* The groove should be located at the very top of the first pin on the front and back (H) *(Fig. 3a).* This way, when the drawer is assembled, you won't see any gaps from the *front* of the drawer. But you will still see them from the *sides,* so I cut small wood plugs to cover the ends of the grooves.

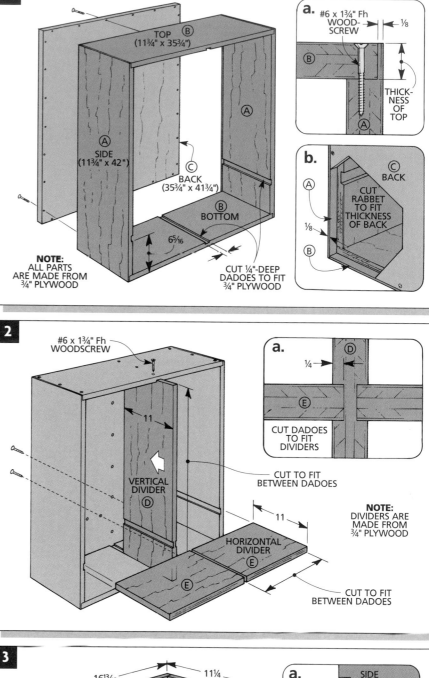
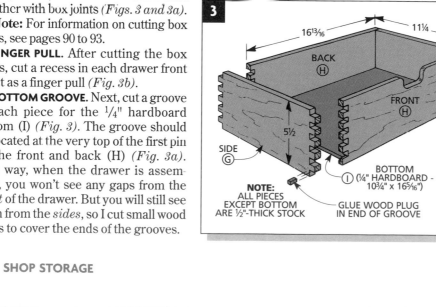

SHELVES

To divide the storage space inside the tool cabinet into compartments, I added four shelves.

CUT TO SIZE. The shelves (J) are cut from ³/₄" plywood *(Fig. 4)*. I wanted to make the shelves wide enough to support a router or belt sander, but narrow enough so I could close the doors of the cabinet without having the tools hanging on them hit the shelves. So I ended up cutting my shelves 7³/₄" wide.

To determine the length of the shelves, measure the opening and subtract ¹/₁₆" for clearance. (In my case, this made the shelves 16¹³/₁₆" long.)

MAKE THEM ADJUSTABLE. Since storage requirements change, I wanted the shelves to be adjustable. But I also wanted them to provide solid support for my power tools.

To hold the shelves securely in place, a groove is cut in each end to fit over shelf pins *(Fig. 4a)*. I used ³/₄"-long pieces of ¹/₄" dowel for the pins.

EDGING. Once the grooves are cut, you can cover the ends of the grooves and the exposed plies by gluing hardwood edging (K) to the front edge of each shelf *(Fig. 4)*.

SHELF PIN HOLES. Now you can drill holes for the shelf pins. To make sure the shelves stay level, I used a template made from ¹/₄" hardboard to locate the shelf pin holes an equal distance from the top and bottom *(Fig. 5)*.

DOORS

All that's left to complete the tool cabinet is to add a pair of doors. The doors (L) are just ³/₄" plywood panels trimmed with hardwood edging *(Fig. 6)*.

HINGES. Each door is attached with three butt hinges. The hinges are screwed into mortises cut in the edging on the case *(Fig. 6a)*.

Note: After mounting the doors, you may need to trim a bit off the edges where the doors meet. What you're looking for here is a consistent ¹/₁₆" gap.

PULLS & CATCHES. To make it easy to open and close the doors, I installed a pair of door pulls and four magnetic catches *(Figs. 6 and 6b)*.

MOUNT ON WALL. First, I measured between centers of the wall studs on which the cabinet would be mounted. I then marked and drilled two pairs of holes through the back of the cabinet, and mounted it using four ¹/₄" lag screws. ■

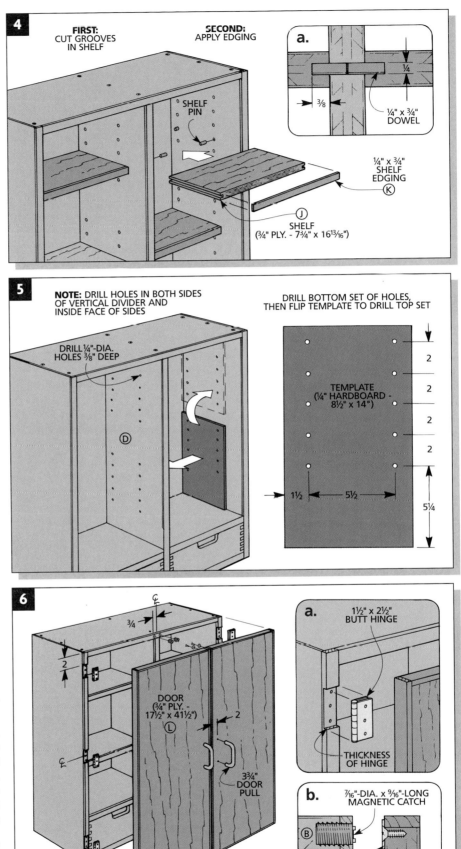

ACCESSORIES.... *Custom Tool Holders*

Before I hung the cabinet doors, I laid out the tools I wanted to mount and marked locations for the holders. It was sort of like a jigsaw puzzle, positioning everything according to size and where it will be most convenient.

TOOL HOLDERS. Once you decide where everything goes, you can make custom-designed holders for all of your tools. Of course, you don't want the tool holders to take up a lot of extra space in the cabinet, but they should hold the tools *securely* when the doors swing open. You don't want nicks, scrapes and gouges in the doors of your brand new tool cabinet.

DIFFERENT DESIGNS. You won't be able to use the same type of design for every holder. That's because each tool has its own special requirements.

Some tools like the mallet or dividers could hang on dowels angled slightly upward. For awkward, bulky tools, like a block plane or framing square, I used $\frac{1}{2}$" or $\frac{3}{4}$" hardwood and $\frac{1}{4}$" hardboard to make little shelves for added support.

In the photos and drawings below and on the next page are a number of ideas you can use to adapt to fit your own tools.

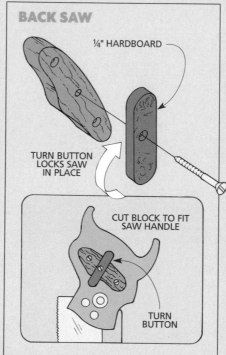

BACK SAW

¼" HARDBOARD

TURN BUTTON LOCKS SAW IN PLACE

CUT BLOCK TO FIT SAW HANDLE

TURN BUTTON

This back saw fits over a block that's cut to match the inside shape of the handle. Twisting a hardboard turn button locks the saw in place.

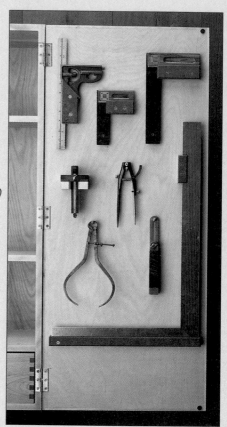

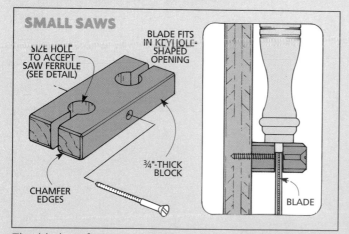

SMALL SAWS

SIZE HOLE TO ACCEPT SAW FERRULE (SEE DETAIL)

BLADE FITS IN KEYHOLE-SHAPED OPENING

¾"-THICK BLOCK

CHAMFER EDGES

BLADE

The blades of gent's and dovetail saws slip into keyhole-shaped openings in the ends of a block. And the ferrules fit down in the holes to secure the saws.

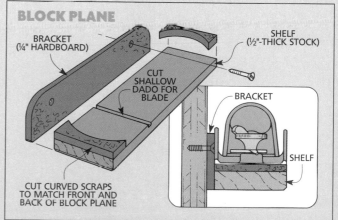

BLOCK PLANE

BRACKET (¼" HARDBOARD)

SHELF (½"-THICK STOCK)

CUT SHALLOW DADO FOR BLADE

BRACKET

SHELF

CUT CURVED SCRAPS TO MATCH FRONT AND BACK OF BLOCK PLANE

Curved scraps of hardboard keep a block plane from falling off a thin wood shelf. Gluing a bracket to the shelf makes the holder easy to mount.

FRAMING SQUARE

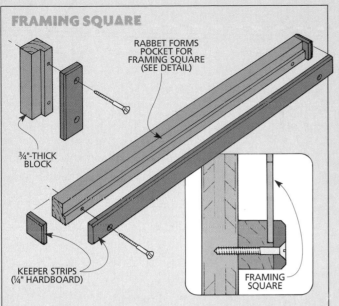

RABBET FORMS POCKET FOR FRAMING SQUARE (SEE DETAIL)

¾"-THICK BLOCK

KEEPER STRIPS (¼" HARDBOARD)

FRAMING SQUARE

Along with a rabbet in each of these two blocks, hardboard "keeper strips" create a pocket to house the legs of a framing square securely.

CHISELS

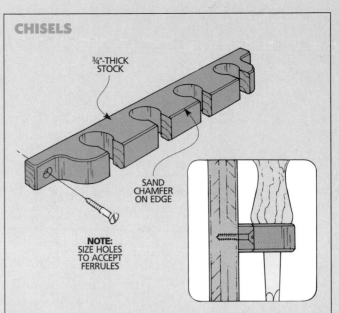

¾"-THICK STOCK

SAND CHAMFER ON EDGE

NOTE: SIZE HOLES TO ACCEPT FERRULES

To hold chisels firmly in place, the open-ended holes in this rack are smaller than the wood handles, but large enough to accept the metal ferrules.

TRY SQUARE

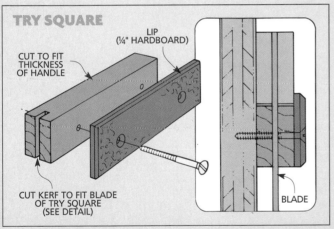

LIP (¼" HARDBOARD)

CUT TO FIT THICKNESS OF HANDLE

CUT KERF TO FIT BLADE OF TRY SQUARE (SEE DETAIL)

BLADE

The handle of a try square rests on top of a block while the blade slips into a kerf cut in one end. A hardboard lip keeps the square from sliding off.

COMBINATION SQUARE

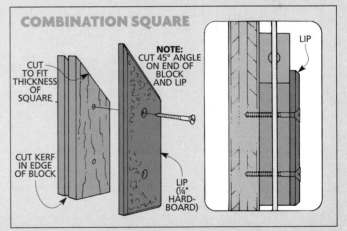

CUT TO FIT THICKNESS OF SQUARE

CUT KERF IN EDGE OF BLOCK

NOTE: CUT 45° ANGLE ON END OF BLOCK AND LIP

LIP

LIP (¼" HARD-BOARD)

A block cut at a 45° angle cradles a combination square. Here again, the blade fits in a kerf and a hardboard lip holds the square snug.

MARKING GAUGE

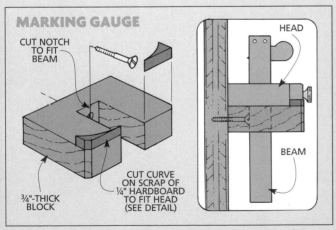

CUT NOTCH TO FIT BEAM

HEAD

¾"-THICK BLOCK

CUT CURVE ON SCRAP OF ¼" HARDBOARD TO FIT HEAD (SEE DETAIL)

BEAM

The beam of a marking gauge slips into the notch of this U-shaped block. And the head of the gauge is secured by curved scraps of hardboard.

BEVEL GAUGE

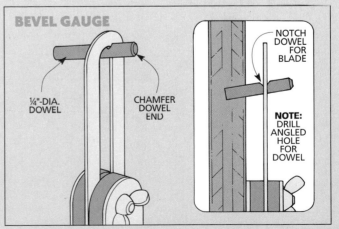

NOTCH DOWEL FOR BLADE

¼"-DIA. DOWEL

CHAMFER DOWEL END

NOTE: DRILL ANGLED HOLE FOR DOWEL

A number of tools (like this bevel gauge) can hang on dowels glued into angled holes. A notch keeps the tool tight against the door.

JOINERY... Box Joints on a Router Table

I've always had a weakness for box joints. I suppose it's the symmetry of the joint — the evenly spaced pins and slots are hard to resist whenever I need to join together the parts of a drawer or a small box. And, in many situations, they "dress up" a project and give it a stately, old-fashioned feel.

But there are reasons other than appearance why I like box joints. The first is their strength. Next to its cousin, the dovetail, the box joint is one of the strongest ways to join wood together. That's because of the alternating pins and slots.

INTERLOCKING FINGERS. The pins and slots on mating pieces interlock like tiny fingers (see the drawing below). This creates a lot of glue surface and makes for a strong joint. In order for it to be really strong, though, you'll need a snug and accurate fit.

The trick to getting a good fit on a box joint is to get the width of the pins to match the width of the slots exactly. It's not really all that difficult. All you need is a jig that uses a small index pin. This index pin determines the width of both the pins and the tails.

WHICH TOOL? The only dilemma I have when cutting box joints is choosing which tool to use — the table saw or router table. The jig for each is essentially the same. On the table saw the jig usually attaches to the miter gauge. On the router table it can attach to a miter gauge, or run between the fence and a straightedge as shown in the photo at right.

As a general rule of thumb, if the stock is thicker than $1/2$", I use the table saw with a dado blade. It works much quicker than a router table, especially when cutting large box joints. (Also, it's not safe to make a cut this wide in a single pass with a router bit.)

But if the stock is $1/2$" thick or less (as on the drawers for the Tool Cabinet), I use the router table. The advantage of using a router table is that a straight router bit produces a perfect slot — smooth sides and a flat bottom (unlike the less-than-perfect cut from a saw blade).

DESIGN CONCERNS. One limitation, though, of using the router table is that the width of the pins must match the thickness of one of your straight router

bits (usually $1/8$", $1/4$", $3/8$", or, as shown here, $1/2$"). This means that the finished width of your drawer or project has to be a multiple of this measurement. Otherwise you will end up with a partial pin on the bottom. That's one thing you'll need to take into consideration when designing a project.

There's one other thing. I think box joints look best if they're balanced. That is, with a pin at the very top and bottom of the front and back of the drawer. This requires that you have an *odd* number of pins. (For the drawer shown here, five.)

Once you have the design all worked out, it's time to build the jig.

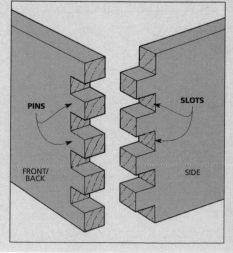

PINS

SLOTS

FRONT/ BACK

SIDE

To cut box joints on the router table, I built this simple jig. It's just a three-piece sled that rides between the fence and a straightedge.

Note: Although this jig is designed to handle stock up to $5^1/_2$" in width, it can be made larger to handle wider stock.

SLED. The sled is made up of a $1/_4$" hardboard sled base and a hardwood backing board (see drawing).

Attached to the backing board is an adjustable fence with a hardwood index pin that allows you to index your workpiece to make evenly-spaced cuts.

PIN. The size of this pin is what determines the width of the box joint. For example, if you're going to cut $1/_4$" box joints, use a $1/_4$" pin. Or for $1/_2$" box joints, use a $1/_2$" pin.

Note: You'll need to make a different adjustable fence for each of the different-sized box joints you're going to cut.

SLOTS. There's one more step to allow for small adjustments. Drill slots in the backing board for the bolts that hold the adjustable fence in place.

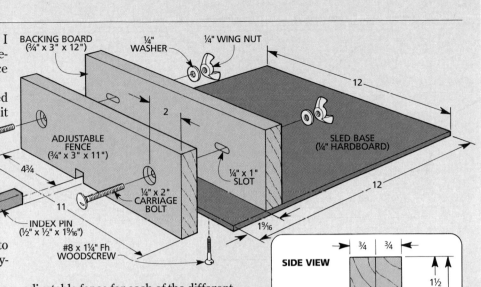

BACKING BOARD ($3/_4$" x 3" x 12")
$1/_4$" WASHER
$1/_4$" WING NUT
12
2
SLED BASE ($1/_4$" HARDBOARD)
ADJUSTABLE FENCE ($3/_4$" x 3" x 11")
$4^3/_4$
$1/_4$" x 2" CARRIAGE BOLT
$1/_4$" x 1" SLOT
12
11
INDEX PIN ($1/_2$" x $1/_2$" x $1^9/_{16}$")
#8 x $1^1/_4$" Fh WOODSCREW
$1^9/_{16}$

SIDE VIEW
$3/_4$ $3/_4$
COUNTERBORE $3/_8$" DEEP
INDEX PIN
$1^1/_2$
3

SETUP

Setting up the box joint jig (shown above) is relatively easy. First, raise the bit *above the sled* to the desired height. The height should equal the thickness of the stock (in our case, $1/_2$").

The next step is to position the index pin. To determine the correct position, simply adjust the router table fence so the gap between the router bit and the index pin matches the width of the index pin itself *(Fig. 1)*.

Next, you'll need a way to keep the jig from shifting during cutting. I clamped a straightedge to the table *(Fig. 2)*. This helps to ensure an accurate cut.

Also, clamp a stop block to the router table fence. This will keep you from routing through the jig's backing board *(Step 3)*.

To "fine tune" the critical distance between the index pin and the router bit, turn on the router and rout into the sled base, stopping just short of the adjustable fence. Then turn off the router and make any adjustments (see Shop Tip at right).

When that distance is right on, make a series of test cuts following the procedure on pages 92 and 93. If you encounter any problems, refer to the troubleshooting section on page 93.

SHOP TIP

Pin Spacing

A $1/_2$" drill bit or the shank of a $1/_2$" router bit makes a handy gauge to set up the $1/_2$" pin spacing.

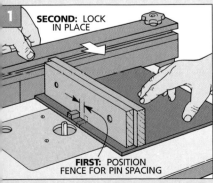

SECOND: LOCK IN PLACE

FIRST: POSITION FENCE FOR PIN SPACING

Position the router table fence so the gap between the bit and the index pin matches the width of the index pin.

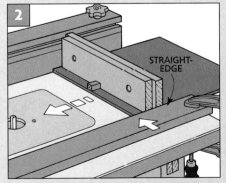

STRAIGHT-EDGE

To ensure an accurate cut, clamp a straightedge to the table top so it's parallel with the fence.

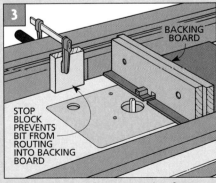

BACKING BOARD

STOP BLOCK PREVENTS BIT FROM ROUTING INTO BACKING BOARD

Position a stop block on the fence to prevent the bit from cutting through the backing board.

With the box joint jig complete, you're ready to get down to business. But just because the jig is set up accurately doesn't mean the process is completely automatic. There are still a few things that can give you trouble.

TEST CUT. One good way to work out the "bugs" is by first cutting a test corner on some scrap pieces, following the steps shown in the drawings below.

TIPS. In addition to following these steps, here are a few extra tips that should result in better box joints:

■ Start with pieces a little wider than needed. Then you can come back later after cutting the joints and trim them right at the last full pin or slot.

■ Keep yourself organized. Start by labeling all of the pieces of the drawer (or project) that will have box joints. Number each mating piece and label the tops of the workpieces. Then you will be sure you're cutting the pin or slot at the right place on each piece.

■ It's important to be consistent when cutting box joints. Even shifting pressure on the pieces slightly can affect the fit of the joint. I hold the workpiece and the jig with two hands and perform each pass exactly the same way.

■ Don't cut the pieces to fit too tight. If they're too tight, the pieces won't go completely together or you'll crack off some pins. But they shouldn't be too

loose, either. They should be tight enough to require a few light taps with a mallet to go together.

ASSEMBLY. After the joints are cut, *dry* assemble and clamp them to make sure you won't have any surprises. Once everything seems to fit, I like to use white glue for the actual assembly. It sets up a little slower than yellow glue so it gives me a little more work time.

Also, to get the glue on quickly, I use cotton swabs or a small artist's brush, dabbing glue onto the *sides* of the pins. You don't want much glue.

When clamping, tighten the clamps just until the joint closes. Don't over-tighten, or the drawer sides may bow.

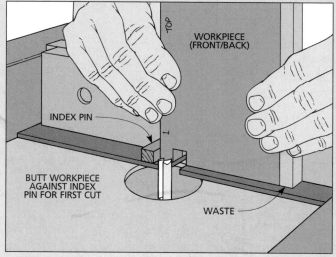

1 Start with the front and back. When routing the first slot in the front (or back), hold the workpiece tight against the jig's index pin and backing board.

2 To rout the next slot, simply lift the workpiece, slip it onto the index pin, and take another pass. Repeat this until all the slots are complete.

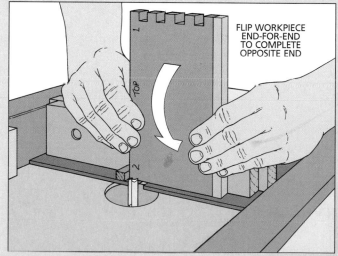

3 To cut matching slots on the opposite end of the work-piece, flip the workpiece end-for-end and repeat the procedure. Once the front and back are complete, work can begin on the sides.

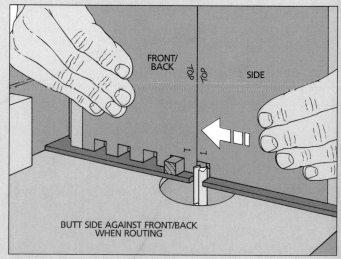

4 The only difference in the side pieces is you use a front (or back) as a reference to offset the slots in the sides. Seat the first slot cut in the front (or back) on the index pin. Then butt one of the side pieces against it and take the first pass.

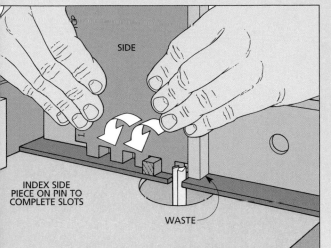

INDEX SIDE
PIECE ON PIN TO
COMPLETE SLOTS

SIDE

WASTE

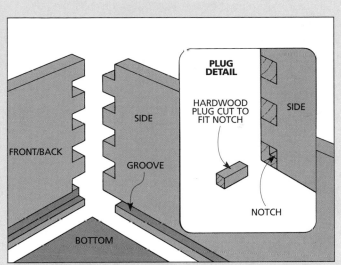

PLUG
DETAIL

HARDWOOD
PLUG CUT TO
FIT NOTCH

SIDE

SIDE

FRONT/BACK

GROOVE

NOTCH

BOTTOM

5 After routing the first slot, set aside the front (or back). Now rout the remaining slots just as you did earlier. Once you've completed one end, flip the workpiece end-for-end and rout the opposite end (remember to offset the first slot).

6 To add a bottom, you'll need to cut a ¹/₄" groove in each workpiece. After assembly, cut ¹/₄" square plugs to fill the notched pins on the ends of the front and back pieces. When the glue dries, trim the plugs flush and sand them smooth.

TROUBLESHOOTING

There are really only a couple of things that cause most of the problems with box joints.

First, the router bit is either set too low or too high. If the pins are too short, it's set too low. And if the pins are too long, it's set too high.

Note: Sometimes I set the bit just a hair high on purpose. Then I can sand the ends of the pins down perfectly flush with the mating piece.

The other common problem is that the joint is too tight or too loose. To solve this problem, make sure that

three things are all *exactly* the same size: the diameter of the router bit, the distance between the bit and the index pin, and the width of the index pin.

The problem is usually in the distance between the bit and the pin. Make a slight adjustment and try again.

PERFECT FIT. *On a perfect-fitting joint, the pins are flush with the sides, and there are no gaps.*

SHORT PINS. *If the router bit is set too shallow, you'll end up with pins that are too short.*

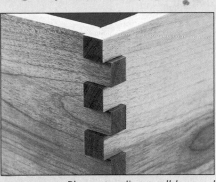

LONG PINS. *Pins extending well beyond the sides are caused by a router bit that's set too deep.*

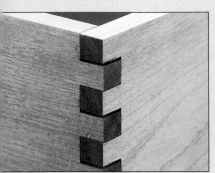

GAP. *A gap between each pin and slot is caused by an index pin that's too close to the bit.*

TOO TIGHT. *If the pins won't fit in the slots, the index pin is set too far away from the router bit.*

OFFSET. *An offset can be caused by not having a workpiece fully seated on the index pin or jig.*

Pegboard System

Here's a tool rack you can customize to fit your needs and hand tools. It features a different approach to using common pegboard and holding your most commonly used tools.

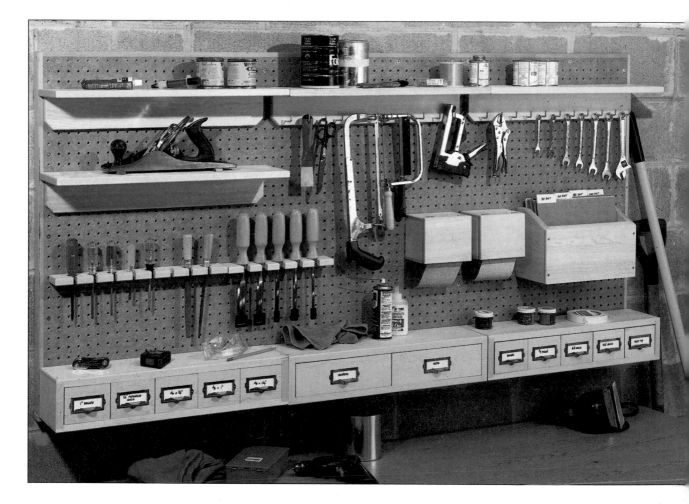

One item common to almost all workshops is a sheet or two of pegboard and an assortment of wire hooks that hold the usual items — screwdrivers, pliers, hammers, and other hand tools.

FALLING HANGERS. One thing that has always bothered me about pegboard storage is that almost every time I reach for a tool, the hook comes off with it or falls to the floor.

To avoid this, I came up with a whole new system of tool racks and storage units that stay put on pegboard. The system uses common L-hooks that are

available at any hardware store or home center. These hooks are screwed to the back of each storage unit. (For more on this, see the Shop Tip box on page 97.)

WASTED SPACE. Another thing that bothered me about traditional pegboard systems is how they waste space. They don't seem to hold as many tools as they should.

So when I designed this new system, I modified some common tool racks to make them more efficient. And I added adjustable shelves and drawers.

CUSTOMIZE. Though this system has a lot of interesting features, the best

part is how you can customize it to *your* needs. You can add more shelv or drawers if you need them. And i easy to move things around to mal them more convenient.

MATERIALS. This entire pegboa system is built with common materi found at most lumberyards or hon centers. To build the frame, I used o six-foot 2x8 and a little less than a f sheet (4x8) of ¼" pegboard.

For all of the shelves, drawers, a different storage units, I simply us ½" and ¾" pine and some small piec of ¼" hardboard.

EXPLODED VIEW

OVERALL DIMENSIONS:
36H x 72W x 6D

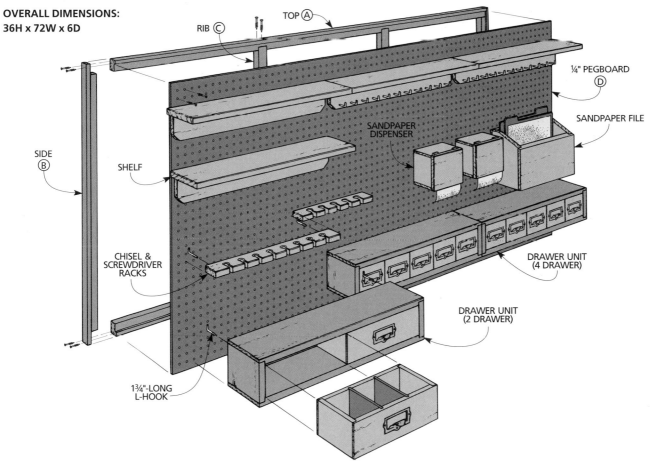

TOP Ⓐ

RIB Ⓒ

¼" PEGBOARD Ⓓ

SANDPAPER FILE

SANDPAPER DISPENSER

SIDE Ⓑ

SHELF

CHISEL & SCREWDRIVER RACKS

DRAWER UNIT (4 DRAWER)

1¾"-LONG L-HOOK

DRAWER UNIT (2 DRAWER)

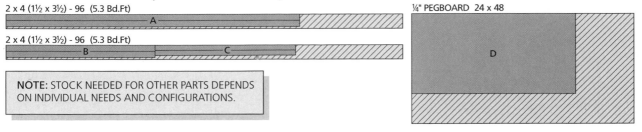

MATERIALS LIST

PEGBOARD FRAME

A	Top/Bottom (2)	1½ x 1½ - 71
B	Sides (2)	1½ x 1½ - 36
C	Ribs (2)	1½ x 1¼ - 34
D	Pegboard (1)	¼ pgbd. - 35 x 71

DRAWER UNIT

E	Frm. Top/Btm. (2)	¾ x 6 - 24
F	Frm. Sides (2)	¾ x 6 - 4¼
G	Frm. Back (1)	¼ hdbd. - 4 x 23
H	Drwr. Sides*	½ x 3⁷/₁₆ - 5½
I	Lg. Dr. Fr./Bk (4)	½ x 3⁷/₁₆ - 11³/₁₆
J	Sm. Dr. Fr./Bk (10)	½ x 3⁷/₁₆ - 4⁷/₁₆
K	Lg. Dr. Btm. (2)	¼ hdbd. - 5¼ x 10¹¹/₁₆
L	Sm. Dr. Btm. (5)	¼ hdbd. - 3¹⁵/₁₆ x 5¼
M	Lg. Dr. Divid. (4)	¼ hdbd. - 2¹⁵/₁₆ x 5¼
N	Sm. Dr. Divid. (5)	¼ hdbd. - 2¹⁵/₁₆ x 3¹⁵/₁₆

SHELF

O	Shelf (1)	¾ x 6 - 24
P	Back (1)	¾ x 3¼ - 23

SANDPAPER DISPENSER

Q	Sides (2)	½ x 3¾ - 4¼
R	Door (1)	½ x 5 - 6
S	Top/Bottom (2)	¾ x 4¼ - 6
T	Back (1)	¼ hdbd. - 4 x 5½

CHISEL & SCREWDRIVER RACKS

U	Chisel Rack (1)	¾ x 2¼ - 12
V	Screwdr. Rack (1)	¾ x 2¼ - 18

SANDPAPER FILE

W	Front (1)	¾ x 6½ - 12¾
X	Back (1)	¾ x 8 - 12¾
Y	Sides (2)	¾ x 5¼ - 8
Z	Bottom (1)	¼ hdbd. - 4⁵/₈ x 11¾
AA	Dividers*	¼ hdbd. - 9¾ x 11

HARDWARE SUPPLIES*

(16) No. 8 x 1¾" Fh woodscrews
(44) No. 12 x 1" Fh woodscrews
⁵/₃₂"-dia. x 1¾"-long L-hooks
No. 4 x ⅜" Fh woodscrews
No. 6 x 1" Fh woodscrews
No. 8 x 1½" Fh woodscrews
1" wire brads
Drawer pulls with label holders
1" x 1" butt hinges w/screws
Hacksaw blade
Toilet paper holder

*Quantities will depend on individual needs

CUTTING DIAGRAM (FOR PEGBOARD FRAME)

2 x 4 (1½ x 3½) - 96 (5.3 Bd.Ft)

A

2 x 4 (1½ x 3½) - 96 (5.3 Bd.Ft)

B   C

NOTE: STOCK NEEDED FOR OTHER PARTS DEPENDS ON INDIVIDUAL NEEDS AND CONFIGURATIONS.

¼" PEGBOARD 24 x 48

D

The frame that the pegboard hangs on is made from standard "two-by" lumber ($1\frac{1}{2}$" thick). I used $\frac{1}{4}$" pegboard instead of $\frac{1}{8}$" pegboard because it will hold the heavy weight of the bins and shelves better.

FRAME. Start by cutting the top/bottom (A) and sides (B) to a width of $1\frac{1}{2}$" and to finished lengths *(Fig. 1)*.

Then cut two reinforcing ribs (C) to finished width and rough length. Also, rip them to finished thickness ($1\frac{1}{4}$").

RABBET. To join the frame, first cut a rabbet on the inside edges of the top, bottom, and sides to hold the $\frac{1}{4}$" pegboard. To do this, I used a dado blade buried in an auxiliary fence on the table saw *(Fig. 2)*.

NOTCH. To join the sides to the top and bottom, cut a notch on both ends of each side *(Fig. 3)*. Cut these notches just wide enough to accept the top and bottom pieces.

DADO. After the sides are notched, the next step is to cut two dadoes in the top and bottom to hold the ribs (C) (refer to *Fig. 5*).

ASSEMBLY. With the dadoes cut, the frame is ready to be assembled. To do this, first drill and screw the sides to the top and bottom *(Fig. 4)*. Then cut the ribs to finished length and screw them in place *(Fig. 5)*.

PEGBOARD. Once the frame is screwed together, cut the pegboard to fit between the rabbets. Cut the pegboard so the holes are about $\frac{1}{2}$" from the edge *(Fig. 6)*. That way the L-hooks in the storage units won't contact the sides or ribs. And the units won't hang over the edge of the frame. It also means you can use the holes in the pegboard as screw holes.

CHAMFER. Finally, rout an $\frac{1}{8}$" chamfer around the outside edge *(Fig. 7)*.

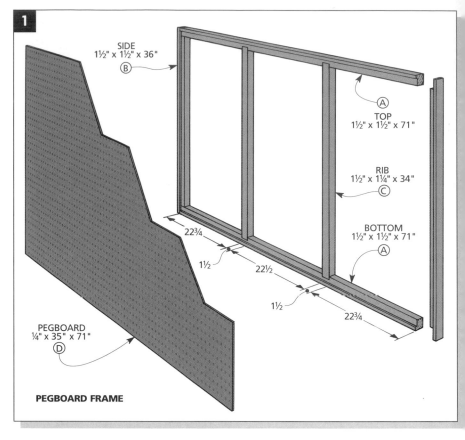

1

SIDE
$1\frac{1}{2}$" x $1\frac{1}{2}$" x 36"
(B)

(A)

TOP
$1\frac{1}{2}$" x $1\frac{1}{2}$" x 71"
(A)

RIB
$1\frac{1}{2}$" x $1\frac{1}{4}$" x 34"
(C)

BOTTOM
$1\frac{1}{2}$" x $1\frac{1}{2}$" x 71"
(A)

$22\frac{3}{4}$

$1\frac{1}{2}$

$22\frac{1}{2}$

$1\frac{1}{2}$

$22\frac{3}{4}$

PEGBOARD
$\frac{1}{4}$" x 35" x 71"
(D)

PEGBOARD FRAME

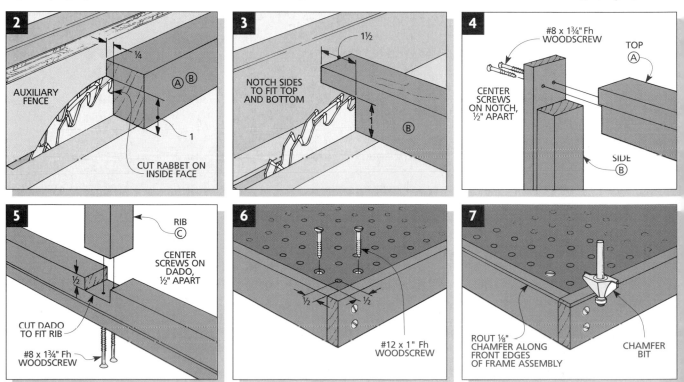

2

$\frac{1}{4}$

AUXILIARY
FENCE

(A) (B)

1

CUT RABBET ON
INSIDE FACE

3

$1\frac{1}{2}$

NOTCH SIDES
TO FIT TOP
AND BOTTOM

1

(B)

4

#8 x $1\frac{3}{4}$" Fh
WOODSCREW

TOP
(A)

CENTER
SCREWS
ON NOTCH,
$\frac{1}{2}$" APART

SIDE
(B)

5

RIB
(C)

CENTER
SCREWS ON
DADO,
$\frac{1}{2}$" APART

$\frac{1}{2}$

CUT DADO
TO FIT RIB

#8 x $1\frac{3}{4}$" Fh
WOODSCREW

6

$\frac{1}{2}$ $\frac{1}{2}$

#12 x 1" Fh
WOODSCREW

7

ROUT $\frac{1}{8}$"
CHAMFER ALONG
FRONT EDGES
OF FRAME ASSEMBLY

CHAMFER
BIT

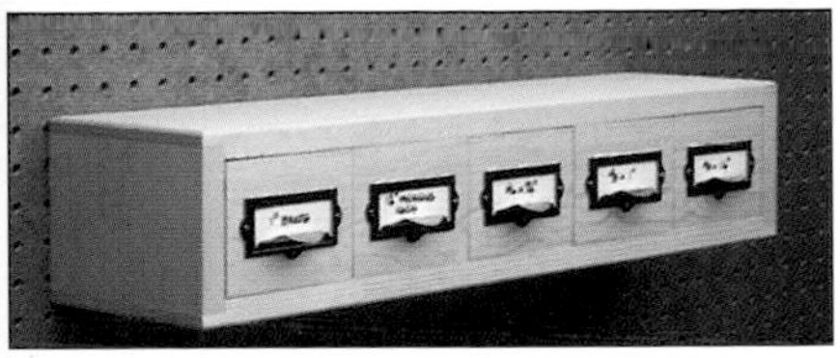

DRAWER UNIT

To help organize some of the hardware scattered throughout the shop, I decided to build five-drawer and two-drawer storage units.

The frames for both drawer units are identical. The only differences are the size and number of drawers.

FRAME. A frame consists of the top and bottom (E), two sides (F), and a back (G). I used 3/4" pine for all of the parts except the 1/4" hardboard back *(Fig. 8)*.

To hold the back, there's a rabbet running along the back edge of each piece *(Fig. 8a)*. Also, rabbets are cut on either side of the top and bottom to hold the sides *(Fig. 8b)*.

Now glue and screw the top and bottom to the sides. Then cut the back to size and glue it in place.

Next, chamfer the top and bottom. Then screw three L-hooks into the back edge of the top. When installing the L-hooks, it's important to install them correctly so the unit hangs properly (see the Shop Tip, below right).

DRAWERS. Now the frames are ready for the drawers themselves. This time, I used 1/2"-thick stock for all of the parts, except the 1/4" hardboard bottoms and dividers *(Fig. 9)*.

When building either size drawer, the basic approach is the same. There are only two differences — the lengths of the fronts and the backs, and the number of dividers.

To begin, cut the sides (H) and fronts/backs (I or J) to size *(Fig. 9)*. Now cut a rabbet on the front and back pieces for the sides. Then cut a groove on the inside face of each piece for the bottom (K or L).

Next, 1/4"-deep dadoes for drawer dividers (M or N) can be cut. For the larger drawers, the dadoes are cut in the fronts and the backs. On the smaller drawers, they're cut in the sides.

Now dry assemble each drawer to determine the size of the bottom and dividers (or divider). Then after they're cut to size, glue and nail the drawers together. Finally, I added drawer pulls that have a slot for a label card.

8

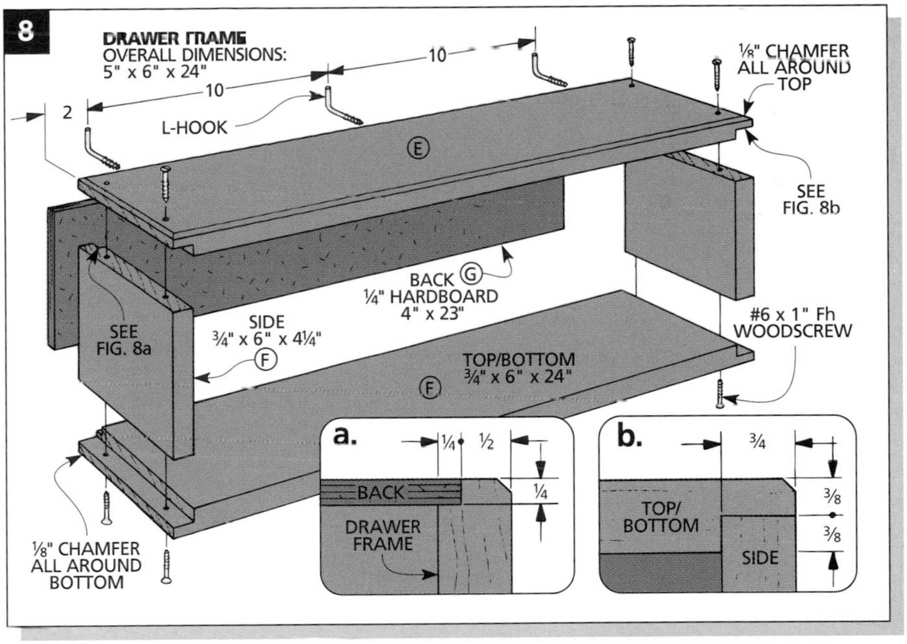

DRAWER FRAME
OVERALL DIMENSIONS:
5" x 6" x 24"
10
10
2
L-HOOK
1/8" CHAMFER
ALL AROUND
TOP
SEE
FIG. 8b
E
BACK G
1/4" HARDBOARD
4" x 23"
SIDE
3/4" x 6" x 4 1/4"
F
SEE
FIG. 8a
#6 x 1" Fh
WOODSCREW
TOP/BOTTOM
3/4" x 6" x 24"
1/8" CHAMFER
ALL AROUND
BOTTOM
a.
1/4
1/2
BACK
DRAWER
FRAME
b.
3/4
3/8
3/8
TOP/
BOTTOM
SIDE

9

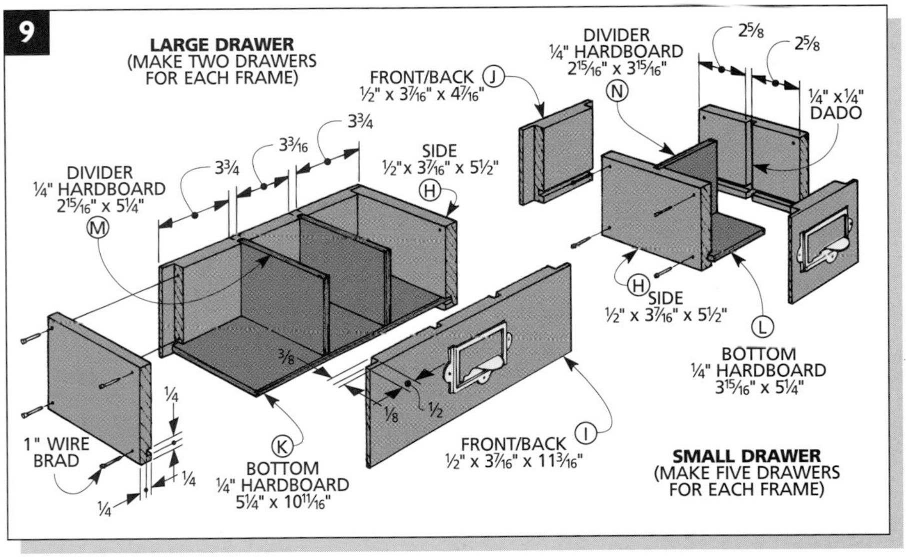

LARGE DRAWER
(MAKE TWO DRAWERS
FOR EACH FRAME)
DIVIDER
1/4" HARDBOARD
2 15/16" x 5 1/4"
M
3 3/4
3 3/16
3 3/4
FRONT/BACK J
1/2" x 3 7/16" x 4 7/16"
SIDE
1/2" x 3 7/16" x 5 1/2"
H
DIVIDER
1/4" HARDBOARD
2 15/16" x 3 15/16"
N
2 5/8
2 5/8
1/4" x 1/4"
DADO
1" WIRE
BRAD
1/4
1/4
1/4
3/8
BOTTOM
1/4" HARDBOARD
5 1/4" x 10 11/16"
K
1/8
1/2
FRONT/BACK
1/2" x 3 7/16" x 11 3/16"
I
SIDE
1/2" x 3 7/16" x 5 1/2"
L
BOTTOM
1/4" HARDBOARD
3 15/16" x 5 1/4"
SMALL DRAWER
(MAKE FIVE DRAWERS
FOR EACH FRAME)

SHOP TIP .... *L-Hook System*

All of the storage units and shelves for this pegboard system hang the same way. And, unlike typical metal pegboard hooks, it's almost impossible for them to fall out.

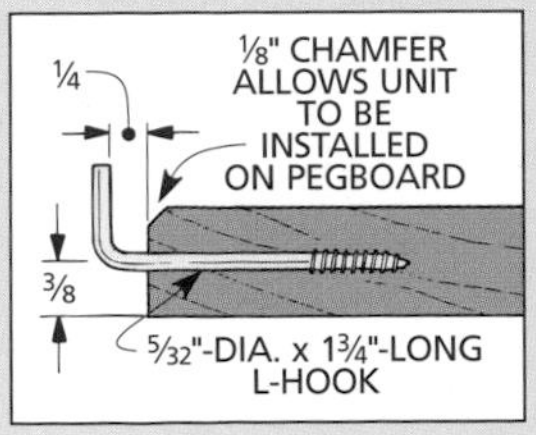

1/4
1/8" CHAMFER
ALLOWS UNIT
TO BE
INSTALLED
ON PEGBOARD
3/8
5/32"-DIA. x 1 3/4"-LONG
L-HOOK

To use this system, first screw 1 3/4"-long L-hooks to the back of each storage unit (see drawing below left).

Then, to hang the unit, tilt it in the pegboard at a 45° angle (see top photo at right).

As the unit is lowered, the weight of the unit pulls the hook tight against the back of the pegboard (see bottom photo at right).

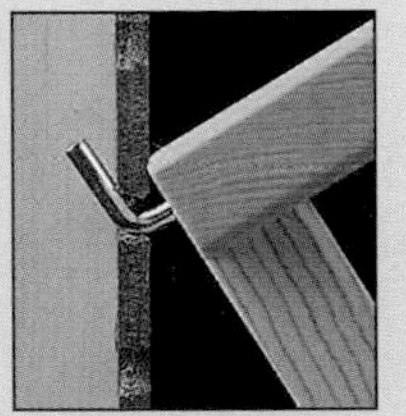

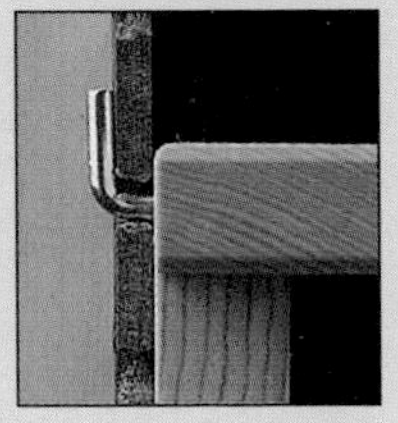

SHELF

When designing this pegboard system, I thought it would be a good idea to have a shelf for holding small items like glue bottles and containers of wood filler.

The simplest shelf to build would have been a board with two mounting hooks screwed in the back. But to add more support to the shelf (O), I screwed a back (P) to the bottom *(Fig. 10)*.

Once I had the back in place, I realized it could be used for more than support. So I screwed L-hooks in the back near the bottom and used them for hanging hand tools *(Figs. 11 and 12)*.

SANDPAPER DISPENSER

One thing we use a lot of in the shop is adhesive-backed sandpaper. When I realized that we go through about as many rolls of it as we do toilet paper, it gave me an idea for a sandpaper dis-

penser — using a toilet paper holder.

Each dispenser is built with $1/2$"-thick stock for the sides (Q) and door (R). But $3/4$"-thick stock is used for the top. This allowed me to screw L-hooks into the top (S) *(Fig. 13)*. And because the top and bottom (also S) have the same size rabbets, it was easiest to use $3/4$"-thick stock for the bottom as well.

Before the parts can be assembled, several things have to be done. First cut $1/4$" rabbets in the top, bottom, and sides for the back (T) *(Figs. 13 & 14)*.

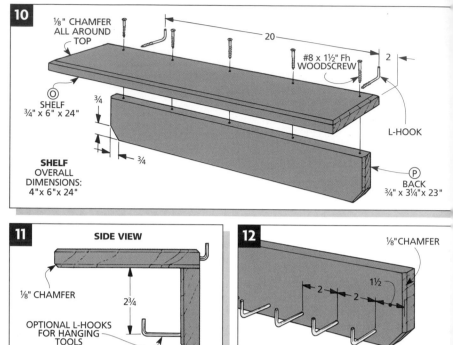

Second, cut mortises in the top for hinges *(Fig. 13)*. Then drill a finger hole in the bottom *(Fig. 14)*. This hole allows a finger to get behind the sandpaper when tearing off a piece.

Next, cut a recess in the bottom edge of the door for a short piece of a hacksaw blade to act as a paper "cutter" *(Fig. 15)*. Then drill a hole in each side for the toilet paper holder *(Fig. 16)*.

Finally, the dispenser can be glued and nailed together.

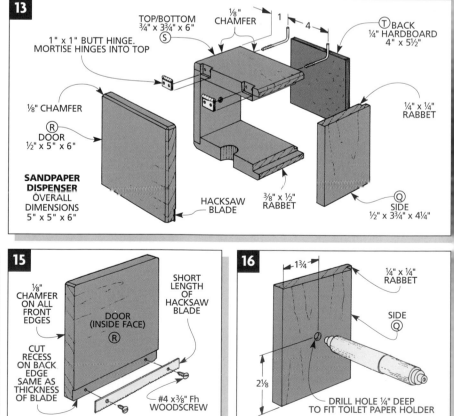

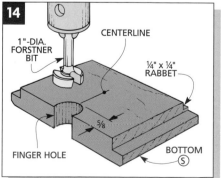

CHISEL & SCREWDRIVER RACKS

No pegboard is complete without a rack for chisels and screwdrivers. Since not all screwdrivers and chisels are alike, use the ideas shown and customize

them to fit your specific tools.

With many tool racks, you have to lift the tool to clear the hole in the rack. This means the space above the rack can't be used for anything else.

Instead, these tool racks have narrow slots in front of the holes, so the tools can be pulled straight out. (You'll still have to lift a little.)

When drilling a hole for a chisel, chamfer the top edge of the hole so the ferrule can't slip out (*Figs. 17 and 17a*). When drilling for a screwdriver, counterbore the hole slightly larger than the handle so the handle sits down into the hole (*Figs. 18 and 18a*).

SANDPAPER FILE

I've always had a difficult time keeping sheets of sandpaper flat. They always want to curl up when the humidity changes. To keep them flat and rela-

tively dry, I made a system that also lets me store them according to grit.

The sandpaper file is simply a pine box with an open top (*Fig. 19*).

Loose dividers made of ¼" hardboard, similar to folders found in a file cabinet, separate different grits of sandpaper and keep them flat (refer to *Fig. 21*).

To build the sandpaper file, first cut a rabbet in the ends of the front (W) and back (X) pieces for the sides (Y). Then cut a rabbet in the front and sides for the bottom (Z).

To make it easier to get the sandpaper out of the file, I cut the sides at an angle on the band saw. Then the top edge of the front is bevel-ripped on the table saw to match the sides (*Fig. 20*).

Once all the parts are glued and screwed together, install two L-hooks in the back. After cutting the dividers (AA) to shape with a little identification "tab" like a file folder (*Fig. 21*), label the tabs for the grits you use. ■

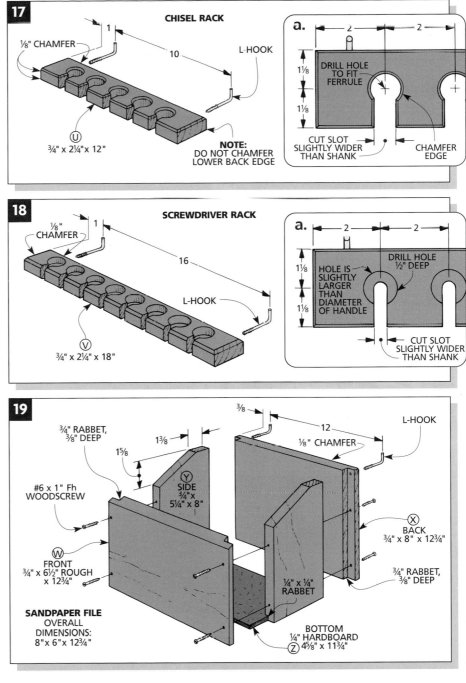

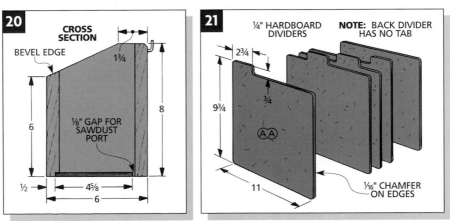

Lumber Rack

This lumber rack is a space-saving storage system that protects yet provides access to long boards, cutoffs, and plywood. You can also add a convenient bin for sheet goods.

When it comes to lumber, I'm like a squirrel storing nuts for the winter. Whether it's a long board, a short cutoff, or a piece of hardwood plywood that's too valuable to throw away, it's all saved for a project I'm going to build "someday."

Needless to say, storage has been a problem. In the past I've always had a stack of wood on the floor, and had to sort through it to find the right board. Not to mention bracing sheets of plywood against my leg while trying to pull out a piece from behind.

To get my lumber and plywood off the floor, I built a simple rack. It provides plenty of storage, but the best thing about it is it organizes and pro-

vides easy access to all the pieces I need.

PIPES. The key is a number of sturdy metal pipes that are supported by a wood frame (see Exploded View). A series of holes allows you to move the pipes up or down so you can customize the rack to fit your needs.

I laid long boards across the top row of pipes. And to keep short pieces from falling through, they're stored on shelves on the other two rows of pipes. To create even more storage, I ran stretch cords across the bottom compartments (refer to page 104).

OPTIONAL BIN. You can also add an optional swing-out bin (see page 105). Resting on casters, it's designed to hold large sheets of plywood and other kinds

of sheet goods on edge. This way, you can sort through the pieces and select the piece you need.

MATERIALS. I used standard construction grade Douglas fir for the frame of the lumber rack. For the bin, shelves, stretchers, and kickplate, I used 1/2" fir plywood. Finally, the edging strips were cut from 1x6 pine.

EXPLODED VIEW

OVERALL DIMENSIONS:
Custom Height x 95½L x 17½D

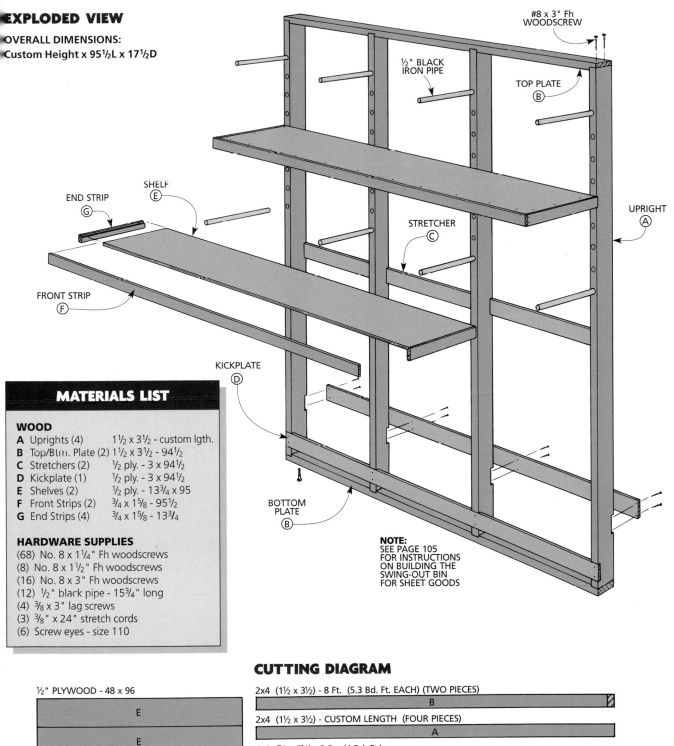

#8 x 3" Fh WOODSCREW

½" BLACK IRON PIPE

TOP PLATE
(B)

UPRIGHT
(A)

END STRIP
(G)

SHELF
(E)

STRETCHER
(C)

FRONT STRIP
(F)

KICKPLATE
(D)

BOTTOM PLATE
(B)

NOTE:
SEE PAGE 105
FOR INSTRUCTIONS
ON BUILDING THE
SWING-OUT BIN
FOR SHEET GOODS

MATERIALS LIST

WOOD

A	Uprights (4)	1½ x 3½ - custom lgth.
B	Top/Btm. Plate (2)	1½ x 3½ - 94½
C	Stretchers (2)	½ ply. - 3 x 94½
D	Kickplate (1)	½ ply. - 3 x 94½
E	Shelves (2)	½ ply. - 13¾ x 95
F	Front Strips (2)	¾ x 1⅝ - 95½
G	End Strips (4)	¾ x 1⅝ - 13¾

HARDWARE SUPPLIES

(68) No. 8 x 1¼" Fh woodscrews
(8) No. 8 x 1½" Fh woodscrews
(16) No. 8 x 3" Fh woodscrews
(12) ½" black pipe - 15¾" long
(4) ⅜ x 3" lag screws
(3) ⅜" x 24" stretch cords
(6) Screw eyes - size 110

CUTTING DIAGRAM

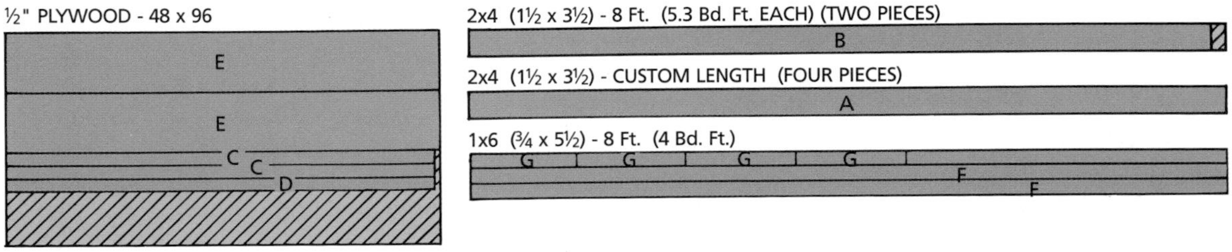

½" PLYWOOD - 48 x 96

E

E

C C
D

2x4 (1½ x 3½) - 8 Ft. (5.3 Bd. Ft. EACH) (TWO PIECES)

B

2x4 (1½ x 3½) - CUSTOM LENGTH (FOUR PIECES)

A

1x6 (¾ x 5½) - 8 Ft. (4 Bd. Ft.)

G G G G F F

The "backbone" of the lumber storage rack is a 2x4 stud wall that supports the pipes. You can build a separate frame for this wall. Or, you can drill holes for the pipes in an existing stud wall (see box below). (This is *not* recommended for a bearing wall unless you add an additional 2x4 to each stud.)

FRAME. The basic frame consists of four uprights (A) that are held together by a top and bottom plate (B) *(Fig. 1)*. I cut these pieces from standard 2x4s.

Before determining the length of the uprights, you'll need to decide the location of the lumber rack. Then measure the shortest distance between the floor and the joists (or ceiling) and subtract $2^{1}/_{2}$". This allows $1/2$" for levelers (added later) and 2" for the tongues on the top and bottom plates *(Fig. 2a)*.

Now the top and bottom plates can be cut to final length. (I cut mine $94^{1}/_{2}$" long, but it will depend on your space.)

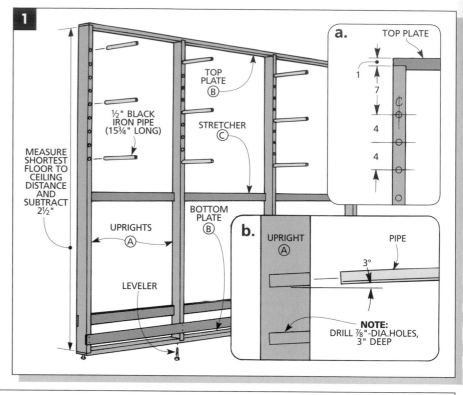

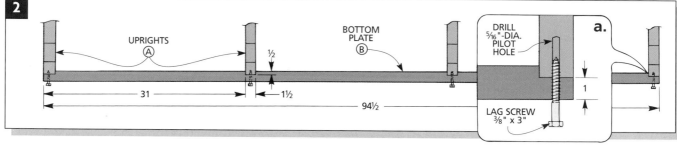

To drill a series of consistently angled holes, I used a simple guide that starts the bit at the correct angle. It's just a scrap block of 2x4 with a piece of hardboard glued to one side.

To make the guide, first drill a *straight* hole through the block. Then cut the back edge at the desired angle (3°). When you clamp the guide to the upright, the back edge tilts the hole at the same angle.

To help position the guide on the uprights, draw a reference mark on the guide (at the center of the hole) and a second one on the upright (where you want the hole). Then just align the reference marks.

After the hole is started in the upright, you can remove the guide and drill the hole to full depth.

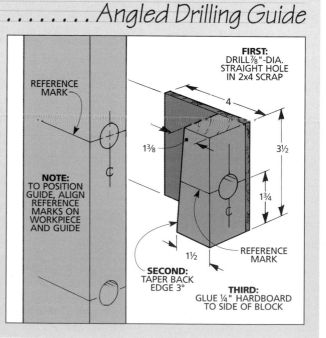

DADOES AND RABBETS. With the top and bottom plates cut to length, a pair of dadoes can be cut in them to accept the inside uprights *(Fig. 2)*.

Next, a 1/2"-deep rabbet is cut at each end of the top and bottom plates to accept the outside uprights *(Fig. 2a)*.

PIPE HOLES. The next step is to drill 3"-deep holes in each upright to hold the pipes. These holes are drilled at a 3° angle *(Fig. 1b* and Shop Tip on opposite page). This way, when you install the pipes, they're raised at a slight angle to help keep your lumber tight against the frame.

The size of the holes to drill depends on the diameter of the pipe. I used 1/2" black iron pipe from the hardware store.

Note: The 1/2" actually refers to the approximate *inside* diameter of the pipe. So I drilled 7/8"-dia. holes to accept the outside diameter of the pipe.

I positioned nine holes on the front edge of each upright so they were 4" apart *(Fig. 1a)*.

STRETCHERS. To keep the frame from racking (and to help secure it against a wall later), the next step is to cut a pair of 1/2"-thick plywood stretchers (C) *(Fig. 3)*. These stretchers fit into shallow dadoes that are cut in the back edge of each upright.

KICKPLATE. While I was at it, I cut a 1/2" plywood kickplate (D) *(Fig. 3)*. It holds short cutoffs in place when you stand them on end between the uprights. Here again, the kickplate fits in dadoes cut on the front edges of the uprights *(Fig. 3a)*.

ASSEMBLY. Now you're ready to assemble the frame. This is just a matter of screwing the uprights to the top and bottom plates *(Fig. 3a)*. Then screw the stretchers and kickplate into the front and back of the uprights.

LEVELERS. To compensate for an uneven floor, I attached a leveler under each upright. These are nothing more than lag screws centered on the bottom ends of the uprights *(Fig. 2a)*.

INSTALLATION

With the frame complete, it can be mounted to the ceiling and wall. The frame is held in place with screws that pass through the top plate into the ceiling joists.

The only problem is if the joists aren't all level across the bottom, the frame will end up out of square. The solution is simple — level the top plate.

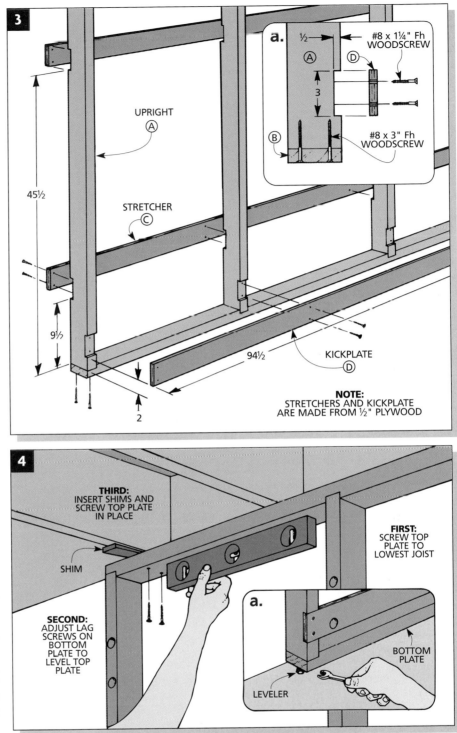

Start by measuring from the floor to the ceiling to determine which joist is the lowest. Then screw the top plate to that joist.

Next, level the top plate by adjusting the lag screws on the bottom of the frame *(Figs. 4 and 4a)*. Now just fit shims between the top plate and the "high" joists, and screw the frame in place with two screws into each joist.

For additional support, you can also screw the plywood stretchers into the existing wall studs or anchor them to a solid wall.

PIPE. All that's left is to add 15 3/4"-long pieces of black pipe. To provide three separate storage sections, I used twelve pieces of pipe.

Note: Most hardware stores will cut the pipe to length for a small charge. Or you can buy longer lengths and cut it yourself with a hacksaw.

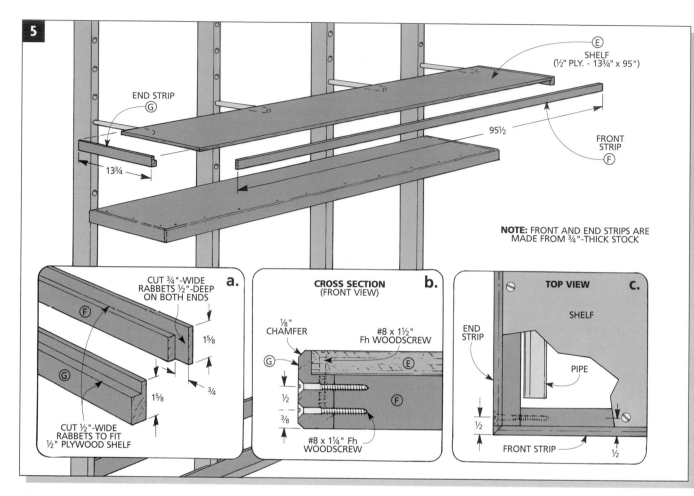

5

END STRIP
G

13¾

SHELF
(½" PLY. - 13¾" x 95")
E

95½

FRONT
STRIP
F

NOTE: FRONT AND END STRIPS ARE MADE FROM ¾"-THICK STOCK

a.

CUT ¾"-WIDE RABBETS ½"-DEEP ON BOTH ENDS

F

1⅝

G

1⅝

¾

CUT ½"-WIDE RABBETS TO FIT ½" PLYWOOD SHELF

b.

CROSS SECTION (FRONT VIEW)

⅛" CHAMFER

#8 x 1½" Fh WOODSCREW

G

E

½

⅜

F

#8 x 1¼" Fh WOODSCREW

c.

TOP VIEW

END STRIP

SHELF

PIPE

½

½

FRONT STRIP

SHELVES

Although long boards can be stored easily across a row of pipes, short pieces can fall between the pipes. So I added two plywood shelves that slide over the pipes.

CUT SHELVES TO SIZE. Each of the shelves (E) is made from a piece of ½" plywood *(Fig. 5)*. Cut the plywood ½" longer than the top and bottom plates.

TRIM. To help strengthen the plywood, and keep the shelves from sliding across the pipes when loading (or removing) a board, I added trim strips on the front and ends of each shelf.

Note: To allow the shelves to sit flat on the pipes, there's no trim fastened to the back edge.

The front (F) and end (G) strips are just pieces of ¾"-thick stock *(Fig. 5)*. (I used pine.) Each strip has a rabbet cut in the top edge to accept the shelves *(Figs. 5a and 5b)*. But before attaching the trim strips to the shelves, there's one more thing to do.

The strips are joined at the corners with a simple rabbet joint. This requires cutting a vertical rabbet across each

end of the front strip (F) to accept the end strips (G) *(Figs. 5a and 5c)*.

ASSEMBLY. Now you're ready to assemble the shelves. After screwing the front and end strips together, just set the shelves down in the rabbets and

screw them in place *(Figs. 5b and 5c)*. Finally, to keep from accidentally "catching" the strips when loading a board, I routed ⅛" chamfers on the top and bottom edges. Then the shelves are just set on the pipes. ∎

DESIGNER'S NOTEBOOK

CONSTRUCTION NOTES:

- The bin has two main parts: an L-shaped frame and two panels.
- Start building the frame by cutting an eight foot-long 2x6 to a finished length of 95" for the bottom (H).
- For the side (I) of the frame, cut another 2x6 to a finished length of 48".
- Cut a ½"-deep rabbet at the bottom end of the side piece to accept the bottom piece (Detail 'a').
- To complete the L-shaped frame, screw the side to the bottom with three No. 8 x 3" flathead woodscrews.
- You will need one full (4' x 8') sheet of ½"-thick plywood for the front and back panels of the bin. Clamp a straightedge across the plywood diagonally and make one pass with a portable circular saw (Fig. 1). The front panel (J) will come off one side of the cut, and the back panel (K) off the other side.

  Note: To make it easy to see what's in the bin, the front panel is smaller than the back.
- Apply a bead of construction adhesive to the edges of the frame and screw on the plywood panels with No. 8 x 1¼" flathead woodscrews.

  Note: The bin, as shown, swings to the right. If it's better for it to swing to the left in your shop, switch the location of the front and back panels and hinge it on the left side of the lumber rack.
- Screw two 2" fixed casters under the open end of the bin (Detail 'b').
- Screw the closed end of the bin to the rack with two T-hinges (Detail 'b').

  Note: To support the weight of the bin when attaching the hinges, place a temporary spacer (the same height as the casters) under the bin.

MATERIALS LIST

SHEET GOODS BIN

H Bottom (1)	1½ x 5½ - 95
I Side (1)	1½ x 5½ - 48
J Front Panel (1)	½ ply. - 42 x 90
K Back Panel (1)	½ ply. - 48 x 96

HARDWARE SUPPLIES

(46) No. 8 x 1¼" Fh woodscrews
(3) No. 8 x 3" Fh woodscrews
(2) 2" fixed casters
(1 pr.) 5" T-hinges with screws

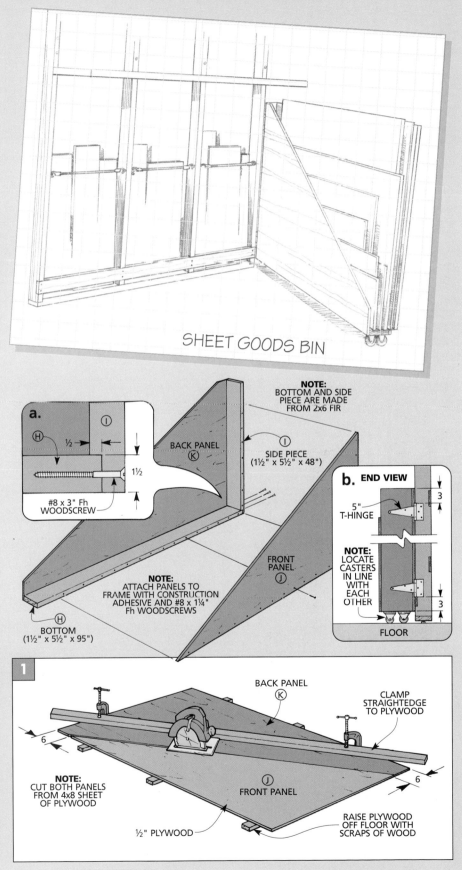

SHEET GOODS BIN

a.
H — ½
#8 x 3" Fh WOODSCREW — 1½

NOTE: BOTTOM AND SIDE PIECE ARE MADE FROM 2x6 FIR

BACK PANEL K

SIDE PIECE I (1½" x 5½" x 48")

b. END VIEW
5" T-HINGE — 3
NOTE: LOCATE CASTERS IN LINE WITH EACH OTHER — 3
FLOOR

FRONT PANEL J

NOTE: ATTACH PANELS TO FRAME WITH CONSTRUCTION ADHESIVE AND #8 x 1¼" Fh WOODSCREWS

BOTTOM H (1½" x 5½" x 95")

1
BACK PANEL K
CLAMP STRAIGHTEDGE TO PLYWOOD
6
6
NOTE: CUT BOTH PANELS FROM 4x8 SHEET OF PLYWOOD
J FRONT PANEL
½" PLYWOOD
RAISE PLYWOOD OFF FLOOR WITH SCRAPS OF WOOD

Finishing Cabinet

This cabinet is more than just a secure place to store all your finishing supplies — it's also a complete finishing station with a removable revolving work table.

When the doors on this finishing cabinet are closed, it may appear that one is on wrong. It looks like the two doors open in opposite directions — and they do.

But once the cabinet is open, you'll see why. Inside the top door is a work table that drops down to rest on the bottom door (see top photo below).

SPECIAL HARDWARE. To attach the work table, all you need is a piano hinge. But there are also two other special kinds of hardware on this project.

A removable lazy Susan makes it easy to rotate a project when applying a finish. It stores away in the bottom door (see bottom photo below). And metal shelf standards hold adjustable shelves.

MATERIALS AND FINISH. I built the project with ¾" maple plywood and solid maple edging. It's finished with three coats of a tung oil and urethane combination finish.

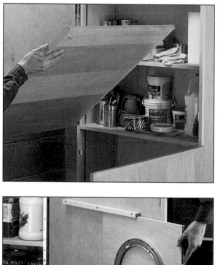

EXPLODED VIEW

OVERALL DIMENSIONS:
74¼H x 32W x 13½D

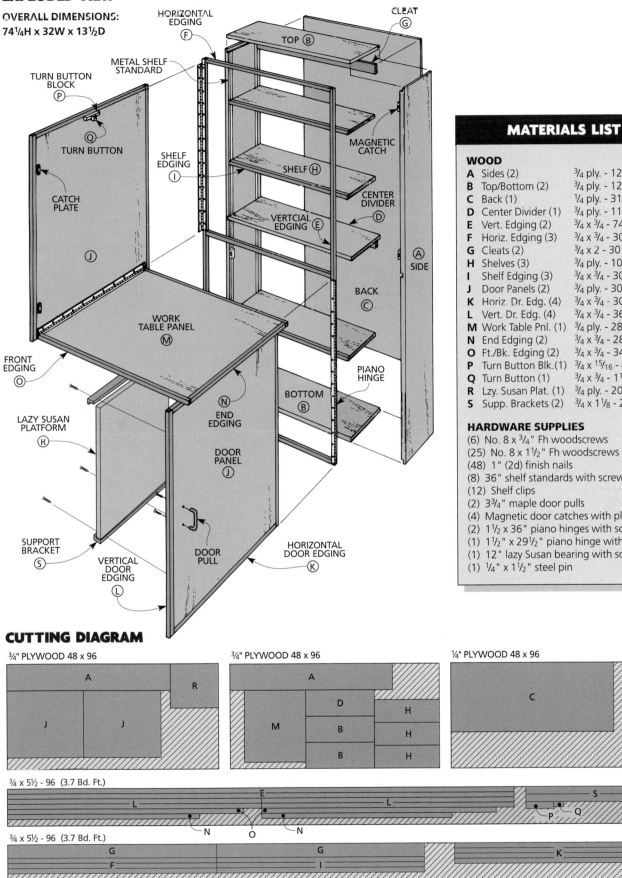

HORIZONTAL EDGING — F
TOP — B
CLEAT — G
METAL SHELF STANDARD
TURN BUTTON BLOCK — P
TURN BUTTON — Q
SHELF EDGING — I
SHELF — H
MAGNETIC CATCH
CATCH PLATE
CENTER DIVIDER — D
VERTCIAL EDGING — E
BACK — C
SIDE — A
— J
FRONT EDGING — O
WORK TABLE PANEL — M
PIANO HINGE
LAZY SUSAN PLATFORM — R
END EDGING — N
BOTTOM — B
DOOR PANEL — J
SUPPORT BRACKET — S
VERTICAL DOOR EDGING — L
DOOR PULL
HORIZONTAL DOOR EDGING — K

MATERIALS LIST

WOOD

A	Sides (2)	¾ ply. - 12 x 74¼
B	Top/Bottom (2)	¾ ply. - 12 x 31½
C	Back (1)	¼ ply. - 31½ x 73¾
D	Center Divider (1)	¾ ply. - 11¾ x 31½
E	Vert. Edging (2)	¾ x ¾ - 74¼
F	Horiz. Edging (3)	¾ x ¾ - 30½
G	Cleats (2)	¾ x 2 - 30½
H	Shelves (3)	¾ ply. - 10½ x 30⅜
I	Shelf Edging (3)	¾ x ¾ - 30⅜
J	Door Panels (2)	¾ ply. - 30½ x 35⅜
K	Horiz. Dr. Edg. (4)	¾ x ¾ - 30½
L	Vert. Dr. Edg. (4)	¾ x ¾ - 36⅞
M	Work Table Pnl. (1)	¾ ply. - 28 x 33
N	End Edging (2)	¾ x ¾ - 28
O	Ft./Bk. Edging (2)	¾ x ¾ - 34½
P	Turn Button Blk.(1)	¾ x ¹⁵⁄₁₆ - 4
Q	Turn Button (1)	¾ x ¾ - 1½
R	Lzy. Susan Plat. (1)	¾ ply. - 20 x 20
S	Supp. Brackets (2)	¾ x 1⅛ - 20

HARDWARE SUPPLIES

(6) No. 8 x ¾" Fh woodscrews
(25) No. 8 x 1½" Fh woodscrews
(48) 1" (2d) finish nails
(8) 36" shelf standards with screws
(12) Shelf clips
(2) 3¾" maple door pulls
(4) Magnetic door catches with plates
(2) 1½ x 36" piano hinges with screws
(1) 1½" x 29½" piano hinge with screws
(1) 12" lazy Susan bearing with screws
(1) ¼" x 1½" steel pin

CUTTING DIAGRAM

¾" PLYWOOD 48 x 96

A · R · J · J

¾" PLYWOOD 48 x 96

A · M · D · B · B · H · H · H

¼" PLYWOOD 48 x 96

C

¾ x 5½ - 96 (3.7 Bd. Ft.)

L · E · L · S · P · Q · N · O · N

¾ x 5½ - 96 (3.7 Bd. Ft.)

G · G · K · F · I

The design of the cabinet is similar to that of a simple bookshelf. The only difference is that a set of doors is added to the front of the cabinet.

SIDES. I started work on the cabinet by cutting two sides (A) from $3/4$"-thick plywood (see *Fig. 1* and the cutting diagram on page 107).

Next, to accommodate a set of metal shelf standards that are added later, two grooves are cut on the inside face of each workpiece *(Fig. 1d)*. Cut these grooves to match the width and thickness of the shelf standards.

The sides of the cabinet are joined to the top and bottom (B) with simple rabbet joints. Cut these $1/2$"-deep rabbets at both ends of each side piece to match the thickness of the top and bottom pieces *(Fig. 1b)*.

There's also a $1/2$"-deep dado needed in the center of each side. These dadoes will accept a center divider that's also added later *(Fig. 1c)*.

TOP AND BOTTOM. Now the top and bottom pieces (B) can be cut to size. They're cut to the same width as the side pieces (12"), and $31 1/2$" long.

Before you can assemble the case, there's one more thing to do. A rabbet for a $1/4$"-thick plywood back is cut on the inside face of each of the four workpieces *(Figs. 1 and 1a)*.

Once the back rabbet is cut, the top and bottom can be glued and screwed to the sides with No. 8 x $1 1/2$" flathead woodscrews.

BACK. Cut the back (C) from $1/4$" plywood to fit between the back rabbets *(Fig. 1a)*. Attach it to the cabinet with glue and 1" finishing nails.

CENTER DIVIDER. Next, to divide the upper and lower sections of the case, I cut a center divider (D) to fit between the dadoes cut earlier in the sides *(Figs. 1 and 1c)*. When you're gluing and clamping this center divider in place, make sure it's flush with the front of the case and tight against the back.

EDGING. Next, I covered all of the exposed front plywood edges by gluing on $3/4$" edging (E, F) *(Fig. 2)*.

CLEATS. To support the weight of the cabinet when it's screwed to the wall, I added a pair of cleats (G) that fit between the sides *(Fig. 2)*. These pieces are glued and screwed to the back, and either the top or the center divider *(Fig. 2a)*.

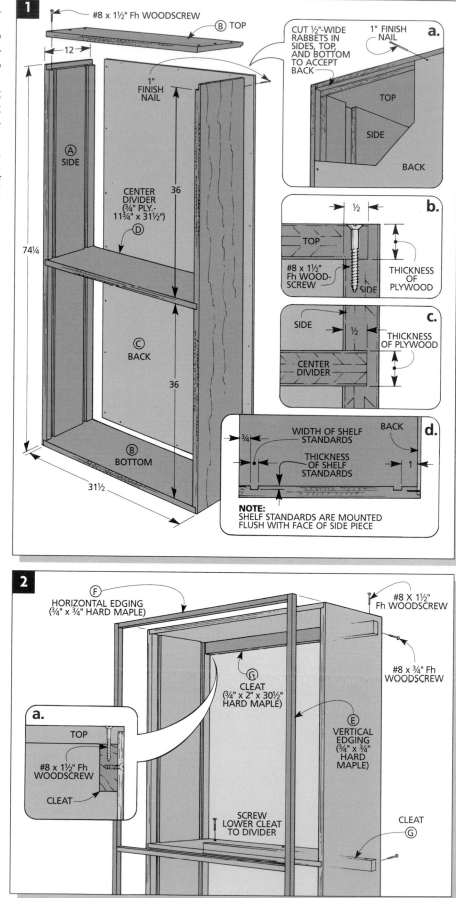

SHELVES

Once the basic case was complete, I started working on the three adjustable shelves to fit inside.

STANDARDS. Before cutting the shelves to final size, the metal shelf standards should be installed. They're screwed into the grooves already cut in the sides *(Fig. 3)*.

CUT SHELVES. To determine the length of the ³/₄"-thick plywood shelves (H), measure the opening and subtract ¹/₈" to allow for ¹/₁₆" clearance on each end *(Fig. 3a)*.

Then, to determine the width of the shelves, measure the inside depth of the case (12¹/₂"). Now subtract ³/₄" for the edging that will be put on the front of the shelf, and another 1¹/₄" to allow clearance for the work table attached to the inside of the door. (In my case, I cut the shelves 10¹/₂" wide and 30³/₈" long.)

Once the shelves are cut to size, cover the front edge of each one with edging (I) *(Fig. 3)*.

DOORS

With the case complete, you can turn your attention to the doors.

DOOR PANELS. Like the case, the exposed edges of the plywood doors are covered with hard maple edging. But before cutting the door panels to size, measure the cabinet for the door sizes (they should be the same).

Note: Take into consideration that you want to end up with a ¹/₄" gap between the two doors and a ¹/₄" gap between the lower door and the floor *(Figs. 4b and 4c)*.

Then subtract 1¹/₂" from each dimension to allow for the maple edging (30¹/₂" x 35³/₈") *(Fig. 4)*.

Once you've cut the panels (J) to final size, the edging (K, L) can be glued in place *(Fig. 4)*.

MOUNTING DOORS. The lower door is mounted on the right side of the case. But because the lower door is used to support the drop-down work table, the top door is mounted on the left side. To support the weight of these doors, piano hinges are used to mount them to the case *(Fig. 4)*.

PULLS. Now door pulls can be mounted *(Fig. 4)*. Mounting these pulls is fairly straightforward. I used 3³/₄" maple pulls and centered the mounting holes 1¹/₂" from the edge of the doors.

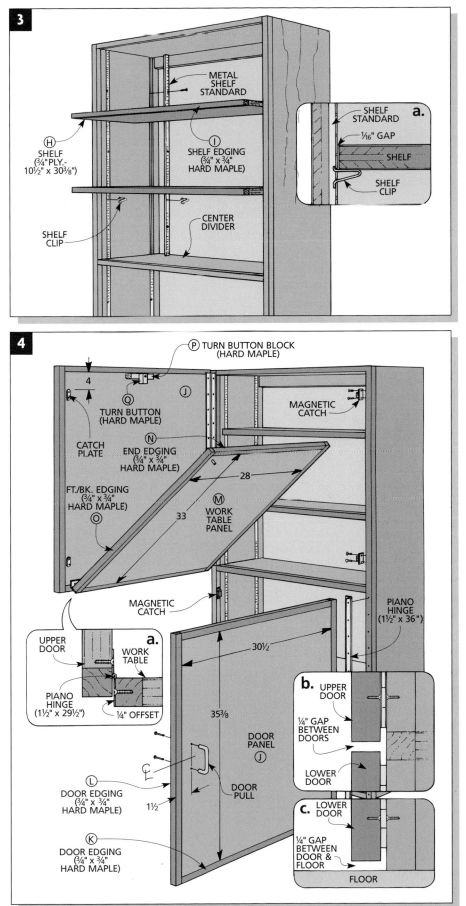

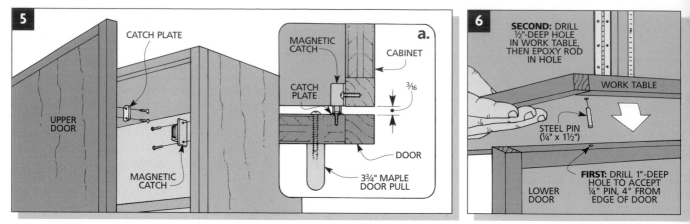

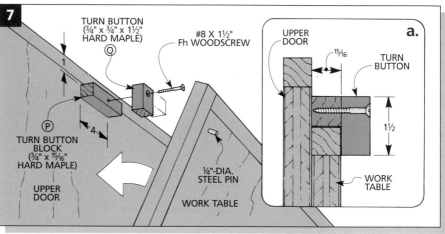

CATCHES. When mounting door catches and plates, it's important to leave a $3/16$" gap between each door and the case *(Figs. 5 and 5a)*. This compensates for the thickness of the hinge, and allows air to circulate inside the case.

WORK TABLE. Now you can move on to the drop-down work table that's mounted to the back of the upper door. Like the doors, the work table consists of a plywood panel (M) with the exposed edges covered with maple edging (N, O) (refer to *Fig. 4* on page 109). A piano hinge is used to mount the table to the upper door (refer to *Fig. 4a*).

Next, to lock the table to the lower door, a steel pin is glued with epoxy into a hole that's drilled in the bottom of the work table *(Fig. 6)*. There's a matching hole in the lower door to receive the pin (see Shop Tip box below).

TURN BUTTON. Finally, a turn button block (P) and turn button (Q) used to lock the table to the back of the door can be mounted to the door *(Fig. 7)*.

LAZY SUSAN

At this point, you could use the storage cabinet just as it is. But to make it easier and more efficient to finish all the sides of a project, I built a lazy Susan for the drop-down work table.

It consists of a $3/4$"-thick plywood platform (R) that's screwed to a lazy Susan bearing *(Fig. 8)*. These bearings are usually available at hardware stores or home centers (or see Sources on page 126).

To store the lazy Susan when it's not being used, a pair of L-shaped support brackets (S) are glued and screwed to the back of the lower door *(Fig. 8a)*. Then the platform slides into place. ■

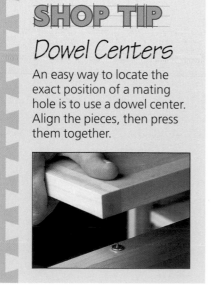

SHOP TIP

Dowel Centers

An easy way to locate the exact position of a mating hole is to use a dowel center. Align the pieces, then press them together.

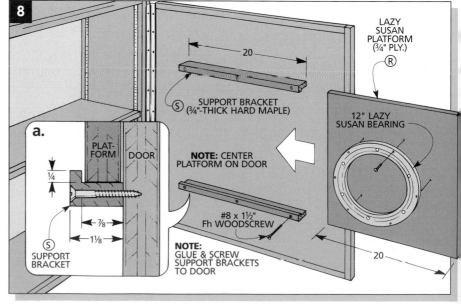

Cleaning brushes is not my favorite pastime. In fact, for most finishing jobs, I use poly-foam brushes. They lay down an even coat and they're so inexpensive you can throw them away.

But at times, I want to use a bristle brush, like when using shellac or lacquer. Or when finishing spindles, moldings and carvings, it's easier to get finish into crevices with a bristle brush.

In these situations, it's important that the brush is clean before you use it. If there are any traces of old hardened finish, they could be deposited in the new finish.

Cleaning a brush right when you're done using it is ideal. If you don't get it clean, it can harden. Then you'll need to soak the brush in a strong solvent to clean it.

ALTERNATIVE. There is an alternative. If you're going to reuse a brush in a day or two, just wrap it in aluminum foil and put it in the freezer. Then when you need it, take it out and allow it to reach room temperature.

IMMEDIATE CLEAN-UP

The most important factor in getting a brush clean is to get to it right away. The longer it sits, the harder it gets.

Start by wiping the brush on some old newspaper or cardboard to remove as much finish as possible. Then pour about 3/4" of solvent in a shallow dish and work the brush back and forth against the bottom. (A small glass bowl with tapered sides works well.)

While working the brush in the solvent, occasionally turn the bristles skyward so the solvent can wash out any finish that's against the metal ferrule.

COMB THE BRUSH. If the brush is really full of crud, I grab my "brush comb." The best one I've found is a heavy metal pet comb. I picked one up at a local pet store. It cleans the brush and straightens out tangled bristles.

When most of the finish is out, pour out the dirty solvent (save it for later use in a capped jar), and pour in clean solvent. Now use your thumb and fingers to work solvent completely through the bristles *(Fig. 1)*.

SOAP AND WATER. Next, put dish-soap on the bristles and run them under warm water. Continue to work the bristles between your fingers until a lather forms. This won't dissolve finish, but it will wash away hardened particles.

After washing the brush with soap and water a few times, rinse it with clear water, and comb it out one more time. Then dry the bristles with a paper towel.

HARDENED FINISH

If the finish on a brush has been allowed to harden, more drastic action has to be taken. Then, I soak the brush in a brush cleaner.

The cleaner I use softens just about any finish because it contains so many different solvents: petroleum distillates for oil-based paint and varnish; toluenes, acetones and ketones for lacquers; alcohol for shellac; and for good measure methylene chloride, the main ingredient in most paint strippers.

OVERNIGHT IN CLEANER. To recondition a hard brush, hang it from a wire in a jar of cleaner *(Fig. 2)*.

Note: Never clean or store a brush with the bristles resting on the bottom of a can or jar. They'll become bent from the weight of the handle.

CLEAN AS BEFORE. After it soaks overnight, clean it with the comb and cleaner, then soap and water (like before).

STORAGE

To help a brush hold its shape and keep dust off it, I wrap it with brown paper from a grocery sack (see first step in *Fig. 3*). Then wrap a rubber band around it (see second step), and hang the brush from a nail with the bristles face down.

Work with fingers. *With most of the finish out, change the solvent and work bristles with your thumb and forefinger.*

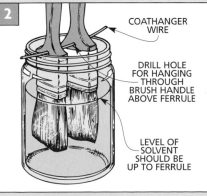

Overnight soaking. *To soak brushes in a small jar, drill a new hole to keep the bristles from resting on the bottom.*

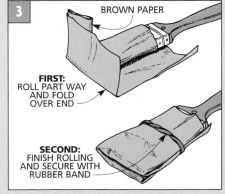

Wrap bristles. *Brown grocery bag paper and a rubber band maintain the bristles' shape and keep dust off the brush.*

Modular Workshop

Based on ordinary "two-bys" and metal conduit, this modular system meets your storage and workspace requirements in the shop or anywhere around the house.

Most woodworkers would probably agree that a good workshop is never actually complete. Space requirements change, you bring in new tools, and sometimes you just need a more convenient layout.

If storage is a constant problem, this modular system is the answer. Convenient and flexible, it puts everything at your fingertips and leaves floorspace for your bench and power tools.

OPTIONS. The design shown here features a work table below a pegboard panel (see photo above) and storage units for power tools. You can add wide or narrow shelves, a dust-proof tool cabinet, and small pull-out bins to create even more storage.

MODULAR. These units are not permanently attached. Each one has a set of shop-made brackets that hang on a con-duit grid (see inset photo). So, as your needs change, you can rearrange them.

VERSATILE. The photos on page 113 show how you can easily customize the system for other areas in the house.

EXPLODED VIEW

OVERALL DIMENSIONS:
72H x 81½W x 20⅝D

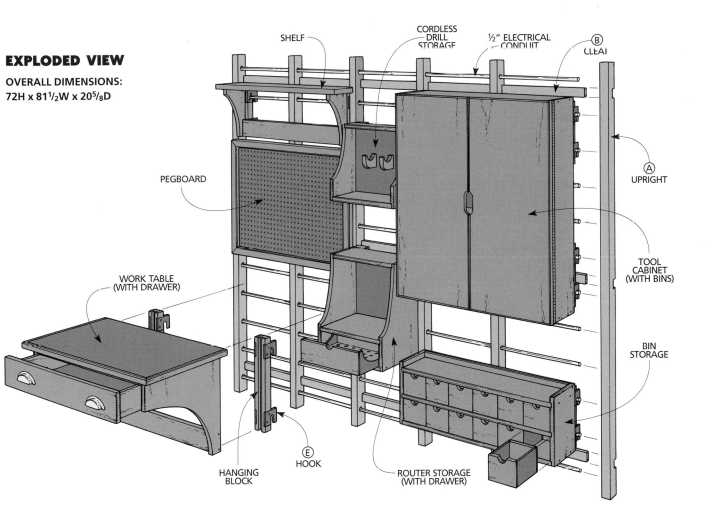

SHELF

CORDLESS DRILL STORAGE

½" ELECTRICAL CONDUIT

Ⓑ CLEAT

PEGBOARD

Ⓐ UPRIGHT

WORK TABLE (WITH DRAWER)

TOOL CABINET (WITH BINS)

BIN STORAGE

HANGING BLOCK

Ⓔ HOOK

ROUTER STORAGE (WITH DRAWER)

DESIGNER'S NOTEBOOK

◄ **IN A KID'S ROOM.** Inexpensive, readily available materials and a sturdy design make a modified version of the modular workshop ideal for a child's room (see photo at left).

A work table with a large drawer acts as a functional study desk, and a couple of wide shelves with dowel peg hooks below the shelves work great to store books and other items.

▶ **IN A LAUNDRY ROOM.** The vertical design of the modular system can also help you get a handle on a cluttered laundry room, even in a limited amount of space (see photo at right).

Once again, the hardboard work table is useful, this time for folding clothes. And since the unit is wall-hung, there's extra room under the table. Meanwhile, the large storage cabinet is perfect for organizing and storing cleaning supplies.

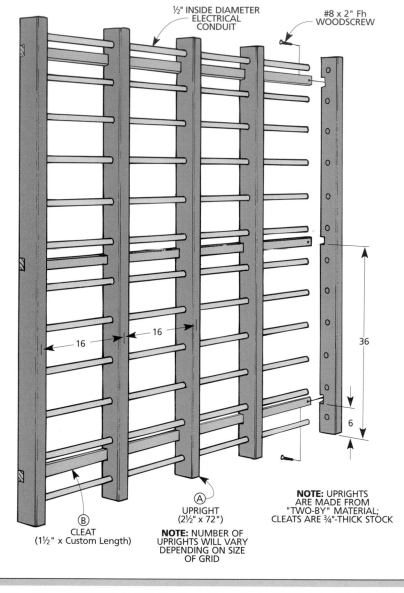

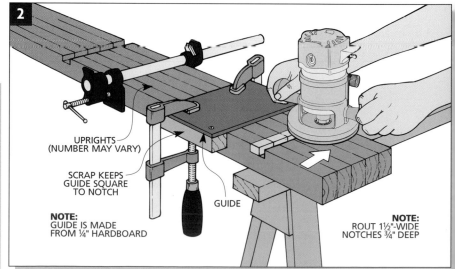

The backbone of this storage system is a grid that attaches to the wall. It consists of a number of vertical uprights with horizontal rows of metal conduit running between (*Fig. 1*).

UPRIGHTS. To provide plenty of support for the conduit, the uprights (A) are located at 16" increments (like wall studs). Each upright is made from "two-by" material that's ripped to a width of $2^1/2$". (I used Douglas fir.)

NOTCHES. To accept a set of cleats (which will be added later), the next step is to cut three notches in the back edge of each upright.

An easy way to ensure that these notches align is to cut them all at the same time (*Fig. 2*). First clamp the uprights together. Then clamp a guide to the uprights and use a router with a straight bit to cut all the notches.

Since you're removing quite a bit of material, it's best to rout one side of the notches by making a series of passes, lowering the bit between each one. Then to increase the width of the notches, move the guide in several small increments and make a full-depth pass at each setting.

DRILL HOLES. Next, you'll need to drill a series of holes in each upright to accept the conduit (refer to *Figs. 1* and *3*). To simplify the assembly of the grid, these holes will be cut slightly (approximately $^1/_{16}$") larger than the conduit. I used $^1/_2$" electrical conduit that has an outside diameter of $^{11}/_{16}$". So I drilled $^3/_4$"-diameter holes (*Fig. 3b*).

One thing to be aware of here is that the holes in the *outer* uprights do not go all the way through (*Fig. 3a*). Instead, these holes form pockets that will prevent the metal conduit from moving side to side.

MATERIALS LIST

GRID
A Uprights* $1^1/_2$ x $2^1/_2$ - 72
B Cleats* $^3/_4$ x $1^1/_2$ - custom lgth.

HARDWARE SUPPLIES*
No. 8 x 2" Fh woodscrews
$^1/_2$" metal electrical conduit ($^{11}/_{16}$" out. dia.)
Wall mounting screws

*Number will vary depending on the size of your grid and number of storage units.

CLEATS. To prevent the grid from racking, I added three 1¹/₂"-wide cleats (B) that fit into the notches in the uprights. Besides adding extra rigidity, these cleats are used to mount the grid to the wall.

To determine the length of the cleats, it's easiest to arrange the uprights on the floor in the same positions they'll have in the final grid. Then measure the total width of the grid and cut the cleats to length.

CONDUIT. Before attaching the cleats, you'll need to cut the conduit to length (1¹/₂" shorter than the cleats) and feed it through the inner uprights. After capping the ends of the conduit with the outer uprights, you can glue and screw the cleats in place.

MOUNT GRID. Now you can mount the grid to the wall. The size of the grid may make it awkward to handle. But a temporary wall cleat will simplify the installation (see Shop Tip below).

(see Shop Tip below).

SHOP TIP

Cleaning Up Conduit

Metal conduit normally comes with black print labelling along the outside, but there is an easy way to remove it so your modular workshop looks cleaner.

All it takes to "erase" the black print on the conduit is to wipe it off with lacquer thinner (see photo below).

3

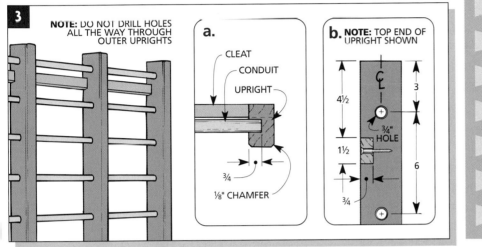

NOTE: DO NOT DRILL HOLES ALL THE WAY THROUGH OUTER UPRIGHTS

a. CLEAT — CONDUIT — UPRIGHT — ³/₄ — ¹/₈" CHAMFER

b. NOTE: TOP END OF UPRIGHT SHOWN — 4¹/₂ — 1¹/₂ — ³/₄ — C L — 3 — ³/₄" HOLE — 6

SHOP TIP . . . . Installing the Grid

Hanging the grid is made easier and more accurate by screwing a temporary cleat to the wall to serve as a support "shelf" *(Step 1)*.

First, make sure the cleat is level and positioned right at the bottom of where you want the grid. You'll need to screw the cleat into studs so it will support the grid's weight. Then you can use those screws as markers to help find the studs again later when you hang the grid.

Next, raise the grid up and set it on the cleat *(Step 2)*. (Have a friend help if it's too heavy.) The whole grid can now be shifted left or right.

Use a level to check that the grid is plumb. Then attach the grid to the wall by screwing through the cleats into the wall studs *(Step 3)*.

Once the grid is secure, the temporary cleat can be removed and the screwholes in the wall filled.

1 *Use a level to position a long strip of wood where the bottom of the grid will be placed. This cleat is temporarily screwed to the wall.*

2 *Raise the grid carefully, using the temporary cleat as a support shelf. Make sure the grid is at the correct height before continuing.*

3 *After checking to be sure the uprights are level and plumb, attach the grid by driving screws through the cleats into the wall studs.*

With the grid in place, you can start on the hanging brackets. There are two different lengths of brackets *(Fig. 4)*. Aside from that, each one is the same. They're made from "two-by" material and hardboard hooks that fit over the conduit on the grid. I used a couple of "mass production" techniques on these for speed and uniformity.

HANGER BLOCKS. For instance, the hanger blocks (C, D) have a pair of notches in each edge, and each notch starts 1" from the end *(Fig. 4)*. So I used the fence on the saw as a stop *(Fig. 6)*.

HOOKS. The hooks (E) must also be uniform, especially the slots that fit over the conduit. So I clamped a framing square to the drill press table as a positioning guide when drilling holes that form the ends of the slots *(Fig. 5)*. Then I completed the slots using a simple jig (refer to Shop Tip below).

Now just glue and screw the hooks into the notches in the hanger blocks.

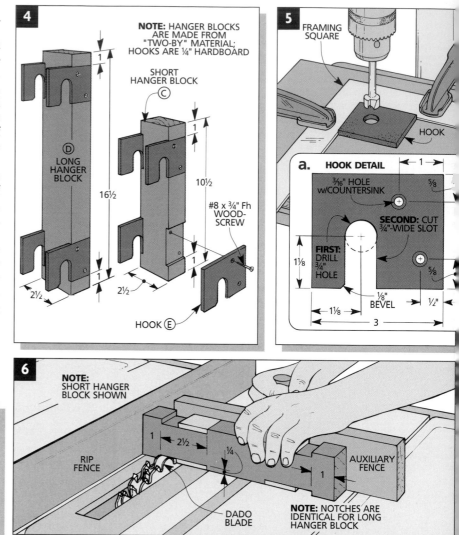

MATERIALS LIST

HANGING BRACKETS

C	Short Hang. Blk.	1½ x 2½ - 10½
D	Long Hang. Blk.	1½ x 2½ - 16½
E	Hooks	¼ hdbd. - 2½ x 3

HARDWARE SUPPLIES
No. 8 x ¾" Fh woodscrews

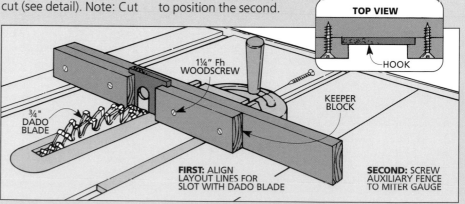

SHOP TIP .... *Slot-Cutting Jig*

Before building the Modular Workshop, I sat down to count the number of hardboard hooks I had to make. I was sitting a long time, because the system had over 100 hooks.

To cut the slots for these hooks, I used a jig with a dado blade mounted in the table saw. The hooks are inserted into the jig like slides in a projector. Then the jig carries the hook through the blade.

The jig has two main parts: an auxiliary fence and a pair of keeper blocks (see drawing). There's a rabbet on one end of each block, which forms a lip to fit over the hook and keep it from falling out as you cut (see detail). Note: Cut these rabbets so the hook slides in with a friction fit.

For assembly, screw one block to the auxiliary fence and use a hook as a spacer to position the second.

Finally, align the layout lines with the blade, screw the fence to the miter gauge, and cut the slots.

One of the things I wanted to include in this modular system was a number of deep shelves. The shelf shown here is 12" deep — deep enough to hold paint cans, jigs, or toolboxes.

Note: If you're planning on hanging a shelf next to the tool cabinet, you'll want to make that shelf (as well as its supports) narrower in order to allow the cabinet door to swing open without hitting the corner of the shelf. On the pattern below we've shown both a wide support and a narrow support.

SUPPORTS. Each shelf is held up by two $^3/_4$"-thick plywood supports (F) *(Fig. 7* and the pattern below). The supports are attached to a pair of short hanging brackets. To accept the supports, a $^1/_2$"-deep groove is cut in each hanging bracket *(Fig. 7)*. Then the sup-

ports are glued and screwed in place with No. 8 x 2$^1/_4$" screws.

STRETCHER. After attaching the supports, the next step is to add a single stretcher (G). It acts as a stiffener.

When determining the length to cut the stretcher, keep in mind that it has to allow the hanging brackets to fit between two uprights. I cut the stretcher for my shelf 27$^1/_8$" long and then screwed it between the supports with No. 8 x 2" flathead woodscrews *(Figs. 7 and 7a)*.

Note: Before screwing the stretcher in place, you may want to drill some angled holes in the stretcher for $^1/_2$" dowel pegs. These provide a good spot for hanging cords, clamps, or other items (refer to the photo of the modular system in a kid's room on page 113).

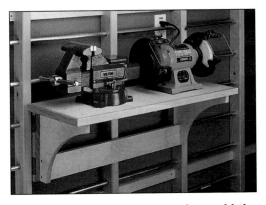

SHELF. Now you're ready to add the shelf (H) *(Fig. 8)*. It's a piece of $^3/_4$" plywood trimmed with strips of solid wood edging (I) on the front and both of its ends *(Fig. 8b)*.

After mitering each strip to length, it's glued flush with the top of the shelf. These shelf edges can take a lot of abuse, but chamfering the top and bottom edges of the strips will help to prevent them from chipping.

ATTACH SHELF. The last step is to attach the shelf to the supports. What works well here is to hang the brackets on the grid first. After centering the shelf on the supports, position it so it's set in 1" from the back edge of the hanger block *(Fig. 8a)*. Then screw the shelf down to the supports with No. 8 x 2" woodscrews.

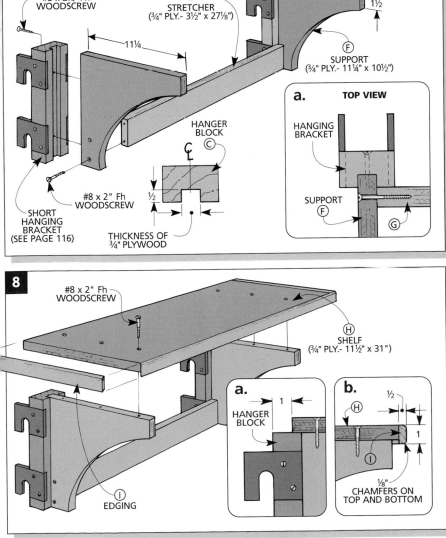

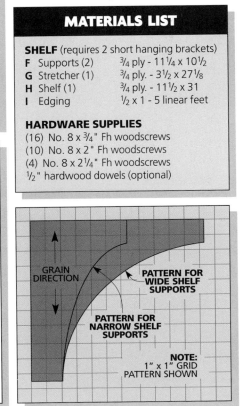

MATERIALS LIST

SHELF (requires 2 short hanging brackets)

F	Supports (2)	$^3/_4$ ply - 11$^1/_4$ x 10$^1/_2$
G	Stretcher (1)	$^3/_4$ ply. - 3$^1/_2$ x 27$^1/_8$
H	Shelf (1)	$^3/_4$ ply. - 11$^1/_2$ x 31
I	Edging	$^1/_2$ x 1 - 5 linear feet

HARDWARE SUPPLIES

(16) No. 8 x $^3/_4$" Fh woodscrews
(10) No. 8 x 2" Fh woodscrews
(4) No. 8 x 2$^1/_4$" Fh woodscrews
$^1/_2$" hardwood dowels (optional)

The tool cabinet is the largest of the storage units. Its three shelves provide plenty of room for tools and supplies (see photo). And the pull-out bins at the bottom are ideal for organizing small parts and hardware.

Because of its size, it's a good idea to hang the cabinet first. Once it's hung on the grid, you can position all the other storage units around it.

CASE. I began work on the cabinet by making an open plywood case that's held together with simple rabbet joints (*Fig. 9*). (I used ³⁄₄" birch plywood.)

To accept the top and bottom (J) of the case, the sides (K) are rabbeted at each end (*Fig. 9a*). You'll also need to rabbet the back edge of each side for the back of the cabinet and the hanging brackets.

In addition to the rabbets, there's a dado near the bottom of each side to hold a fixed shelf (L) (*Fig. 9e*). Also, it's easiest to drill holes now for the shelf supports to be added later (*Figs. 9 and 9d*).

ASSEMBLY. At this point, you're ready to assemble the case. It's held together with glue and screws. To help square up the case during the glue-up, I cut a ¹⁄₄" hardboard back (M) to fit and nailed it in place (*Fig. 9b*).

SHELVES. All that's left to complete the case is to add two adjustable shelves (N). After cutting these shelves to length to allow ¹⁄₈" clearance, I glued a ¹⁄₄"-thick strip of hardwood edging (O) to the front of each one (*Fig. 9c*). This creates a durable edge that's not as likely to chip as an exposed plywood edge.

DOORS. With the case complete, I added a pair of doors. These are just plywood panels "wrapped" with hardwood edging (*Fig. 10*).

The doors (P) lay completely over the front of the cabinet. So the easiest way to determine the size of the doors is to measure the case. Just be sure to allow for a ¹⁄₈" gap between the doors and the ¹⁄₈"-thick door edging (Q) that runs all the way around.

PULL. After gluing on the edging, I cut an opening centered on the inside edge of each door to act as a door pull (*Fig. 10d*). Once the edges of these openings are sanded smooth, it's just a matter of attaching the doors.

MATERIALS LIST

TOOL CABINET (requires 4 short hangers)

J	Top/Bottom (2)	³⁄₄ ply. - 7¹⁄₄ x 29⁷⁄₈
K	Sides (2)	³⁄₄ ply. - 8 x 36
L	Fixed Shelf (1)	³⁄₄ ply. - 7¹⁄₄ x 29⁷⁄₈
M	Back (1)	¹⁄₄ hdbd. - 30³⁄₈ x 36
N	Adj. Shelves (2)	³⁄₄ ply. - 6³⁄₄ x 29¹⁄₄
O	Shelf Edging (2)	¹⁄₄ x ³⁄₄ - 29¹⁄₄
P	Doors (2)	³⁄₄ ply. - 15¹⁄₈ x 35³⁄₄
Q	Door Edging	¹⁄₈ x ³⁄₄ - 18 linear ft.
R	Cabinet Edg. (3)	³⁄₁₆ x ³⁄₄ - 29³⁄₈
S	Bin Frts./Bcks. (12)	³⁄₄ ply. - 3¹⁵⁄₁₆ x 4⁷⁄₈
T	Bin Btms. (6)	³⁄₄ ply. - 6³⁄₄ x 4³⁄₈
U	Bin Sides (12)	¹⁄₄ hdbd. - 6³⁄₄ x 3¹⁵⁄₁₆

HARDWARE SUPPLIES
(32) No. 8 x ³⁄₄" Fh woodscrews
(8) No. 8 x 1¹⁄₂" Fh woodscrews
(8) No. 8 x 2" Fh woodscrews
(150) 1" brads
(2) 1¹⁄₂" x 36" piano hinges
(4) ⁷⁄₁₆" magnetic catches w/strike plates & screws
(8) ¹⁄₄" shelf supports

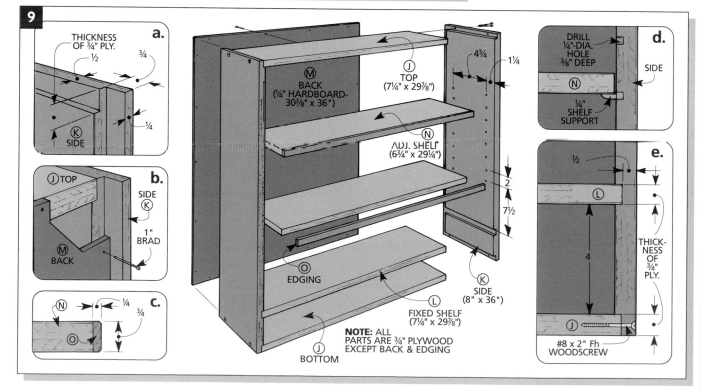

9

a. THICKNESS OF ³⁄₄" PLY. — ¹⁄₂ — ³⁄₄ — ¹⁄₄ — (K) SIDE

b. (J) TOP — SIDE (K) — 1" BRAD — (M) BACK

c. (N) — ¹⁄₄ — ³⁄₄ — (O)

BACK (¹⁄₄" HARDBOARD- 30³⁄₈" x 36") — (M)
TOP (7¹⁄₄" x 29⁷⁄₈") — (J) — 4³⁄₄ — 1¹⁄₄
ADJ. SHELF (6³⁄₄" x 29¹⁄₄") — (N)
2 — 7¹⁄₂
(O) EDGING
SIDE (8" x 36") — (K)
FIXED SHELF (7¹⁄₄" x 29⁷⁄₈") — (L)
(J) BOTTOM
NOTE: ALL PARTS ARE ³⁄₄" PLYWOOD EXCEPT BACK & EDGING

d. DRILL ¹⁄₄"-DIA. HOLE ³⁄₈" DEEP — SIDE — (N) — ¹⁄₄" SHELF SUPPORT

e. ¹⁄₂ — (L) — 4 — THICKNESS OF ³⁄₄" PLY. — (J) — #8 x 2" Fh WOODSCREW

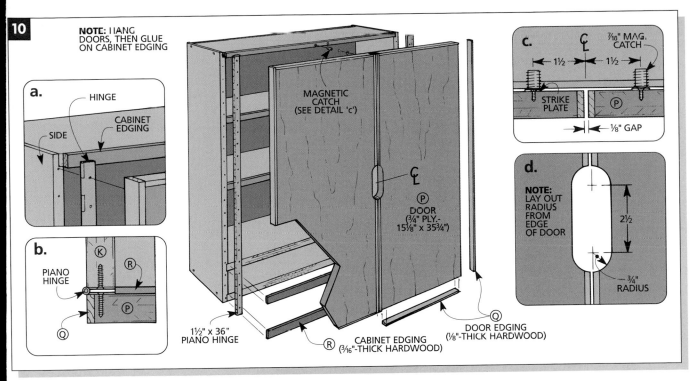

10 NOTE: HANG DOORS, THEN GLUE ON CABINET EDGING

a. HINGE · SIDE · CABINET EDGING

b. PIANO HINGE · K · R · P · Q

MAGNETIC CATCH (SEE DETAIL 'c')

DOOR (3/4" PLY.- 15⅛" x 35¾")

CL · P

1½" x 36" PIANO HINGE

CABINET EDGING (R) (3/16"-THICK HARDWOOD)

DOOR EDGING (⅛"-THICK HARDWOOD) · Q

c. CL · 7/16" MAG. CATCH · 1½ · 1½ · STRIKE PLATE · P · ⅛" GAP

d. NOTE: LAY OUT RADIUS FROM EDGE OF DOOR · 2½ · ¾" RADIUS

HANG DOORS. The doors are hung with piano hinges *(Fig. 10b)*. The problem is that they create a gap between the doors and the case. So to fill the gap (and cover the edges), I glued strips of ³/₁₆" edging (R) to the top/bottom (J) and fixed shelf (L) *(Fig. 10)*.

CATCHES. To keep the doors closed, I added magnetic catches and installed strike plates on each door *(Fig. 10c)*.

HANGING BRACKETS. Once the cabinet is filled with tools, it's going to be quite heavy. To support this weight, I attached four short hanging brackets to the back *(Fig. 11 and page 116)*. These brackets are glued and screwed ¾" from the top and bottom of the cabinet and tight against the sides *(Fig. 11a)*.

BINS. To keep small parts organized, I added six pull-out bins *(Fig. 12)*.

Each bin consists of a ³/₄"-thick plywood front/back (S) and bottom (T), and a pair of ¼" hardboard sides (U) *(Fig. 12)*. (To add labels to the front of the bins, see the Shop Tip on page 122.)

Cutting or drilling a half-circle in the front piece is all that's needed as a pull *(Fig. 12a)*. Then all of the bin parts are assembled with rabbet joints, glue, and brads *(Figs. 12b and 12c)*.

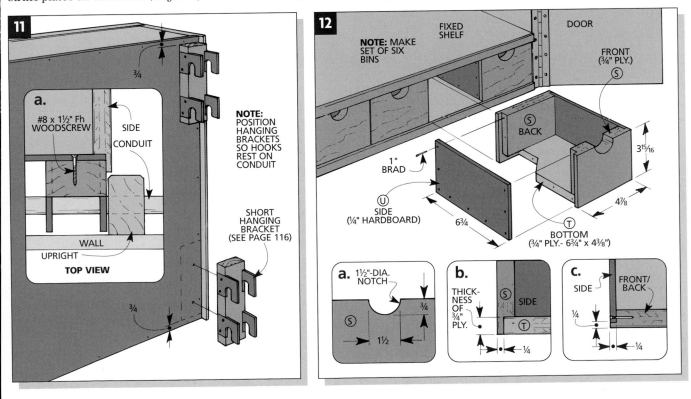

11

a. #8 x 1½" Fh WOODSCREW · SIDE · CONDUIT · WALL · UPRIGHT · **TOP VIEW** · ¾

¾ · ¾

NOTE: POSITION HANGING BRACKETS SO HOOKS REST ON CONDUIT

SHORT HANGING BRACKET (SEE PAGE 116)

12 NOTE: MAKE SET OF SIX BINS

FIXED SHELF · DOOR

FRONT (¾" PLY.) · S

BACK · S

1" BRAD

U SIDE (¼" HARDBOARD) · 6¾

3¹⁵/₁₆

4⅞

T BOTTOM (¾" PLY.- 6¾" x 4⅜")

a. 1½"-DIA. NOTCH · S · ¾ · 1½

b. THICKNESS OF ¾" PLY. · S · SIDE · T · ¼

c. SIDE · FRONT/ BACK · ¼ · ¼

This work table is a perfect place to sketch a drawing, spread out a plan, or tackle a small project. And when you're ready to close up shop for the day, there's a drawer underneath that provides a convenient place to hold tools and supplies (see photo).

SUPPORTS. To provide a sturdy work surface that won't tilt or wobble under weight, the table is held up by two matching supports (V). These are just pieces of $3/4$"-thick plywood that are cut and sanded to a gentle curve (*Fig. 13* and pattern below).

HANGING BRACKETS. Like the other units, these supports are attached to a pair of hanging brackets. But this time, because of the weight of the table, I used a pair of the long (16½") brackets to provide extra strength.

In addition to making the long brackets, a ½"-deep groove has to be cut into the face of each bracket to accept one of the supports. After fitting the supports into these grooves, they're simply glued and screwed in place (*Fig. 13a*).

STRETCHERS. To add even more rigidity to the table, I added three stretchers (W) that bridge the supports. One of them is screwed to the bottom of the supports. The other two are screwed flush with the top edge of the supports.

TOP. At this point, work can begin on the table top. It's made up of two separate layers. A plywood core creates a flat, stable base (*Fig. 14*). And a

MATERIALS LIST

WORK TABLE (requires 2 long hangers)

V	Supports (2)	$3/4$ ply. - $16^3/4$ x $16^1/2$
W	Stretchers (3)	$3/4$ ply. - $3^1/2$ x $27^1/8$
X	Core (1)	$3/4$ ply. - $17^1/2$ x 31
Y	Cover (1)	$1/4$ hdbd. - $17^1/2$ x 31
Z	Table Edging	$1/2$ x 1 - 6 linear feet
AA	Drwr. Fr./Bk. (2)	$1/2$ ply. - $3^{15}/16$ x $25^5/8$
BB	Drwr. Sides (2)	$1/2$ ply. - $3^{15}/16$ x 16
CC	Drwr. Btm. (1)	$1/4$ hdbd. - $15^1/2$ x $25^5/8$
DD	False Front (1)	$3/4$ ply. - $4^{11}/16$ x $28^5/8$

HARDWARE SUPPLIES

(4) No. 8 x $1/2$" Fh woodscrews
(16) No. 8 x $3/4$" Fh woodscrews
(6) No. 8 x $1^1/2$" Fh woodscrews
(12) No. 8 x $2^1/4$" Fh woodscrews
(2) No. 8 x $2^1/2$" Fh woodscrews
(4) No. 8 x 3" Fh woodscrews
(16) 1" brads
(2) Nickel-plated drawer pulls
(1 pr.) 16" full-extension drawer slides

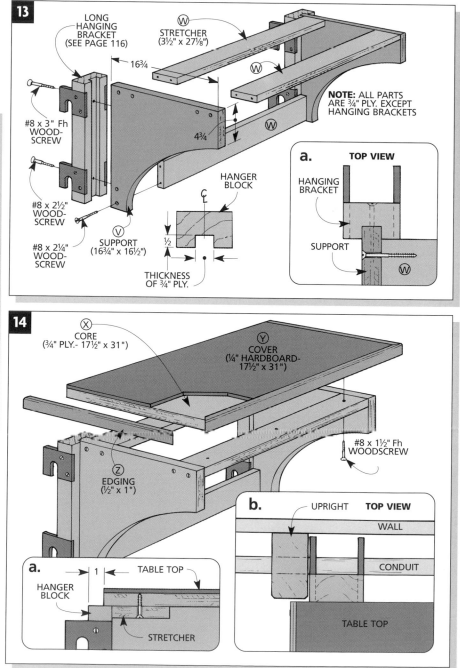

13 LONG HANGING BRACKET (SEE PAGE 116) — STRETCHER (3½" x 27⅛") — $16^3/4$ — #8 x 3" Fh WOODSCREW — #8 x 2½" WOODSCREW — #8 x 2¼" WOODSCREW — SUPPORT ($16^3/4$" x $16^1/2$") — $4^3/4$ — NOTE: ALL PARTS ARE $3/4$ PLY. EXCEPT HANGING BRACKETS — HANGER BLOCK — ½ — THICKNESS OF $3/4$" PLY.

a. TOP VIEW — HANGING BRACKET — SUPPORT

14 CORE ($3/4$" PLY.- $17^1/2$" x 31") — COVER ($1/4$" HARDBOARD- $17^1/2$" x 31") — EDGING ($1/2$" x 1") — #8 x $1^1/2$" Fh WOODSCREW

a. HANGER BLOCK — 1 — TABLE TOP — STRETCHER

b. UPRIGHT TOP VIEW — WALL — CONDUIT — TABLE TOP

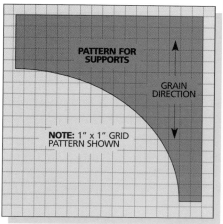

PATTERN FOR SUPPORTS — GRAIN DIRECTION — NOTE: 1" x 1" GRID PATTERN SHOWN

hardboard cover provides a smooth, durable work surface.

Note: An easy way to get the edges of these pieces perfectly aligned is to cut the plywood core (X) to final size first. Then, after gluing on a slightly oversize cover (Y), you can just trim the overhanging edges with a flush trim bit and a hand-held router (refer to page 16).

EDGING. The edges of the table top are bound to get nicked up with use. So I added $1/2$"-thick strips of hardwood edging (Z) to protect the ends and the front edge *(Figs. 14 and 16a)*. These strips are mitered to length to fit around the table top. Then they're simply glued in place.

ATTACH TABLE TOP. Now you can attach the table top. It's centered over the supports, 1" in from the back edges of the hanger blocks *(Fig. 14a)*. This way, the back of the table top won't bump into the uprights as it hangs on the grid *(Fig. 14b)*.

Once the top is positioned on the supports, it's secured with screws. These screws pass through countersunk shank holes drilled in the bottom of the stretchers.

DRAWER. The space under the table top provides a perfect place to add a

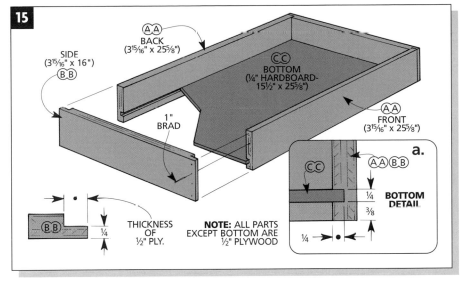

large drawer. For easy access to the stuff that "migrates" to the back corners, I mounted the drawer on full-extension slides.

Note: To help determine the overall size of the drawer, you'll need to have your slides in hand before you begin building the drawer.

The drawer is actually quite simple. The front, back, and sides are all made from $1/2$" plywood and joined with rabbet joints *(Fig. 15)*.

Each of these drawer pieces is the same width ($3^{15}/16$"). But to determine their final length, you have to figure out the overall width of the drawer.

To do this, measure the distance between the supports ($27^1/8$" in my case). Then subtract the combined thickness of the slides (1").

Once you know the overall width, cut the front and back (AA) of the drawer $1/2$" shorter to allow for the rabbets. Then cut the sides (BB) 16" long.

JOINERY. Once all the drawer parts have been cut to final size, it's just a matter of rabbeting both ends of each side to accept the front and back (Detail in *Fig. 15*).

Before assembling the drawer, you'll need to cut a groove near the bottom of each piece for the hardboard bottom (CC) *(Fig. 15a)*. Then glue and nail the drawer together.

FALSE FRONT. To complete the drawer, I screwed a false front (DD) to it *(Fig. 16)*. This is just a piece of $3/4$" plywood that's cut to size so it covers the front edges of the supports (V) and the front stretcher (W).

Note: To provide clearance under the table top when you open and close the drawer, the false front should be $1/16$" shorter ($4^{11}/16$") than the fronts of the supports.

PULLS. After attaching the false front with screws, I added two nickel-plated drawer pulls. Each pull is mounted with two short screws *(Fig. 16b)*.

INSTALL SLIDES. Finally, all that's left to complete the work table is to install the drawer slides *(Fig. 16a)*. As usual, it's best to follow the instructions that came with your drawer slides.

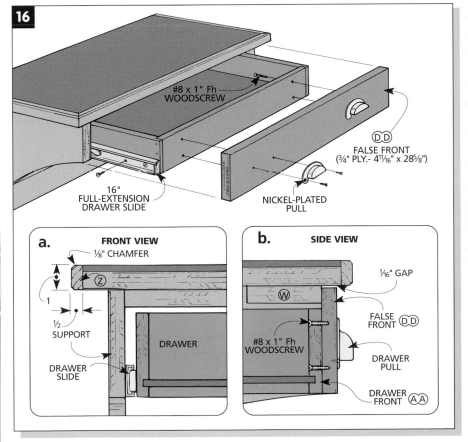

BINS

I can never have enough places to store and separate all the small pieces of hardware around my shop. Even with the bins in the tool cabinet I think I would be pushing it.

If you need extra storage bins, this small case may be just the ticket. It houses another dozen small bins that are identical to the ones in the tool cabinet you built earlier.

The basic construction of the case is also very similar to that of the tool cabinet. However, here the sides (EE) and the back (FF) extend above the top of the case (*Fig. 17*). This extension creates a shallow storage tray on top (see photo at right).

The openings for the bins are formed by two fixed shelves (GG), and the bottom (HH) of the case. These pieces fit in dadoes and rabbets that are the same size as those in the cabinet (refer to page 118).

BINS. Now the twelve bins can be made following the same procedure as on the tool cabinet (refer to Page 119).

SUPPORT STRIP. To add rigidity where the back extends beyond the top of the case, I glued a support strip (II) behind it. This is just a piece of ½" hardwood

cut to the same length as the back.

HANGING BRACKETS. Finally, a pair of short hanging brackets supports the case on the grid.

MATERIALS LIST

BIN STORAGE (requires 2 short hangers)

EE	Sides (2)	¾ ply. - 8 x 11¼
FF	Back (1)	¼ hdbd. - 11¼ x 30⅜
GG	Fixed Shlvs. (2)	¾ ply. - 7¼ x 29⅞
HH	Bottom (1)	¾ ply. - 7¼ x 29⅞
II	Suppt. Strip (1)	½ x ¾ - 30⅜
JJ	Bin Fr./Bks. (24)	¾ ply. - 3¹⁵⁄₁₆ x 4⅞
KK	Bin Btms. (12)	¾ ply. - 6¾ x 4⅜
LL	Bin Sides (24)	¼ hdbd. - 6¾ x 3¹⁵⁄₁₆

HARDWARE SUPPLIES

(16) No. 8 x ¾" Fh woodscrews
(4) No. 8 x 1½" Fh woodscrews
(8) No. 8 x 2" Fh woodscrews
1" brads

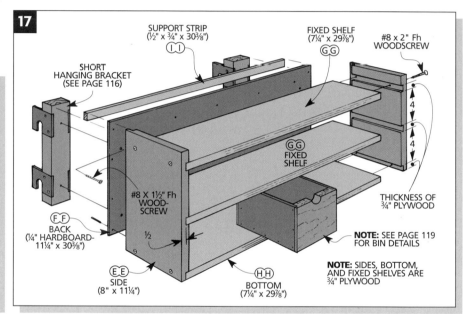

17

SUPPORT STRIP (½" x ¾" x 30⅜") — II

FIXED SHELF (7¼" x 29⅞") — GG

#8 x 2" Fh WOODSCREW

SHORT HANGING BRACKET (SEE PAGE 116)

GG FIXED SHELF

THICKNESS OF ¾" PLYWOOD

#8 X 1½" Fh WOODSCREW

FF BACK (¼" HARDBOARD- 11¼" x 30⅜")

½

NOTE: SEE PAGE 119 FOR BIN DETAILS

EE SIDE (8" x 11¼")

HH BOTTOM (7¼" x 29⅞")

NOTE: SIDES, BOTTOM, AND FIXED SHELVES ARE ¾" PLYWOOD

SHOP TIP .... Adding Bin Labels

One way to identify what goes in each bin is to add thin cardboard labels.

The labels slide in dovetailed slots cut across the front of the bin. A label can be easily removed and replaced if the contents of a bin changes.

I cut the slots using a ½" dovetail bit on the router table. Set the bit ⅛" deep and use a fence. For safety and to prevent chipout, back up the workpiece with a piece of scrap as a push block.

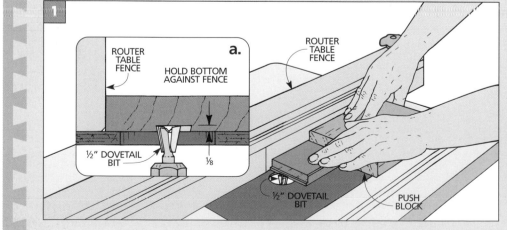

1

a.

ROUTER TABLE FENCE

HOLD BOTTOM AGAINST FENCE

½" DOVETAIL BIT

⅛

ROUTER TABLE FENCE

½" DOVETAIL BIT

PUSH BLOCK

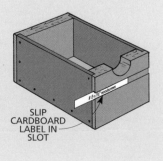

SLIP CARDBOARD LABEL IN SLOT

PEGBOARD STORAGE

A wall storage system wouldn't be complete without a place to hang tools. So I decided to add this simple pegboard storage unit. (Or, it could become a bulletin board, see box below.)

PEGBOARD. It's just a pegboard panel (MM) surrounded by a wood frame *(Fig. 18)*. The pegboard is cut to size so the centerpoints of the holes are $1/4$" in from each edge (see Detail). Once the project is assembled, this will effectively provide even spacing between the holes and the outer frame.

FRAME. After cutting the pegboard to final size, I built a mitered frame to fit around it. It consists of two rails (NN) and two stiles (OO). All of these pieces are made from "two-by" material. (I used Douglas fir.)

To accept both the pegboard and a pair of long hanging brackets, you'll need to cut a rabbet in the back of each frame piece *(Fig. 18a)*.

HANGING BRACKETS. The easiest way I found to mount the brackets to the pegboard is to countersink the pre-drilled holes in the corners of the pegboard first. Then you can simply screw the pegboard in place.

MATERIALS LIST

PEGBOARD (requires 2 long hangers)
MM	Pgbd. Panel (1)	$1/4$ pgbd. - $22\frac{5}{8}$ x $30\frac{3}{8}$
NN	Rails (2)	$1\frac{1}{2}$ x $1\frac{1}{2}$ - $31\frac{7}{8}$
OO	Stiles (2)	$1\frac{1}{2}$ x $1\frac{1}{2}$ - $24\frac{1}{8}$

HARDWARE SUPPLIES
(16) No. 8 x $3/4$" Fh woodscrews
(6) No. 8 x $1\frac{1}{4}$" Fh woodscrews
(4) No. 8 x 2" Fh woodscrews

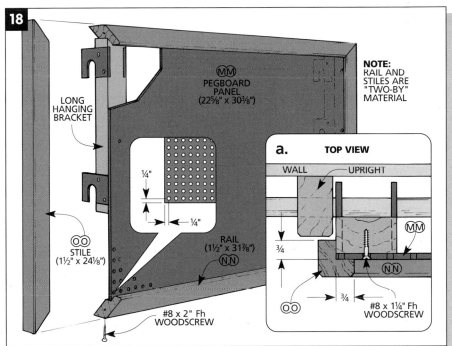

18

LONG HANGING BRACKET

MM
PEGBOARD PANEL
($22\frac{5}{8}$" x $30\frac{3}{8}$")

$1/4$"

$1/4$"

OO
STILE
($1\frac{1}{2}$" x $24\frac{1}{8}$")

RAIL
($1\frac{1}{2}$" x $31\frac{7}{8}$")
NN

NOTE: RAIL AND STILES ARE "TWO-BY" MATERIAL

a. **TOP VIEW**

WALL   UPRIGHT

$3/4$

MM

$3/4$

OO

$3/4$

#8 x $1\frac{1}{4}$" Fh WOODSCREW

NN

#8 x 2" Fh WOODSCREW

DESIGNER'S NOTEBOOK

BULLETIN BOARD

CONSTRUCTION NOTES:

■ To add a bulletin board, cut a slightly deeper rabbet ($7/8$") in the frame for a (soft but still secure) combination of materials. Glue a thin layer of cork over $1/4$" mahogany underlayment with contact cement (see drawing below). This assembly is then set into the frame, and the underlayment glued to the hanging brackets.

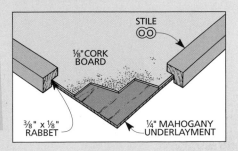

$1/8$" CORK BOARD

STILE
OO

$3/8$" x $1/8$" RABBET

$1/4$" MAHOGANY UNDERLAYMENT

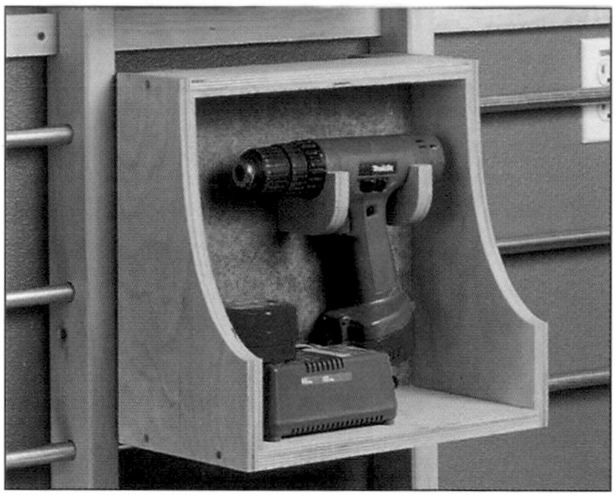

CORDLESS DRILL STORAGE

My cordless drill is one tool I always like to have handy — and charged up. So I decided to build a storage unit that would be big enough to hang the drill and also hold the battery charger (see photo at left).

The top (PP) and bottom (QQ) fit in $^1/_4$"-deep rabbets cut in the sides (RR) *(Fig. 19)*. To make it easy to grab the drill, there's a curved "scoop" in the sides (see pattern below). I cut the flat area at the front of the sides to match the height of my charger.

Also, I drilled a hole in the hardboard back (SS) for the power cord on the charger to pass through *(Fig. 19)*.

CRADLES. The drill hangs on two $^3/_4$"-thick plywood cradles (TT) screwed to the back *(Fig. 19a)*.

Note: When making the cradles, cut a scrap template first to see if the body of your drill will fit in the cradles.

Finally, glue and screw the sides to the top and bottom. Then glue and nail the back in place. And screw two short hanging brackets to the back *(Fig. 19)*.

MATERIALS LIST

DRILL UNIT (requires 2 short hangers)

PP	Top (1)	3/4 ply. - 3 1/4 x 13 7/8
QQ	Bottom (1)	3/4 ply. - 7 1/4 x 13 7/8
RR	Sides (2)	3/4 ply. - 8 x 14
SS	Back (1)	1/4 hdbd. - 14 x 14 3/8
TT	Cradles (2)	3/4 ply. - 2 1/2 x 3 1/2

HARDWARE SUPPLIES

- (16) No. 8 x 3/4" Fh woodscrews
- (2) No. 8 x 1" Fh woodscrews
- (4) No. 8 x 1 1/2" Fh woodscrews
- (8) No. 8 x 2" Fh woodscrews
- (16) 1" brads

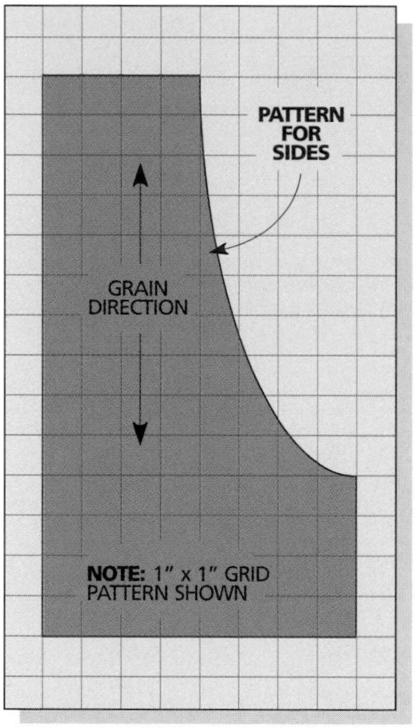

PATTERN FOR SIDES
GRAIN DIRECTION
NOTE: 1" x 1" GRID PATTERN SHOWN

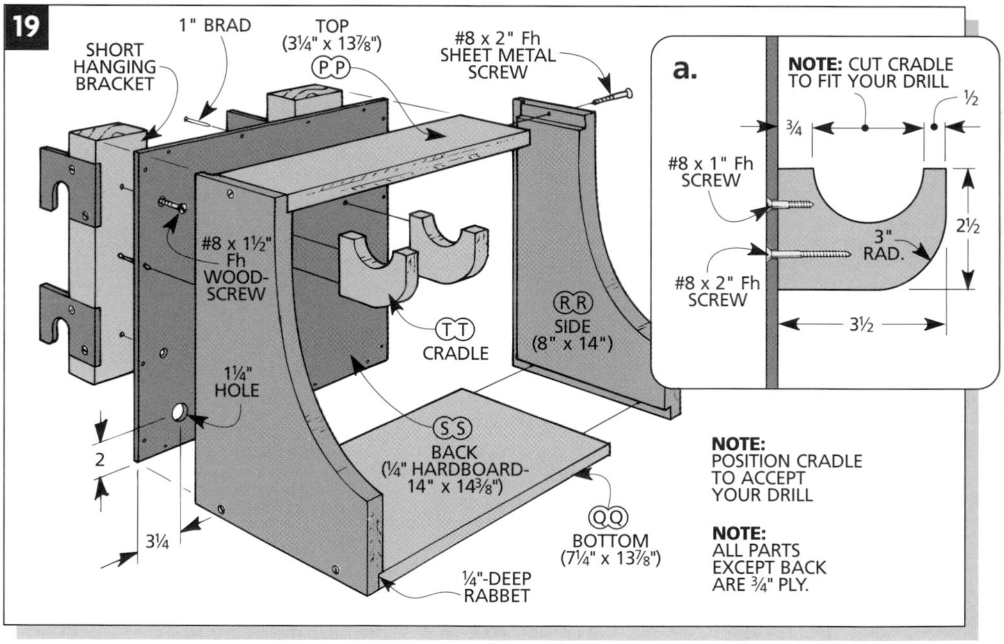

19
SHORT HANGING BRACKET
1" BRAD
TOP (3¼" x 13⅞")
PP
#8 x 2" Fh SHEET METAL SCREW
#8 x 1½" Fh WOOD-SCREW
TT CRADLE
RR SIDE (8" x 14")
1¼" HOLE
SS BACK (¼" HARDBOARD- 14" x 14⅜")
QQ BOTTOM (7¼" x 13⅞")
¼"-DEEP RABBET
2
3¼
a.
NOTE: CUT CRADLE TO FIT YOUR DRILL
¾
½
#8 x 1" Fh SCREW
#8 x 2" Fh SCREW
3" RAD.
2½
3½
NOTE: POSITION CRADLE TO ACCEPT YOUR DRILL
NOTE: ALL PARTS EXCEPT BACK ARE ¾" PLY.

SHOP TIP .... Preventing Stuck Bits

A common method for storing router and drill bits is to drill holes in a piece of wood to accept the shank of the bit. But if the wood swells up with changes in humidity, the holes can close up around the bit.

One solution is to drill *oversized* shank holes in the wood. Then, to hold the bits tight, drill holes that match the shank in a piece of acrylic plastic or hardboard *(Fig. 1)*.

Another solution is to use nylon sleeves (see photo). These were used on the router storage unit.

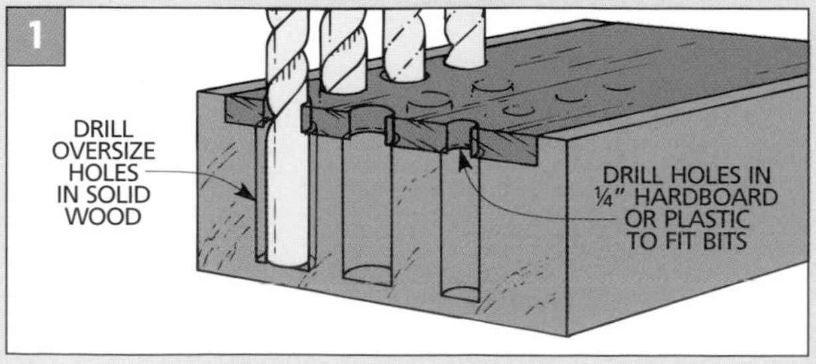

1
DRILL OVERSIZE HOLES IN SOLID WOOD
DRILL HOLES IN ¼" HARDBOARD OR PLASTIC TO FIT BITS

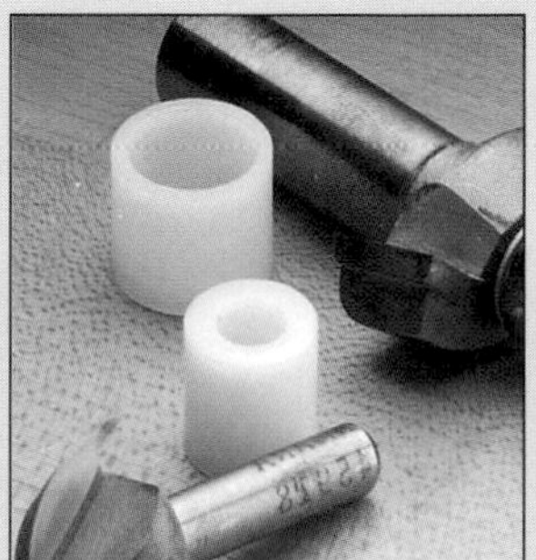

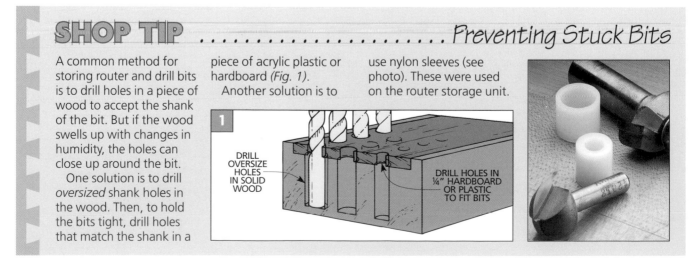

ROUTER STORAGE

This storage unit provides a handy place to set my router. But what I like even better is the drawer underneath that lets me safely store my router bits (see photo at right).

To hold even a large plunge router, this storage unit is a bit deeper and taller than the drill unit. But the basic design is almost the same.

The sides (UU) are rabbeted at each end to accept the top (VV) and bottom (WW) *(Fig. 20)*. And a rabbet in the back edge holds the hardboard back (XX) and a pair of short hanging brackets.

SHELF. But one difference in this storage unit is there's a dado in each side to hold a shelf (YY) *(Fig. 20a)*. Besides supporting the router, the shelf forms an opening for the drawer.

CURVED PROFILE. All that's left to do before assembling this unit is to cut a

curved profile on the front edge of each side (see pattern below).

DRAWER. Now you're ready to add the drawer that holds the router bits. It's a simple box that fits the opening at the bottom of the storage unit.

The front and back (ZZ) of the drawer are just pieces of 3/4" plywood *(Fig. 21)*. A deep rabbet holds the bottom (AAA) of the drawer *(Fig. 21a)*. And shallow rabbets on each end accept the hardboard sides (BBB) *(Fig. 21b)*. These sides are dished out along the top edge to make it easy to remove a bit (or put one back).

NYLON SLEEVES. To hold the bits, I used nylon sleeves that I picked up at the hardware store (see Shop Tip on opposite page). The sleeves are glued into 1/2"-deep holes in the drawer bottom with "instant" glue. ■

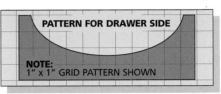

PATTERN FOR DRAWER SIDE

NOTE:
1" x 1" GRID PATTERN SHOWN

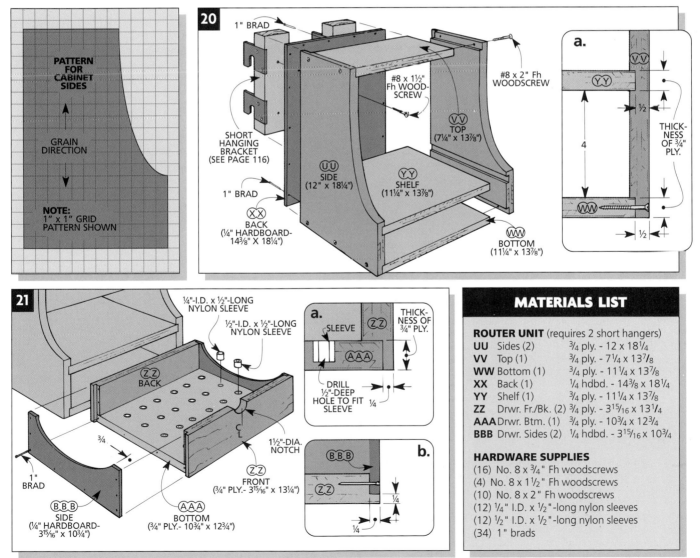

20

PATTERN FOR CABINET SIDES

GRAIN DIRECTION

NOTE:
1" x 1" GRID PATTERN SHOWN

1" BRAD

SHORT HANGING BRACKET (SEE PAGE 116)

1" BRAD

XX BACK (1/4" HARDBOARD- 14 3/8" X 18 1/4")

#8 x 1 1/2" Fh WOOD-SCREW

UU SIDE (12" x 18 1/4")

YY SHELF (11 1/4" x 13 7/8")

VV TOP (7 1/4" x 13 7/8")

#8 x 2" Fh WOODSCREW

BOTTOM (11 1/4" x 13 7/8")

a.

THICKNESS OF 3/4" PLY.

21

1/4"-I.D. x 1/2"-LONG NYLON SLEEVE

1/2"-I.D. x 1/2"-LONG NYLON SLEEVE

ZZ BACK

3/4

1" BRAD

BBB SIDE (1/4" HARDBOARD- 3 15/16" x 10 3/4")

AAA BOTTOM (3/4" PLY.- 10 3/4" x 12 3/4")

1 1/2"-DIA. NOTCH

ZZ FRONT (3/4" PLY.- 3 15/16" x 13 1/4")

a.

SLEEVE

ZZ

THICKNESS OF 3/4" PLY.

AAA

DRILL 1/2"-DEEP HOLE TO FIT SLEEVE 1/4

b.

BBB

ZZ

1/4

1/4

MATERIALS LIST

ROUTER UNIT (requires 2 short hangers)

UU	Sides (2)	3/4 ply. - 12 x 18 1/4
VV	Top (1)	3/4 ply. - 7 1/4 x 13 7/8
WW	Bottom (1)	3/4 ply. - 11 1/4 x 13 7/8
XX	Back (1)	1/4 hdbd. - 14 3/8 x 18 1/4
YY	Shelf (1)	3/4 ply. - 11 1/4 x 13 7/8
ZZ	Drwr. Fr./Bk. (2)	3/4 ply. - 3 15/16 x 13 1/4
AAA	Drwr. Btm. (1)	3/4 ply. - 10 3/4 x 12 3/4
BBB	Drwr. Sides (2)	1/4 hdbd. - 3 15/16 x 10 3/4

HARDWARE SUPPLIES
(16) No. 8 x 3/4" Fh woodscrews
(4) No. 8 x 1 1/2" Fh woodscrews
(10) No. 8 x 2" Fh woodscrews
(12) 1/4" I.D. x 1/2"-long nylon sleeves
(12) 1/2" I.D. x 1/2"-long nylon sleeves
(34) 1" brads

One of the first things we take into consideration when designing projects at *Woodsmith* is whether the hardware is commonly available. Most of the hardware and supplies for the projects in this book can be found at local hardware stores or home centers. Sometimes, though, you may have to order the hardware through the mail. If that's the case, we've tried to find reputable national mail order sources with toll-free phone numbers (see box at right).

In addition, *Woodsmith Project Supplies* offers hardware for some of the projects in this book (see below).

WOODSMITH PROJECT SUPPLIES

At the time of printing, the following project supply kits and hardware were available from *Woodsmith Project Supplies*. The kits include hardware, but you must supply any lumber, plywood, or finish. For current prices and availability, call toll free:

1-800-444-7527

Fold-Down Work Center
(pages 18-26) .... No. 6814-300

Maple Workbench
(pages 27-43)
front vise ....No. 785-110
end vise ....No. 785-120
wooden bench dogs ....No. 750-130

Router Table
(pages 60-71)
phenolic insert...........No. 4502-228
fence kit......................No. 6801-200
bit guard
(requires fence kit or attachment
kit below) ....No. 4502-206A
large featherboard
(requires fence kit or attachment
kit below) ....No. 4502-526
attachment kit............No. 6801-250
freehand guard ....No. 6801-220
dust hood ....No. 6801-230

Lumber Rack
(pages 100-105)..........No. 6817-200

KEY: TL02

MAIL ORDER SOURCES

Some of the most important "tools" you can have in your shop are mail order catalogs. The ones listed below are filled with special hardware, tools, finishes, lumber, and supplies that can't be found at a local hardware store or home center. You should be able to find many of the supplies for the projects in this book in one or more of these catalogs.

It's amazing what you can learn about woodworking by looking through these catalogs. If they're not currently in your shop, you may want to have them sent to you.

Note: The information below was current when this book was printed. Time-Life Books and August Home Publishing do not guarantee these products will be available nor endorse any specific mail order company, catalog, or product.

WOODCRAFT

P.O. Box 1686
Parkersburg, WV 26102-1686
800–225–1153
A must! Has just about everything for the woodworker including tools, vises, leg levelers, casters, magnetic tool bars, hardware, and finishing supplies.

ROCKLER WOODWORKING AND HARDWARE

4365 Willow Drive
Medina, MN 55340
800–279–4441
One of the best all-around sources for general and specialty hardware. They carry drawer pulls, full-extension drawer slides, leg levelers, casters, and lazy Susans. Also a variety of tools, finishes, and lumber.

GARRETT WADE

161 Ave. of the Americas
New York, NY 10013
800–221–2942
The "Bible" for hand tools but also one of the best sources for finishing supplies and high quality power tools and accessories. This catalog is filled with useful information and tips for your shop. It reads like a good woodworking book.

THE WOODSMITH STORE

2625 Beaver Avenue
Des Moines, IA 50310
800–835–5084
Our own retail store filled with tools, hardware, books, and finishing supplies. Though we don't have a catalog, we do send out items mail order. Call for information.

CONSTANTINES

2050 Eastchester Road
Bronx, NY 10461
800–223–8087
One of the original woodworking mail order catalogs. Good collection of hardware and finishing supplies.

WOODWORKER'S SUPPLY

1108 N. Glenn Road
Casper, WY 82601
800–645–9292
Excellent source for power tools and accessories, folding leg brackets, hardware, and finishing supplies.

TRENDLINES

135 American Legion Highway
Revere, MA 02151
800–767–9999
Another complete source for power tools and accessories. Some hardware and supplies.

INDEX

ABC

Bench dogs, wooden, 33
Benchtop
    Building, 16, 25, 29-37, 42-43, 63
    Mounting, 16, 41
Benchtop Tool Cabinet, 17
Bins for hardware, 122
Bit storage, 124-125
Box joint jig, 90-93
Brushes, cleaning, 111
Bulletin board, 123
Cabinets
    Finishing, 106-111
    Laundry room, 113
    Miter saw, 72-81
    Table saw, 52-59
    Tool, 18-26, 84-93, 118-119
    Workbench, 44-49
Cabinets and Bench, 8-17

DEF

Desk, for kid's room, 113
Door
    Catch, 15, 87, 109-110
    Fold-down into bench, 25
    Making, 14-15, 47, 49, 87, 109
    Pulls, 14, 87, 109, 121
    Sliding, 49
Drawers, 12 13, 24, 48, 56, 86, 97, 119,
        121, 122, 125
    Dividers, 22, 97
    Labels for, 122
    Joint options, 13
    Pulls, 14, 48, 121
    Unit for pegboard, 97
Drill storage unit, 124
Dust bin/collector, 56
Featherboard, 71
Fences
    Miter saw, 79-81
    Router table, 66-69
Finishing Cabinet, 106-111
Flush trimming, 16, 63
Fold-Down Work Center, 18-26

GHIJK

Guards, for router table, 70
Hardware
    Bins for, 122
    Casters, 55, 76, 105
    Draw catch, 25
    Drawer pulls, 121
    Folding leg brackets, 26
    Inset door hinges, 15
    Knobs, 68-71, 80
    L-hooks, 97
    L-shaped brackets, 16
    Lazy Susan, 110
    Leg levelers, 26, 55, 76, 102-103
    Lid support, 25
    Magnetic catch, 23, 87, 119
    Piano hinge, 25, 78, 109, 119
    Self-adhesive tape measure, 81
    Sources, 126
    Threaded inserts, 41, 43, 67
Joinery
    Box joints, 36, 48, 86, 90-93
    Butt joint (nailed), 13
    Drawer joint options, 13
    Half-blind dovetails, 13
    Locked rabbet, 13
    Sliding dovetails, 13
    Stub tenon and groove, 10, 54-55

LMNO

Lumber Rack, 100-105
Magnetic toolbars, 23
Maple Workbench, 27-43
Miter gauge bracket, 58
Miter Saw Station, 72-81
Modular Workshop, 112-125
Mounting a tool cabinet, 26, 87, 118-119
Outfeed support, 59

PQR

Pattern router bit, 63-65
Pegboard System, 94-99, 123
Plastic laminate, 63
Plywood
    Cutting, 74
    Edging, 23, 46-47, 63, 86-87, 104,
        108-110, 119, 120
    Storage of, 105
Push stick and holster, 58
Racks, chisel and screwdriver, 99
Rip fence bracket, 58
Router and bit storage unit, 125
Router Table, 60-71
    Accessories, 70-71
    Base, 62
    Fence, 66-69
    Insert plate, 64
    Miter gauge slot, 65
    Top, 63

STU

Sandpaper storage, 98-99
Scrap bin, 77
Sheet goods bin, 105
Shelves
    For kid's room, 113
    For laundry room, 113
    For lumber rack, 104
    For modular workshop, 117
    For pegboard, 98
    For tool cabinet, 24, 87, 108-109, 118

Metal standards, 109
Template for rests, 24, 87
Shop Tips
    Adding a miter gauge slot, 65
    Adding bin labels, 122
    Angled drilling guide, 102
    Clamping blocks, 48
    Cleaning up conduit, 115
    Customizing to your saw, 79
    Cutting a slab to length, 31
    Cutting plywood without chipout, 74
    Dowel centers, 110
    Drawer rails and filler strips, 11
    Dust collector hook-up, 56
    Installing the grid, 115
    Installing threaded inserts, 67
    L-hook system, 97
    Leg levelers, 55
    Making a push stick, 58
    Making your own drawer pulls, 14
    Pattern bit, 63
    Pin spacing, 91
    Preventing stuck bits, 124
    Preventing vise rack, 38
    Routing chamfers on edges, 76
    Slot-cutting jig, 116
    Using brackets, 16
    Using a story stick, 22
    Using stretch cords, 104
    Wooden dogs, 33
Splines, 35, 69
Stop block, 80
Story stick, 22
Table saw accessories, 58-59
Table Saw Cabinet, 52-59
Table saw outfeed support, 59
Tool boards, 23
Tool Cabinet, 84-93, 118-119
    Accessories, 88-89
    Fold-Down Work Center, 18-26
    For benchtop tools, 17
Tool holders, 88-89
Tool tray, 37

VWXYZ

Vacuum attachment
    Router table, 71
    Table saw cabinet, 56
Vises
    End vise, 37
    Front vise, 38-39, 43
Wall grid system, 114-116
Workbench Cabinet, 44-49
Workbenches, 8-43
    Base, 40-41
    Cabinet, 44-49
    Top, 16, 17, 29-37
Work centers, 17, 18-26

AUGUST HOME
PUBLISHING COMPANY

President & Publisher: Donald B. Peschke
Executive Editor: Douglas L. Hicks
Art Director: Steve Lueder
Creative Director: Ted Kralicek
Senior Graphic Designers: Chris Glowacki, Cheryl Simpson
Assistant Editors: Joseph E. Irwin, Craig Ruegsegger
Graphic Designer: Vu Nguyen

Designer's Notebook Illustrator: Mike Mittermeier
Photographer: Crayola England
Electronic Production: Douglas M. Lidster
Production: Troy Clark, Minniette Johnson, Susan Rueve
Project Designers: Ken Munkel, Kent Welsh, Kevin Boyle
Project Builders: Steve Curtis, Steve Johnson
Magazine Editors: Terry Strohman, Tim Robertson
Contributing Editors: Vincent S. Ancona, Tom Begnal, Jon Garbison,
Bryan Nelson
Magazine Art Directors: Todd Lambirth, Cary Christensen
Contributing Illustrators: Mark Higdon, David Kreyling, Erich Lage,
Roger Reiland, Kurt Schultz, Cinda Shambaugh, Dirk Ver Steeg

Controller: Robin Hutchinson
Production Director: George Chmielarz
Project Supplies: Bob Baker
New Media Manager: Gordon Gaippe

For subscription information about
Woodsmith and *ShopNotes* magazines, please write:
August Home Publishing Co.
2200 Grand Ave.
Des Moines, IA 50312
800-333-5075
www.augusthome.com/customwoodworking

Woodsmith® and *ShopNotes®* are registered trademarks of August Home
Publishing Co.

ISBN 0-7835-5951-8

Printed in U.S.A   10 9 8 7 6 5 4 3 2

TIME
LIFE ®
BOOKS

Time-Life Books is a division of Time Life Inc.

TIME LIFE INC.
President and CEO: Jim Nelson

TIME-LIFE BOOKS
Publisher/Managing Editor: Neil Kagan
Senior Vice President, Marketing: Joseph A. Kuna
Vice President, New Product Development: Amy Golden

CUSTOM WOODWORKING
The Home Workshop
Editor: Glen B. Ruh
Design Director: Kate McConnell
Assistant Art Director: Patricia Bray
Cover Concept: Phil Unetic/3R1 Studios

Director of Marketing: Wells P. Spence
Marketing Manager: Jennifer C. Williams

Correspondents: Maria Vincenza Aloisi (Paris), Christine Hinze (London),
Christina Lieberman (New York)

Executive Vice President, Operations: Ralph Cuomo
Senior Vice President and CFO: Claudia Goldberg
Senior Vice President, Law & Business Affairs: Randolph H. Elkins
Vice President, Financial Planning & Analysis: Christopher Hearing
Vice President, Book Production: Patricia Pascale
Vice President, Imaging: Marjann Caldwell
Director, Publishing Technology: Betsi McGrath
Director of Editorial Administration: Barbara Levitt
Director of Photography and Research: John Conrad Weiser
Director, Quality Assurance: James King
Manager, Technical Services: Anne Topp
Senior Production Manager: Ken Sabol
Manager, Copyedit/Page Makeup: Debby Tait
Chief Librarian: Louise D. Forstall

School and library distribution by Time-Life Education, P.O. Box 85026,
Richmond, Virginia 23285-5026.